AF480751

PRAISE FOR MEMORIAL

In her latest memoir, Nita Sweeney leans in close to show the reality of a difficult year. Then, she drops us all the way in. Whether in a golf cart, the psych ward, or at the edge of her dying father's bed, when everything in her wants to flee, she stays in the room. With MEMORIAL, Nita has done the real work, creating a book that will echo with you long after you close the cover.

—Natalie Goldberg, bestselling
author of *Writing Down the Bones*
and *Writing on Empty*

As someone who has spent most of his adult life speaking publicly about mental illness, I know how rare it is for a person to tell the whole story without making themselves sound better—in other words, without sanding down the rough edges. In MEMORIAL, Nita Sweeney doesn't sugarcoat the mental health struggles she faces. It's a heartbreaking (yet sometimes comical) story that is brutally honest about suicidal ideation, grief, love, and what it actually takes to keep going. I wholeheartedly recommend this book to anyone.

—Gabe Howard, Webby award-winning
podcaster and author of *Mental Illness
Is an Asshole and Other Observations*

Nita Sweeney has produced a glorious memoir that will touch you deeply and resonate for many years after its last page. Her account of placing life on hold to share her dying father's final days reminds all of us about the obligations to being a son or daughter and giving up the pointless habit of keeping score in life, choosing instead to share love in the heart of grief and loss.

—James Dodson, award-winning
author of *Final Rounds* and
The Road That Made America

Nita Sweeney's MEMORIAL is an emotional tribute to the power of sports in forging unbreakable bonds. Using the metaphor of golf's rhythms—the approach, the front and back nines, the greens—she recounts the tender but tumultuous year spent with her dying father, transforming fairways into pathways of reconciliation and unconditional love. This is a must-read for anyone who has found solace and strength, nine to eighteen holes at a time.

—Leif H. Smith, Psy.D, Clinical &
Sports Psychologist and author of
Sports Psychology for Dummies

MEMORIAL is more than an inspiring and hopeful memoir about fathers and daughters, healing familial relationships, or recovering from mental illness. It's also about golf! And it's a darned good read! Highly recommended for anyone who's ever been a child, a parent, or ever got too caught up in keeping score.

—Sean Murphy, recent National
Endowment for the Arts Fellow in
Creative Writing, award-winning
author of *The Time of New Weather*

Nita Sweeney's new memoir, MEMORIAL, is a fitting tribute to her father while showing his significance in her life. The touching, funny, poignant, and honest book effectively weaves different timelines with many vivid scenes on and off the golf course. It would make a terrific movie!

—James Kingsland, author of
Am I Dreaming? and *Siddhartha's Brain*

MEMORIAL is a touching exploration of the mind and heart. Over a series of golf dates with her dying father, Nita Sweeney eloquently captures the complexities around their relationship, her struggles with depression and her coming to terms with her own life—as a reflection of her father's. Just as with her award-winning *Depression Hates a Moving Target*, Sweeney holds nothing back as she shines a light on mental illness, self-destruction, and grief, all in a way that compels our compassion. A gift for anyone who's navigated difficult family relationships.

—Debbie Russell, award-winning author of
Crossing Fifty-One: Not Quite a Memoir

In MEMORIAL, Nita Sweeney details her journey with her father after his terminal cancer diagnosis, as she attempts to draw closer to him, resolve their differences, and come to terms with his approaching death by bonding with him on the golf course. Her reflections also tackle her history of anxiety and depression, including struggles with suicidal ideation and psychiatric hospitalization, against the backdrop of a woman who feels she's never measured up to her father's expectations. Sweeney's prose is straightforward and to the point, sharing her vulnerable emotions as she examines how her father's sickness impacts her own self-image as well as her future. The memoir offers interesting parallels between Sweeney's battle with mental illness and her father's terminal cancer, offering up insights on the pair's similarities (both often fall back on critical self-talk and tend to check out of uncomfortable conversations) and differences. Sweeney's depression is intensely rendered, sweeping readers into her emotions and thought processes, and her inner monologues when spending time with her father—reflecting on her insecurities, fear of losing him, and frustration that nothing can be done to save him—will strike a chord with readers.

—*Publishers Weekly* BookLife Prize Critic

More from Nita Sweeney

Depression Hates a Moving Target: How Running with My Dog Brought Me Back from the Brink

You Should Be Writing: A Journal of Inspiration and Instruction to Keep Your Pen Moving (co-created with Brenda Knight)

Make Every Move a Meditation: Mindful Movement for Mental Health, Well-Being, and Insight

A Daily Dose of Now: 365 Mindfulness Meditation Practices for Living in the Moment

MEMORIAL

MEMORIAL

The Year My Dad and I Stopped Keeping Score

a mental health memoir

NITA SWEENEY

Mind, Mood, and Movement

Published by Mind, Mood, and Movement
Cover design: 100 Covers
Photo Credit: Nita Sweeney
Copy editing: James Kingsland
Layout and design: 100 Covers

For privacy reasons, some names, locations, and dates have been changed.

For permission requests, please contact the publisher at:

Mind, Mood, and Movement
5650 Blazer Parkway, #178
Dublin, Ohio 43017 USA
info@mindmoodandmovement.com

For special orders, quantity sales, course adoptions and corporate sales, please email the publisher at info@mindmoodandmovement.com. For trade and wholesale sales, please contact Ingram Publisher Services at customer.service@ingramcontent.com or 1.800.509.4887.

Memorial: The Year My Dad and I Stopped Keeping Score

Publisher's Cataloging-in-Publication Data

Names: Sweeney, Nita, author.
Title: Memorial : the year my dad and I stopped keeping score , a mental health memoir / Nita Sweeney.
Description: Dublin, OH: Mind, Mood, and Movement, 2026.
Identifiers: LCCN: 2026903854 | ISBN: 979-8-9880744-3-4 (hardcover) | 979-8-9880744-4-1 (paperback) | 979-8-9880744-5-8 (ebook)
Subjects: LCSH Sweeney, Nita. | Mentally ill--United States--Biography. | Fathers and daughters. | Grief. | Fathers--Death--Psychological aspects. | Bereavement. | Golf. | BISAC BIOGRAPHY & AUTOBIOGRAPHY / Memoirs | FAMILY & RELATIONSHIPS / Death, Grief, Bereavement | HEALTH & FITNESS / Mental Health | SPORTS & RECREATION / Golf
Classification: LCC HQ755.85 .S94 2026 | DDC 306.874--dc23

Printed in the United States of America

To Jim and Amy, the best siblings a ~~spoiled brat~~
baby sister could have.

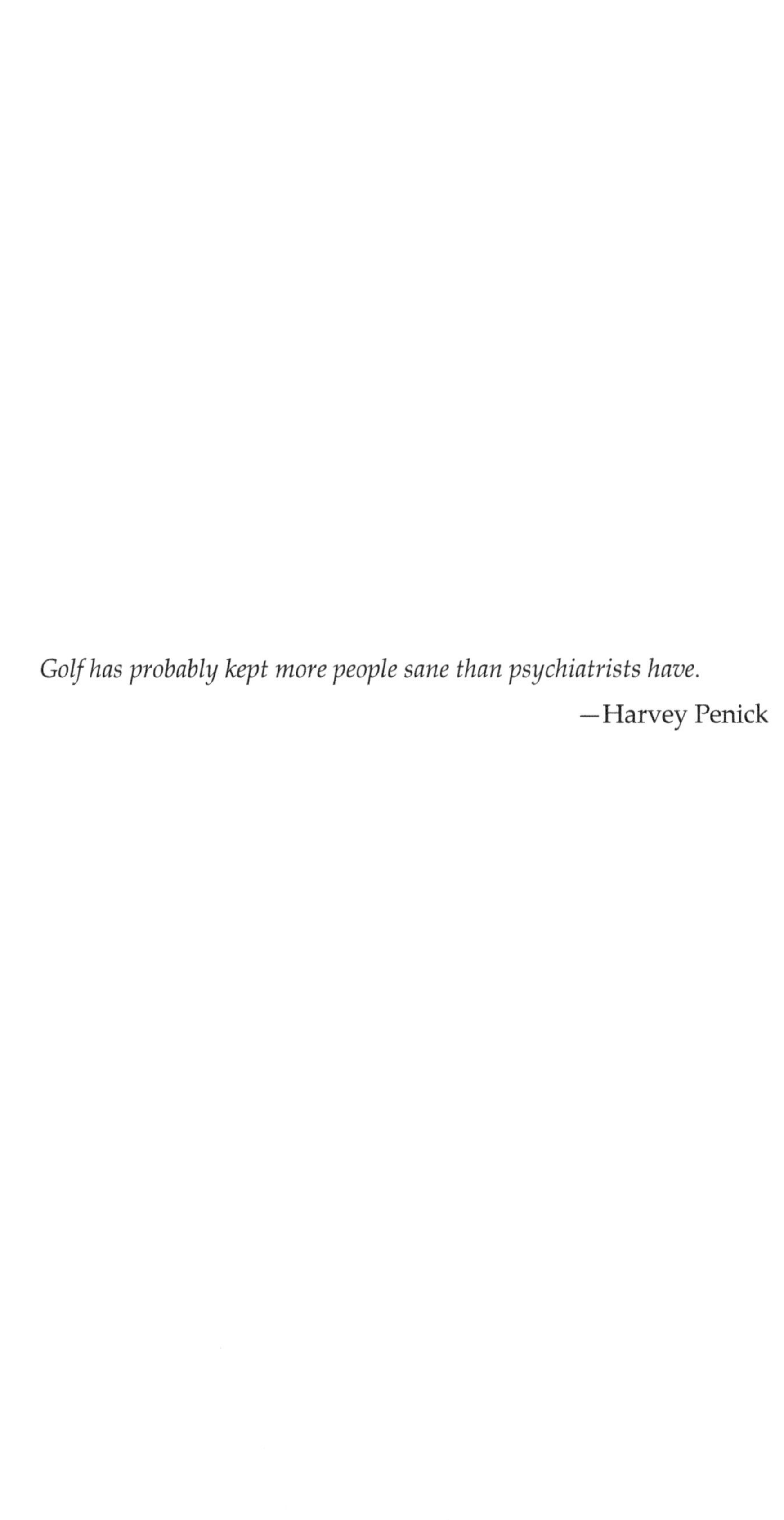

Golf has probably kept more people sane than psychiatrists have.

—Harvey Penick

CONTENTS

PROLOGUE xvii

THE APPROACH: JANUARY 1995 to JUNE 1995

Chapter 1: We've Got All Summer 3

Chapter 2: Road Lawyer 14

Chapter 3: Your Father Took a Nap 22

Chapter 4: Synchronized Crying Club 35

Chapter 5: The Course that Jack Built.........................40

Chapter 6: The Only Daughter You Can Be.....................46

Chapter 7: Really Crappy Odds 57

Chapter 8: Accidental Stepmother 63

Chapter 9: Trip of a Lifetime 83

THE FRONT NINE: JUNE 1995 to SEPTEMBER 1995

Chapter 10: Repairing Divots....................................103

Chapter 11: Mind if I Have a Beer? 119

Chapter 12: Certifiable 123

Chapter 13: Sprinkle Me on the Back Forty 131

Chapter 14: Singing 145

Chapter 15: Go Home and Live Your Dreams...................150

Chapter 16: Lazy 156

Chapter 17: Dummy 165

Chapter 18: Running Against Time.........................170

THE TURN: SEPTEMBER and OCTOBER 1995

    Chapter 19: End of the Season 181

    Chapter 20: Cancer Commune..194

THE BACK NINE: NOVEMBER 1995 to JANUARY 1996

    Chapter 21: I Need My Glasses..215

    Chapter 22: All Dogs Go to Heaven.....................................227

    Chapter 23: Funereal Sprite..231

    Chapter 24: Family Conference 236

    Chapter 25: Turkey Day 242

    Chapter 26: Ice Storm 249

    Chapter 27: Quite a Gal...256

    Chapter 28: A Very Private Act...265

    Chapter 29: He Knew How to Do Things Right................271

EPILOGUE 275

ACKNOWLEDGMENTS 281

ABOUT THE AUTHOR 287

A GIFT AND A REQUEST...287

SENSITIVE CONTENT

This work of nonfiction explores sensitive topics and includes graphic descriptions that some readers might find disturbing. Reader discretion is advised.

If you or a loved one is experiencing significant distress, is having thoughts about suicide, or needs emotional support, call or text 988 to reach the 988 Lifeline. Free, confidential support is available 24-7.

If you need immediate help, call 911.

PROLOGUE

The crowd on the television roared as our family huddled around the set in my father's room at the hospice facility where he would die a few days later. We cheered on The Ohio State University Buckeyes against Tennessee in the 1996 Citrus Bowl. In his hospital bed, my ailing father struggled to take tiny sips of Budweiser—his final beer—that my mother had bought and smuggled in for him.

When the hospice nurse came to administer the liquid morphine Dad usually took diluted in store-brand root beer, I made a joke.

"Hey! Why not put the morphine in your Budweiser?"

Banter between us was normal. I expected him to laugh or retort.

Instead, he spat: "What the hell business is it of yours!"

The room fell silent.

My cheeks burned hotter than they would have if he'd slapped me.

I was three, thirteen, nineteen, thirty—every age at which his scorn had previously stung.

Was everyone staring? I was too ashamed to look.

Hours on golf courses in three states. Days traveling together during his "trip of a lifetime." Weeks at his bedside. Our bond evaporated in a blink.

You idiot! I thought as the inner scaffolding I'd built during our nine months together threatened to collapse.

I stole a hopeful glance at my father, but his eyes had closed.

I stood and walked out.

THE APPROACH

JANUARY 1995 TO JUNE 1995

Golf is a game of inches. The most important are the six inches between your ears.

— Arnold Palmer

CHAPTER 1

WE'VE GOT ALL SUMMER

From the men's tee at the first hole of Wilson Road Golf Course in Columbus, Ohio, my father studied his target: the flag 323 yards away. When he tugged the bill of his John Deere ball cap, smooth tufts of sandy hair peeked out and lay against the back of his tanned neck. From the cart path, I scrutinized my 66-year-old dad for signs of illness. I saw none. Instead, I saw a strong man intent on achieving his goal, the father I'd known for my entire thirty-three years.

Dad slid his long fingers into his shorts pocket and pulled out a tee and ball. He palmed the ball on the tee then bent his six-foot, two-inch frame to stick the tee in the ground with the dimpled sphere balanced on top. He straightened up and positioned his feet near the ball. After another look at the flag, he glanced at his feet and nodded. Each movement tugged at me. Invisible threads connected his arms, head, and hands to my heart.

Next came the practice swings. One. Two. Three. The heavy-headed driver swooshed through the grass at his feet. Then he stepped forward until his shoes were a few feet from the ball and turned to consider the flag again. Not satisfied with his stance, he inched closer before placing his driver. With the club in place, he checked the flag one final time.

When he looked, I looked with him. When he turned back, so did I. He stared down for a second with monk-like stillness. Finally, he swung the club in a smooth arc away from and then back toward the ball until the club face hit the small white orb with enough force to send it hurtling through the air.

Dread tinged the joy of watching him. On any ordinary Thursday in early May, I would have been at my desk at the small law firm where I was a partner, or perhaps driving to visit a client at their office. My father would have been two thousand miles away on his home golf course in Bullhead City, Arizona. My snowbird parents never returned to Ohio before June.

But this was no ordinary Thursday. This was no ordinary year.

Dad and Mom had driven from Arizona to Ohio early so my father could see a cancer specialist at The Ohio State University Medical Center. For my part, I was recovering from a depressive episode that had nearly killed me.

* * *

In the months leading up to this unusually timed golf outing with my father, my mother and I had continued our decades-old ritual of her calling, she and I exhausting all topics, her handing Dad the phone, and he and I spending three-and-a-half minutes with me saying, "Mom just told me that . . ." or "As I just told Mom . . ."

As the weeks passed, my mother's calls grew more serious and she stopped putting Dad on the phone.

First, he was having a chest x-ray. Then, the test revealed a pea-sized tumor on his lung. Finally, in her most recent call, she explained that a biopsy had declared it malignant.

While this stream of news shocked me, I let Mom's calm demeanor guide my emotions. She didn't say the dreaded "C" word. Instead, she offered matter-of-fact details. In a few weeks, she explained, after the pair arrived back in Ohio as scheduled, Dad would have surgery and recover. She sounded confident and strong. In a month, I would see him for myself.

A few days after that call, I sat in my home office at a desk my father had built while I was in law school. He had fashioned the seven-foot expanse from plywood then covered it with a sheet of faux mahogany Formica salvaged from the back room of Arco Linoleum. I absentmindedly ran my fingers along the smooth edges Dad had perfected as I looked over the manuscript of a feature article I had written for *Dog World* magazine.

I returned the article to the corner of my desk and pulled out a handout that contained a list of "feeling words" with accompanying facial expression graphics: homework for the group therapy I now attended three days a week. My assignment was to circle my current emotion for the following morning's group session.

The phone rang once, then stopped.

Pride about the magazine article welled up. I'd researched medicines that veterinarians use to calm unruly dogs and written an extensive piece "on spec." If the *Dog World* editor liked the piece, the magazine would buy it. If they bought it, that would be my first article in a national publication, a major accomplishment. A pleasant glow filled my chest as I circled the face for "happy."

Then my husband, Ed, leaned in the doorway. "It's your dad."

A chill ran through me.

"What?" I stammered. "Dad never . . ."

But Ed had returned to the kitchen to finish preparing dinner.

". . . calls."

Trembling, I lifted the receiver.

Dad's voice sounded mechanical. He spoke slowly, struggling to make his meaning clear.

"It's in my bones . . . my ribs."

What moments before had been a pea-sized, operable lump in his lung, was now a mass in his bones. He did not speak about odds, survival or treatment.

On my desk, the list of feeling words taunted me. Where was the face for "I refuse to believe this?"

An empty space opened in my chest.

"What's next?" I asked.

"We're coming home . . . right away."

I ran my fingertips over the desktop and imagined his fingers on that same surface. Then I hauled myself out of my chair and forced myself toward the kitchen. Ed's knife pounded against the wooden cutting board as he chopped vegetables.

He looked up and set down the knife. "What?"

I couldn't answer. My wobbly body aimed itself across the kitchen toward the family room sofa. The walls looked wavy. If I didn't say Dad's words out loud, didn't tell Ed, maybe the cancer wouldn't have already spread?

When my thigh bumped the sofa arm, I bounced onto the cushions hoping they might swallow me in comfort. Instead, my body met rough, unforgiving fabric. I wrapped my arms around my shoulders, shut my eyes, and rocked, willing the world to recede. Ed's arms enveloped and steadied me. His strong embrace reminded me I wasn't alone and gave me the courage to whisper in his ear.

"It's in his bones."

⁂

I don't know what you call the soft whoosh of a well-hit golf ball, but that's the sound Dad's ball made as it flew above the fairway, sailed over the creek, bounced in the fringe at the edge of the green, and rolled within a foot of the hole. I stared.

How will we get through this?

Dad turned toward me and beamed.

To get through that moment, I resorted to our familiar family tool: sarcasm. Instead of apologizing in advance for the poor golf I would soon demonstrate, or running over to hug him, I lifted my chin and smirked.

"That is simply not the way a sick man is supposed to hit."

He laughed and shrugged. "Don't feel sick today."

He didn't look sick, either. The sun shone against the broad sides of his face and the skin near the corners of his eyes wrinkled behind his glasses. With his hat jauntily placed and his enormous grin, he looked radiant.

"I don't know if I want to play with you or not," I said, continuing to fake petulance. Bravado hid my urge to please him. While I didn't look forward to being embarrassed by my lousy golf skills, nothing could have torn me from that course.

My stomach gnawed with need for his approval, for accolades he hadn't offered when I was growing up. *How much longer did I have to get this right?* If I had to earn his love on the golf course that's what I'd do, but I wouldn't let the insecurity show.

Dad feigned the stern parent and waved his arm toward the women's tee.

"Go hit the ball, young lady!"

In his humor, I found calm. I stuck out my lower lip and marched to the tee.

"Birdie gonna shit on that lip," he said to my back. We both laughed out loud.

As I began to pull a club from my bag, he asked, "You sure about that?" I looked at the driver I'd chosen, the longest, heaviest club in my bag. Not sure in the least, I waited.

"From the women's tee, this hole is about 250 yards," he said.

I pondered the tee boxes. In 1995, when we were playing, most courses referred to the tee closest to the hole as the "women's tee." Three decades later, courses would designate tees by the color of their markers and suggest golfers choose whichever tee suited their game, regardless of gender.

I didn't care what they called the tees. I would hit from the box closest to the hole. I needed every yard I could get.

I'd been playing on and off since my last quarter of college when I took golf as an elective after I knew I was going to law school. I didn't want to be excluded from what I imagined would be important client-development opportunities that happened on the links. But I hadn't played in nine months and the medicines I took to combat depression hampered my concentration.

I inhaled deeply, trying to release the self-deprecation. "Dad, I'll be lucky to hit the ball at all."

He made a zipping motion across his lips with his fingers and tightened his mouth.

I winced, put the driver back in my bag, and pulled out an iron. I took a few practice swings then looked at him. His lips remained clenched.

"What?"

"You keep lifting your head."

"I'm trying to see where I'm hitting."

He shook his head, walked toward me, and gently put his hand on the back of my head.

"Take a few practice swings," he said.

As I lifted the club, his hand held my head in place. His touch was warm, the pressure firm but tender.

"Don't look up from the ball until you've swung all the way through." As he held my head, I swung the club.

"Good," he said, releasing me. "Now, don't bend your elbow."

I stared at the ground until I had the courage to ask, "How can I swing without bending my elbows?"

He replied, "Only bend the right one. Keep the left one locked."

His familiar efforts at "improvement" stirred my angry inner teenager and I stifled a grumble.

"Just try it." He put his hand back on my head.

I locked my left elbow and swung the club.

"Good. Now, line up."

I walked to the ball, put my club head near it, then tried to line up the way he had earlier.

He put his hands on my shoulders and turned my body slightly to the left. I tensed, then forced myself to relax. Part of me enjoyed this attention while another wished he would just let me play. We were wasting what precious little time we might have left together.

"Now, line your feet up with your body."

He told me to imagine a straight line running from the point of the right toe to the left toe and on down the fairway across the green to the hole.

"Jack Nicklaus explained it in a video," he said. "Simple geometry."

My high-school valedictorian father was an excellent golfing student. Once, when I visited my parents, Mom and I looked on from the dining room table while Dad, wearing giant headphones, stood to watch a golf lesson video in the living room. His gaze intent, he held his arms exactly as Mr. Nicklaus instructed, leaned forward to capture every word, and shifted his body weight to mimic Jack on the screen.

I turned my feet slightly to line them up with my body. He walked a few feet away from me and sighted the hole from behind me. "Looks good. Now, hit the ball."

My head. My elbow. My body.

So much to remember. I gritted my teeth.

I wanted to ask him not to watch. Instead, I froze.

"What's wrong?" he asked.

I wished I could tell him how afraid I was to disappoint him, but we didn't talk that way. With the torrent of information swirling in my brain, I pulled my club back then swung wildly. When the club head made contact, the ball barely flew twenty yards.

Dad shrugged.

My heart sank.

"We've got all summer," he said.

Then he walked to my cart, grabbed it, turned it around, and began pushing both carts with a brisk, long stride toward my ball. A chiropractor in Arizona had recommended Dad push his cart instead of pulling. Always eager to try something new, my father followed the instructions. "Easier on the back," he explained to curious onlookers. A decade later, ads for "pushcarts," the latest ergonomic device, would remind me of this afternoon.

I trotted down the fairway after him. Tall, blond, and lean, Dad still resembled the state-champion track star I'd seen in his high-school photos. His shoulders made a sturdy square and his midsection had thickened, but his long arms, graceful hands, and lanky legs gave him the look of a marathoner.

None of this computed.

It's in my bones.

Dad watched while I hit and hit. He continued to make suggestions. My mind continued to yell as I tried to follow. When thoughts of his illness crept into my consciousness, I pushed them aside, stared at the little white ball, and begged myself to be patient with my lack of golf acumen. Eventually, I hit my ball over the creek and onto the green. Dad hit his ball into the hole in one stroke. It took me three.

Dad made par on the second hole. I stopped counting strokes at twelve.

As we walked to the third tee, he chatted about the sandwiches he packed for his golf teammates in Bullhead City. My mouth tightened.

When we headed to four, he said, "Two of those guys had never eaten fried bologna!"

Wondering if he had forgotten why he and my mother had come home early, I interrupted, "When do you see the doctor?"

He continued toward the tee markers as if he hadn't heard. He teed up his ball and hit it. As he watched it sail down the fairway, he said, "Monday," and walked away.

We played the rest of the hole in silence.

"What's the doctor's name?" I asked as we walked toward number five.

He shrugged. "Your mother's handling the details."

A Canada goose stood near a shrub on the fairway. He pointed and asked, "Remember when that goose bit Chad?" speaking of my brother Jim's youngest son, then nine. "He didn't believe me when I told him they would bite."

I remained silent, assuming he had intentionally changed the subject.

"They're just protecting their young," he added, then pointed out trees he had missed over the winter. "She's lovely," he said of one enormous oak that shaded the cart path.

To me, the trees Dad admired looked tired and ragged, their branches sagging under the weight of heavy leaves. I didn't care about them; I only cared about how he felt. I wanted to crawl inside his head, his heart. When he talked about fried bologna and trees instead of cancer, I wanted to scream.

Dad motioned toward a bare spot on the fairway. "I forgot my grass seed." My father was forever tending the courses as he played. While I marveled at how normal he acted, I also bristled. He didn't want to talk about his illness, the most important topic. It was as if a balloon was blowing up in my chest.

We'd both always wanted more from each other than either could give. I wanted him to confide in me, to share his emotions and speak of things we didn't name.

He wanted action. He wanted me to work, be steady and secure.

I wanted empathy. He wanted logic.

We both fell short.

I pretended to be emotionally stable. He pretended to be physically healthy. In fact, as soon as Dad had arrived back in Ohio, he insisted on playing golf before he even saw a doctor. Meanwhile, I hung on his every word.

The way he dodged questions showed me what he wanted: to play golf as if nothing had changed. And I wasn't sure of my place. Should I challenge him? Should I go along with what seemed like a ruse?

I rubbed my eyes and tried to focus.

Could I just play golf, just be his daughter, now, today, without needing him to talk about his illness?

I struggled to bring my mind into the present the way I was learning to do in meditation. For an instant, I sensed my heels against the soft insoles of my shoes. Then, my mind spun with images of hospital beds and the nagging question of how a daughter who is struggling herself should act after cancer has invaded her father's bones.

When Dad drove the green again on number seven, I asked, "Do you want me to just drop my ball where yours lands and play from there?" The macramé stroke counter on my belt held twelve beads, and I needed every last one to keep my score.

The game took all afternoon. The grass, persistent beneath my feet, helped me refocus as I continued to hit, and walk, and hit.

At the next tee, the questions swelled in my throat as my lack of golf skill compounded the agony. The biggest question, one I hadn't let myself think, edged into consciousness.

How do little girls live without their daddies?

Something snapped. I snatched the ball off the grass, hurled it at the green with a grunt, then froze.

"No cheating!" he yelled.

I pivoted toward him as the word "fuck" formed on my lips.

But he was laughing, glowing like a man at complete ease, happy and calm in the moment. I swallowed, caught myself, and began to laugh, too. The pressure in my chest eased as I folded myself back into the small, peaceful shape we both knew.

I putted the ball into the hole and we both drove again. With each stroke, I noticed myself waiting for him to say something positive. He did not, so I trained my eyes on the deep green grass. When my mind began to spin, I focused on the shape of the little white orb and the joy that radiated inside me from the simple experience of being near my dad. My game didn't improve, and the questions continued to nag, but I kept playing.

On we played to the ninth and final tee.

After carefully setting up the shot and taking his three prac-tice swings, Dad hit a long, straight drive that bounced on the fringe and landed high on the green, an easy putt away from the hole.

I shouted, "No wonder you won that championship. You're unstoppable!"

He continued to stare toward the ball he'd just hit. I thought he hadn't heard me. When he slowly turned, he glared at the ground near my feet as if inspecting a spot in the grass. Without lifting his head, he said in a low, gravelly voice, "You know, I've got the curse."

"Curse?"

"The Chaparral Golf Club Championship Curse."

I leaned on my cart. Chaparral was the course in Arizona on which my parents lived. When he looked up, his eyes were dark. He gazed into the distance over my right shoulder.

"I thought I'd broken it."

A pit formed in my stomach.

"Every year for the past few years the winner has gotten sick and died."

I stared at the smooth green fairway, noticed a patch of dry grass I hadn't seen before, then looked at him.

He shifted his weight from one foot to the other. His voice cracked.

"Guess I'll have to beat it."

Chapter 2

Road Lawyer

With our game complete, Dad and I loaded our clubs and ourselves into Mom and Dad's Honda station wagon, and he pointed the car toward the house where Ed and I lived.

Long before Dad's diagnosis, my parents had reserved a tiny Airstream trailer at an RV park near Johnstown, Ohio, down the road from the fifty-acre farm where I grew up. They had rented out the house on the farm to my sister, Amy, when they moved to Arizona. She lived there with her twelve-year-old daughter, Jamey. The small house, still cluttered with Mom's possessions, wasn't sufficiently large for the four of them to stay together over the summer. But the RV park was close enough for Dad to fix things and for Mom to watch Jamey while Amy worked full time in Columbus at The Ohio State University, where she also took classes to finish her bachelor's degree.

When my parents came home early for Dad's medical appointments, however, the Airstream wasn't ready. So, for a few months after they returned to Ohio, Mom and Dad stayed with Ed, me, and our two dogs. Our house was only ten minutes from The Ohio State University Medical Center, whereas the farm was a forty-five-minute drive. Mom and Dad could more easily manage the initial flurry of doctor and clinic visits from our home.

As Dad drove their Honda wagon back to our house—not too fast, not too slow, and always centered in the proper lane—I marveled at the spring green. Four months ago, my depression would have reduced these colors to dull shades of slate and brown.

I also marveled at life's timing.

Had my father's cancer sprouted even one year earlier, before my career fell apart, I would have taken his call on the speakerphone in my Volvo wagon as I gulped coffee while passing a semi-tractor trailer on the right at eighty miles per hour. If I hadn't quit smoking a decade before, I would have been steering with my knees, a coffee in one hand and a cigarette in the other. Like my father, I would have steadied the vehicle in the center of the lane, but traveling at a much faster pace than he would have approved of.

At the firm, we called ourselves "Road Lawyers" because we met our clients at their offices instead of asking them to come to us. When I wasn't racing along Ohio roadways, I was in the law library or my own office doing "important" things. I would have shrugged off Dad's invitation to play golf on a Thursday with, "I'd love to, but . . ." and instead spent the day poring over labor contracts, policy manuals, and marriage dissolution paperwork. Too busy to spend more than a few weekends with my family, I occasionally visited my parents on Sunday afternoons. While my father's medical situation would have slowed me enough to find more time than usual to spend with them, it would not have included a weekday golf outing that didn't involve clients.

As Dad drove along, neither of us spoke. Tired from both the physical and emotional exertion of our game, I closed my eyes. He was a man of few words and I rarely knew what to say to him. That had always been true. But now, the specter of his diagnosis and the brain fog from my mental illness widened the wedge between us. *Is he afraid? What does he need from me?* The thoughts bubbled in my chest and sometimes made their way to my throat where they stuck like sand.

When the turn signal began to click, I opened my eyes. Dad made the left onto Riverside Drive and Scioto Country Club came into view. The well-manicured lawn, clubhouse set high on a hill up a long driveway, and tall trees shrouding it in secrecy reminded me of what I had thought being an attorney would mean.

But I never played that course, never belonged there, and now couldn't imagine wanting to. Dad drove on, eyes fixed ahead, and the Country Club disappeared behind us.

While I loved my father and knew he loved me, I never thought I measured up to his standards. I'm not sure what my father wanted me to be when I grew up, but it wasn't a lawyer. It also wasn't a writer.

⌣ ⌣ ⌣

On an autumn evening during my grade school years, I greeted Dad at the side door carrying the "book" I'd written. He'd just gotten home and barely had a chance to remove his coat and set down his briefcase before I shoved the thing into his hands.

Our teacher had shown us how to bind our manuscripts and create something resembling the library books I devoured in my spare time. For the project, I'd eagerly rewritten my favorite horse story. I didn't yet believe that the tales I made up on my own were worth telling. So, I changed names and details, titled it "Sheeshak the Wild Stallion," and typed it up.

Binding the work proved more difficult than the teacher had made it look and the results showed my lack of precision and effort. On the title page, my teacher wrote that she wished I had spent more time on the binding, but praised the story, noted that I had typed it myself, and gave the work an "A–."

Brimming with pride, I handed the book to my father and proclaimed, "I'm going to be a writer when I grow up."

He turned my "masterpiece" over in his hands, examining the shoddy binding and uneven edges. He rifled through the pages without reading them then pointed out the mismatched edges and crooked lettering.

"Writing is an excellent skill," he said. "It will serve you in whatever profession you choose." He handed the book back and asked Mom what was for dinner.

I swallowed salty tears, wordlessly trotted down the hall to my room, and put the book in the back of my closet.

When it came time for college, my father's admonition that writing was a "skill" not a "profession" pushed me away from the "frivolous" creative writing my heart wanted toward the seeming safety of journalism and, eventually, law.

Continuing a long-time pattern of keeping things from my parents, I did not talk to them about going to law school until I'd made the decision. One weekend during my final year of college, when Dad and I visited his parents, I chose the two-and-a-half-hour drive as the time to tell him. We would be alone, uninterrupted, and I wouldn't have to look at him.

It rained the entire drive up, all during our short visit, and continued to pour as we headed home. While the dark Ohio skies unleashed their fury, I thought about what to say.

Half an hour from the farm, I mustered the courage to speak. Staring at the rain-blurred dotted white line down the middle of the road, I flatly said, "I've decided to go to law school."

The car hydroplaned slightly and Dad righted it.

"Law school?" he chortled.

I stared at the water-logged road.

"I just can't see you . . ." his voice trailed off.

Trying to sound upbeat, I said, "I did really well on the LSAT."

Out of the corner of my eye, I caught his shrug. "It's just a test," he said. "Doesn't mean anything."

I turned and stared at his profile. His hair was combed back from his wide forehead, the same wide forehead I see when I look in the mirror.

"What do you want me to do?" I said, my voice rising.

"Graduate! Get a job!" he shouted.

"I don't want to be a journalist!" I shouted back.

His voice dropped. "You don't know what you want."

This was true, but I didn't respond.

"And who do you expect to pay for this?" he added darkly.

My voice cracked, "I'll get another job, another student loan, take a year off and work to save money if I have to."

"If you take a year off, you'll never go back."

I clamped my jaw. His doubt steeled my determination. In my mind I whispered, "I'll show you. I'll show you. I'll show you," in time with the wiper blades.

Perhaps Dad couldn't imagine me in law school because while Mom and Dad had both attended college, neither had finished. And the jobs they later held were unrelated to their studies. Mom, a home economics education major, first worked in "traffic" at the Ford Motor plant overseeing shipments, but was most successful selling cosmetics. Dad, an industrial arts education major, became a lineman then a manager and then an executive at the phone company from which he retired more than three decades later.

Dad had completed all of his college work except for student teaching. When I asked why he hadn't finished, he flatly replied, "I was afraid I'd kill the children." Mom dropped out after Dad got a job in Sandusky and they moved there. Dad sometimes regaled us with tales from the diner where he worked as a short-order cook. And Mom still bore a grudge against a roommate who wore her clothes without asking. Otherwise, they rarely spoke of their college years.

My father's skepticism fueled me. I applied for and received student loans and scholarships, worked several part-time jobs, finished my undergraduate degree in three years, attended law school, and spent the next decade building the kind of career I thought would make him proud.

For a while, it worked. I became what I thought he wanted: successful, professional, important. I spent so many hours at the office and talked about it so frequently that a friend finally said, "You think your last name is 'Attorney at Law.'" She hadn't intended it as a compliment, but her words made me glow.

My job sometimes required me to spend weekends at the office. But my Saturday and Sunday hours were more about proving my work ethic, satisfying the internal scorekeeper that ruled my psyche. Because the empty halls of the office building echoed, I brought along Maxine, our black Labrador retriever. She was tall for her breed and quietly protective, but stayed out of sight, lying on the carpeted floor between the two side chairs.

One night, when a male consultant stepped through my open doorway, Maxi silently stood to her full height and peered over my desk, dark eyes daring him to step closer. When, at first, he didn't see her, a low growl warned him to stop.

"Shit!" he exclaimed, and stepped back into the hallway.

"Maxine, down," I said.

She slowly folded her sleek, black body back onto the carpet while keeping him in sight.

"She's actually quite friendly," I said. "You can come in."

"I'll stay right here," he said and we continued our conversation under her watchful eye with him still in the hallway.

"Left here?" Dad asked, interrupting my lapse into memory.

"No!" I replied, my voice sharp in my ears. I took a deep breath then added, "That's the way to the office."

Dad nodded. He steered the car to the right and my throat relaxed.

As my career progressed, Dad softened. One weekday, Mom and Dad picked me up at my office. When I greeted them in the lobby, Dad pointed to the large window which bore the firm's name. My last name, along with those of the other partners, was emblazoned in gold letters on the glass.

"Nice!" he said.

Then he gestured toward my attire: a silk blouse beneath a well-made suit, pearls, and pumps.

"You look so professional," he said. "They must be paying you well."

I blushed.

I had never relaxed into attorney garb. The clothes served as armor. I preferred farm girl jeans, but wanted to look the part. Dressed to the nines, I felt strong and important, things I rarely believed of myself. Dad's appreciation mattered. To him, whether on the golf course or in the boardroom, the appropriate clothes marked success.

In my Volvo station wagon, speeding to law libraries, administrative agencies, and clients' offices, I was comfortable. That car suited me: fancy, but practical. Expensive, but useful. The senior partner suggested I add a car phone. I had arrived.

Out of all my legal tasks, I most enjoyed research and writing, advising clients, and speaking at conferences. The law library and the podium felt like home.

Then, one morning when I was riding with the senior partner in his BMW sedan to visit a client an hour away, he brought up my position at the firm.

"How would you feel about taking on some trial work?" he asked. The senior partner always had more faith in me than I had in myself. And I did my best not to let him think otherwise. But the idea of trial work made my stomach lurch.

I fixed my eyes on the road ahead and clasped my hands together to still their trembling, terror shivering through me.

"I could try," I said with a shrug.

"Good. The clients like you. It'll be great," he said.

I did not think it would be great.

Instead of letting me stay in the background, he wanted me to leave my comfort zone. It meant being the lead attorney at trial, a role I did not want and for which I did not believe I was suited. The paper chase battles I fought when researching cases, writing documents, advising clients, and speaking at conferences may not seem that different from in-person conflict. But I already knew I was especially sensitive to anything with a face. In journalism school, I had balked when asked to push sources for juicy information. In law school, I'd nearly fainted during a mock interview. A deep part of me knew I was not up to this task.

But I lacked the fortitude to tell the senior partner about my fear. In the same way I had always wanted to please my father, I wanted the senior partner to admire me as well. I told myself I would do my best and see what happened.

Dad drove the rest of the route home the way he always did—at a continuous pace, hands steady on the wheel. Attention and evenness were what he offered, and, especially right now, what we both needed. As I watched him navigate the familiar streets with his characteristic precision, I wondered if he knew how much of my life had been shaped by trying to prove myself to him.

He expertly parked the station wagon in the drive at our house, then he and I unloaded the clubs. Watching him heft the golf bag and easily roll the cart into the corner of the garage, I caught myself thinking, *Is he really that sick*?

I also wondered how, in my sometimes frail, still very depressed state, I could be present for him and my family. The term "try" has a bad reputation, but that's what popped into my mind—the same "try" I had promised the senior partner.

Mental illness had shattered me. But standing in our driveway, watching Dad stow the golf gear in the garage with the same careful attention he brought to everything, I knew my time to figure out how to talk to him was limited. I didn't know if I could do it, but vowed to do my best. I vowed to try.

CHAPTER 3

YOUR FATHER TOOK A NAP

A few days after my father and I played that earlier-than-usual first round of golf of the season, Mom and I went to lunch at one of our favorite Columbus restaurants, La Chatelaine.

As we supped on the French bistro's specialty, Caesar salad, French onion soup, and sourdough bread with salted butter, I brought up Dad's health.

"When did you notice something was wrong?" I asked, lifting my spoon.

Mom set down her cup of decaf.

"Your father took a nap," she said.

I nearly dropped my spoon.

Mom explained.

One sunny Arizona day five months before, Dad had returned home after playing nine holes instead of his usual eighteen. Rather than sit at the table for a cold drink to rest before returning to the course, he'd told her, "I think I'll lie down for a little while."

Mom said, "I stared at him with my mouth open."

I understood why. My father was notoriously anti-nap. Throughout my childhood, pointedly within my napping mother's earshot, Dad would explain: "If I lie down during the daytime, I can't sleep at night." His message was clear. Anyone worth their salt stayed up. If he took a nap, it was a clear sign of distress.

Once, on a Sunday afternoon when I was eight, Dad had a rare cold—one of the few ailments that previously ever plagued him. When Mom asked me to wake him for dinner, I timidly entered the dark bedroom and stood by the bed, listening to him snore. He lay on his back, arms folded over his chest like a dead giant.

I watched his chest rise and fall a few times before summoning the courage to mutter, "D-dad?" When he stirred, I tried again, louder. "Dad? It's time for dinner."

He startled awake, raised himself on one arm, and stared into the dim room. He rubbed his eyes and his face screwed up as he registered my presence. I stood frozen.

Dad wasn't the kind of father who yelled or hit. But my internal radar was finely tuned to his emotions. A raised eyebrow from him stung the way I imagined a smack from someone else's parent might. Whether he reared me that way or whether I was naturally hypersensitive, I don't know—likely a combination of both, and a precursor to the mood instability that would plague my adult years.

Dad rolled toward the nightstand, reached for his rectangular wire-rimmed glasses, and shook his head. "Damn. I hate to sleep in the daytime." He swung his legs over the side of the bed, stood, and strode past me into the hallway. When he disappeared into the bathroom, I exhaled.

Mom responded to Dad's anti-napping proclamations by ignoring him. She was so much shorter than him that if she wanted to look him in the eye she had to step back and crane her neck. Her small stature made it easier to avoid his intensity. Instead of facing him, she took a nap. Or, she waited until he left the house and complained to me about his criticism.

Dad's illness caught our family off guard. Our mother, not our father, had been the family napper and the one frequently ill. The more Dad complained about Mom's napping, the more time she spent in bed. Her medicine, herb, and vitamin bottles lined the kitchen counters while remedy jars clogged the refrigerator. As a child, I accompanied her to countless doctors including general practitioners, osteopaths, chiropractors, naturopaths, and specialists for her catalog of chronic ailments. Much to my father's consternation, every practitioner recommended supplements and rest, aka "naps." Mom was rarely acutely ill, but always chronically under the weather, while my father remained hearty and hale.

As I recall, the only earlier scrape my family had with the possibility of my fit-as-a-fiddle father's mortality came when I was in my late twenties. Mom called me at the law office to explain that he'd been struck with Bell's palsy. "It looks as if half his face slid downhill," Mom said.

I drove to the farm to see them. Mom's description did not prepare me for the racing heart and light-headed spin that hit me when I saw Dad's drooping eye and lip. Bell's palsy had transformed my handsome father's face into an unrecognizable mask. We sat at the kitchen table drinking coffee and I tried to laugh with them about it, but I could understand little of what he said. I drove home weeping. I didn't know what risks Bell's palsy carried and in those days before the internet, I couldn't research it. For the first time, I wondered what it would be like to lose him.

In the days that followed, I sat at my law office desk waiting for Mom to call with news. Already struggling to focus at work, I aimed my obsessive anxiety toward my father and fought to squelch fears that the paralysis would spread to the rest of his body.

When I visited Dad a few weeks later, he was again the smiling man I remembered. His doctor had received a "sample" electrical nerve stimulator in the mail shortly before Dad consulted him. "Something from California," Dad said, demonstrating. Ever the good student, my father had used the device religiously to jolt the muscles and keep them from atrophying while the virus ran its course. His muscle tension returned with no lasting impairment.

Grateful and relieved, I slid behind the wheel of my car, back into my lawyer life and the daughterly illusion that my beer-drinking, poker-playing, post-hole digging, electric-fence fixing, telephone-pole climbing, Catholic-mass-on-occasional-Sundays father, would live forever.

⚬ ⚬ ⚬

Lifting my own cup of decaf, I asked Mom, "Was there anything else?" I hungered for clues as to how our family missed what now seemed obvious about my father's cancer.

"Oh yes," she said, as her long, slender fingers lifted the white ceramic cup to her gloss-pink lips.

As a young woman, my mother had been a beauty. Photos show her with dark brown hair and pale olive skin that contrasted sharply with Wedgwood-blue eyes and tiny features. When I was little, Mom sold cosmetics successfully enough to rise to manager with the Beauty Counselor line. Even after we moved to the farm and she no longer worked the accounts, she walked around the house with her face slathered in light pink "pick-up cream."

"People used to say I looked like Elizabeth Taylor," she often reminded me as she layered a second coat of mascara onto her long eyelashes. She manicured her nails at the kitchen table with the tools you might see at a salon. When Dad joined the Catholic men's group, the Knights of Columbus, formal events gave her an opportunity to display her finery.

Now, at sixty-five, snow-white hair framed her heart-shaped face. Polished nails had given way to a well-buffed manicure, but Mom still shone.

Her second and biggest clue about Dad's illness, as she told it, had come a few weeks after the alarming nap and a few months before his diagnosis.

The pair had played their usual Fun Sunday golf with other couples who lived near the course. The Arizona sky shone a glorious blue, but the typical winter winds blew hard through the palm trees. Even Mom's matching fuchsia windbreaker and rain pants hadn't kept her warm.

Golf never captured Mom the way it had my father and her frequent illnesses reduced her stamina. She played no more than nine holes once a week and worried the women who played every day thought less of her for it.

"We finished our first trip around the course," Mom said. "And I told him I was going home. I'd had enough of that damned wind for one day."

I pictured her turning her full five-foot-one frame toward my tall father, looking up at him from beneath her pink visor and saying, *I'm done.* She expected him to reprove her, as was his habit. She anticipated the familiar lecture about how she would never improve if she didn't play all eighteen.

Instead, he touched the right side of his chest.

"I've got a pain in my ribs," he said. "I think I'll quit too."

Mom said he looked stooped.

"Should I call a doctor?" she asked.

"Naw," he said, shaking his head. "I probably just swung the club wrong."

He put his putter away and they rode the cart back to their house on the fourth tee.

Contrast that nine-hole day to a Sunday from a few years earlier when my parents lived in Oceanside, California. Ever the salesperson, Mom worked as a hostess at Oasis Country Club showing expensive condos to prospective buyers. As a perk, Dad had free access to the well-groomed course and one of the club's gray Mercedes carts.

While Mom and the manager, Dottie, worked, Dad played. The cart path passed the office, allowing Mom to see him every time he finished a round.

As the hours passed, Dad drove by again and again. Eventually, he stopped in.

With Dottie in earshot, Mom asked him how many holes he'd played.

"Your father beamed," she said. "'After the next hole, it'll be fifty-two.'"

Dottie nearly spat out her dentures. "That's got to be a course record!"

Dad just nodded and headed back out.

That was the father we knew.

⚬ ⚬ ⚬

As Mom continued, my meal began to taste bland and flat. *Why hadn't I known what was happening with my father?* Naturally hypervigilant, I'd long played the role of family mediator and fixer. I tried to ward off problems before they happened, resolve conflicts once they arose, and shield everyone from sadness and fear.

In high school, these instincts kicked in after my directionally-challenged older sister, Amy, was cited in a car accident. Intending to turn left, she mistakenly activated her right signal. The man behind her began to pass her on the left as she turned into his path. The officer faulted Amy.

I was studying for the Ohio driver's test at the time. When I learned it is illegal to pass a car in an intersection, I told my sister. She argued this and was cleared. Despite her having a part in causing the accident, I stepped in to ensure the conflict would be resolved in her favor: to protect her. Only later did I realize that I held onto this family role as a way to protect myself as well.

While I pushed the onions around in my soup, spooning up the broth, thoughts ricocheted through my mind. If I had known Dad was sick, maybe I could have convinced him to see a doctor earlier. I'd been so consumed with my own struggles. Had I not wanted to see the obvious signs? Playing protector meant I should not fall apart, but I was already on a downward spiral.

And was his delay my fault, too? In the months before Dad's diagnosis and their early return to Ohio, he'd been preoccupied in ways Mom hadn't known at the time.

When Dad turned fifty, Mom pulled off an incredible surprise party for him at the farm. In the years since, she dropped hints that she wanted a party of her own. So far, she hadn't gotten one. On March 1st of 1995, the year Dad's cancer would later be discovered, Mom would turn sixty-five. I decided she was past due.

In January, two months ahead of her birthday, I called Dad when I believed Mom would be out. I asked him to plan the surprise. My siblings, my husband, and I would fly to Vegas and drive to Arizona to join them for a party at the clubhouse if he would organize it.

Dad hesitated. "I'm not good at that type of thing."

Still, he agreed. In a later call he admitted, "I'm so nervous. I'm afraid I'll spoil the surprise."

"You won't," I assured him. "She doesn't have a clue."

I often forgot what a worrier he was beneath that rough exterior: concrete outside with a jelly center. What I didn't tell him was that I couldn't plan the party myself because I continued to struggle emotionally. Therapy appointments filled my calendar and I required frequent naps. Between that and the medication, I had neither the focus nor the energy for details. I needed him to handle this.

I insisted that we arrive at my parents' house on Mom's actual birthday. But because of my siblings' work schedules, we didn't land until late evening. By the time we walked into their house, it was 2:00 am on March 2nd.

We stood around Mom's bed, waking her from a sound sleep.

"Am I dying?" she cried.

Our showing up in the middle of the night had been a mistake. We reassured her, hugged and kissed her, and all headed for bed.

Once the secret was out, Dad relaxed and celebrated thoroughly. The whole family played golf and, on the weekend, Ed and our extended family joined us. In the photos, Dad beams with pride at having helped plan something he would never have done without my push.

Still, I wondered: had this extra strain caused him to put off seeing a doctor? If he hadn't been so anxious about spoiling the surprise, would he have attended to that pain in his ribs sooner? Had it really needed to be a surprise?

I reminded myself that by the time he sensed that pain, the cancer was already in his bones.

Until our conversation at La Chatelaine, Mom had told me nothing about Dad's uncharacteristic nap or her suspicion that something might be wrong. As I fished out the bits of baguette from my comforting soup, I considered asking why she hadn't told me. I'd long served as confidante to both parents. Her silence was unusual.

But I swallowed the urge. I wouldn't add to her burden.

Perhaps she'd watched him walk down the hall, his shoulders stooped. Perhaps she tucked her fears away. Perhaps she expressed it to an Arizona neighbor. More likely, she busied herself painting shirts and playing piano at the nearby senior center to fill her days and mind. But she hadn't pushed Dad to see a doctor and she hadn't told me or my siblings what she suspected.

After Mom's birthday party, I had stayed on in Arizona for a few days. One morning, Dad and I drove to Albertsons grocery. The smell of rotisserie chicken and fresh baked bread filled the store.

Dad's eyes caught a plate of smoked sausage samples. In retirement, he and Mom grazed their lunches here. We split up to shop.

When I finished, I waited on a bench near the entrance. Dad returned coughing and rubbing his throat. His skin looked gray and his eyes watery.

A wave of panic surged in me. "Should I call the squad?"

He shook me away. "A piece of sausage went down the wrong pipe."

He kept coughing and trying to swallow, then sat.

"I just need to sit a minute."

I left to get a cup of water from a cart at the back of the store. As I returned, Dad passed me.

"Bathroom," he said, choking out the word. "Back in a minute."

I waited. I told myself he'd be *fine as frog hair* hearing his voice in my head.

I took a gecko-printed t-shirt from my bag and traced the raised design. Refolded it. Put it back.

Should I call the manager? No. He'd be fine.

Five minutes passed. Then ten.

My heart hammered against my ribs as my mind spun with familiar rules. *Don't make a scene. Don't embarrass him.*

A gray-haired man with a name tag reading "Bob" walked past. I asked if he would check on Dad.

"Sure, hon. What's his name?"

"Gene." I shivered.

I imagined Dad slumped on the floor, blue. Why hadn't I asked sooner? I hadn't wanted to "make a big deal out of it." I closed my eyes and tried to focus on my breath as the seconds ticked away in my head.

Bob returned.

"That sausage got stuck," he said. "He threw it up. Happens to us old folks."

A few minutes later, Dad emerged, walking slowly from the back of the store. I rushed to him, forgetting to act calm.

He raised his hand. "I'm fine. Just trouble swallowing."

"Bob told me you threw up," I said. I wanted more from him, but feared asking.

"Has to go down or come up, and it wouldn't go down."

His face was red and his eyes bloodshot. I thought about asking if he needed me to take him to the urgent care, but his downturned mouth and the familiar wall of his height kept me from pushing further.

"I need to go home and lie down," he said.

Lie down? The nap alarm sounded in my head, but I stayed quiet.

After a wordless five-minute drive to their house, he said, "Let's not worry your mother."

On the farm, a decade before, Dad had asked the same thing of me.

I'd ridden into the woods on the back fender of the Allis-Chalmers tractor to help him pull down dead trees that had landed on their healthy neighbors. He stopped at a fallen tree and I jumped off.

The tree leaned at a forty-five-degree angle against a larger, healthy maple. Dad maneuvered the tractor up to the fallen tree's root ball, jumped down, and wrapped the log chain around the trunk. His leather-gloved hands worked quickly and a shock of his light hair fell across his brow from beneath his black International Harvester baseball cap.

With the chain secure, he motioned. I walked far enough away that I could barely see the tractor, then turned as Dad put the Allis in gear and slowly released the clutch. While the tractor edged forward, Dad faced backward toward the trunk of the fallen tree to watch it come down.

The Allis pulled the tree nicely for a foot or so. Every other tree I had seen him fell had cooperated. The roots of those trees pulled free and the trunk gently slid until it and the branches lay peacefully on the ground. Confident this tree would behave the same, I gazed down at the thick leaves that formed a fall-colored carpet on the woods' floor.

A loud crack and a sharp swoosh snapped me back to attention. The front of the tractor jumped and the chain tightened. The top of the tree flew into the air over its roots as if someone was trying to stand it up again. It landed sideways on the tractor with a sickening crack. Branches and browning leaves shrouded my view.

I ran toward the tree-covered machine.

"Dad!"

Silence.

"Daaaaaaaaad!"

Once I reached the tractor, I grasped the nearest branch and pulled. It gave way and I fell to the ground.

Then I heard laughter as he came into view, brushing leaves from his hair.

"That didn't go the way I'd planned," he said, retrieving his cap.

"Why didn't you answer me?"

"I was looking for my hat," he said, helping me up.

"For Christ's sake! Are you okay?"

"Hat's okay. Everything's fine," he said and tugged it over his head.

I dusted myself off and pointed at the tractor. The smokestack was bent into a U-shape.

"Oops," he said. "I can fix that." He started to reach for the hot pipe then reconsidered.

"I suppose you could say the tree is down," I said.

"You could say that."

When the smokestack had cooled, he bent it back using both hands, but a large crease and a wide dent remained.

As we rode back to the barn, he pointed at the pipe and shouted, "Think your mother will notice?"

"Don't know."

"Let's not worry her."

The secrets Dad and I shared were usually small: a new Craftsman wrench, a few too many beers at the local tavern, or the "mad money" he kept in his wallet. I imagined myself special to him because he trusted me.

Mom and I also had secrets, but they were different. With her, I was both accomplice and beneficiary. She never told Dad about our new outfits, our dinner at an expensive restaurant, or the boy's name she caught me writing in a tiny journal.

I didn't understand the dynamic. I only knew it was comfortable, like my well-worn jeans. It's what we did.

"No problem, Dad."

But in their driveway in Arizona after he'd been unable to swallow that sausage sample, I reacted differently. Our bond of secrecy didn't hold up against the waves of dread that had filled my body while I'd waited on that bench.

Instead of nodding the way I had when I was younger, I acted on the urgent throbbing at my temples.

"You gonna get that checked?" I asked.

"She'll just worry."

"Should I tell her, or do you want me to call the doctor?"

He sat, thinking. Then, sensing the change in me, he said, "Okay." Then added, "But I'm fine now."

After I returned home to Ohio from my Arizona visit, a test for Dad's swallowing problem revealed the "spot" on his lung. Further tests led to his cancer diagnosis.

⬤ ⬤ ⬤

I'd never been involved in Dad's health matters the way I'd been with Mom's. Distance, my own life, and their adulthood made it easy not to know. Still, guilt flooded me. I berated myself for not recognizing my father's decline and putting together the pieces of his illness.

While Mom and I put on our coats, I replayed the Albertsons scene in my head. In my parents' Arizona driveway, I'd broken our agreement to keep things from Mom. As a result, they'd found the spot on his lung. I wished I'd seen the signs sooner. Mom had, but didn't recognize them as signals. Because Dad was rarely sick, any of us might have pushed away that tug of fear. In protecting each other, we were all complicit in his delay.

When we reached the car, she turned to me.

"Besides," she said, tilting her chin and clenching her jaw, "he wouldn't go to a doctor until he was damned well good and ready."

She was right, of course. I reached for her and we hugged deeply, two women who loved the same stubborn man.

CHAPTER 4

SYNCHRONIZED CRYING CLUB

"Wait 'til you see this room!" Dad said. "It has the best view of campus anywhere."

The week after Mom and I dined at La Chatelaine, she, Ed, and I accompanied Dad to his first session of a cancer support group. The pleasant and familiar scent of Old Spice cologne wafted past me as I followed Dad off the elevator to the top floor of the James Cancer Hospital at The Ohio State University.

Mom, Dad, and Amy had toured the hospital when he saw the first of several cancer doctors and began radiation. While a scan had shown cancer in his bones, he did not yet have a prognosis or a full treatment plan. We all believed radiation would be the next of many steps.

Dad confidently pointed our group toward the door and we filed into a room filled with soft chairs around a table. While the others folded themselves into the chairs, I walked to one of the large windows that overlooked the "Horseshoe" stadium, St. John Arena, and the Scioto River beyond. The elevated view reduced the towering buildings that had dwarfed me during my law school years on this campus to miniatures I might pick up and move with my bare hands.

After a few minutes, a kind-faced blonde woman, one of the hospital's social workers, joined us. In a low, modulated voice, Kind Face explained that the group ordinarily included several families and patients, but today it was just us.

She turned to him. "Are you comfortable telling us a little bit about how you're feeling?"

When Dad opened his mouth to speak, his cheerful expression crumpled and his eyes filled.

I shifted in my chair. *Be supportive,* my mind said. I wanted him to express his feelings and his refusal to talk about it during our Wilson Road golf outing had frustrated me to no end.

But now, watching him cry, I squirmed. I don't remember seeing him in tears ever before, not even at his mother or father's funerals. Fathers were not supposed to cry, especially not my father.

Dad took a deep breath, stared down at the table, and rearranged his face to force away the tears.

When he looked up and spoke, his voice was clear. "I just feel so sorry for what I'm putting my family through."

Now, I was confused. Sure, he was our rock, but wasn't he afraid? Mad? Depressed? Where were those "feelings" worksheets from my therapy group? If he could circle the corresponding face, I might have a clue about the kind of daughter he needed me to be.

The social worker also looked puzzled. "Would you be willing to say more about that?"

Dad continued. "I'm supposed to be the one who looks after my family. Now they're going to have to look after me."

She let space surround his words.

My insides jiggled like gelatin. I'd spent years wanting him to soften. Now that he had, I couldn't look at him.

I noticed my leg bouncing and stopped it. Why couldn't I be steady like him or let the thoughts and body sensations flow through me the way my meditation teachers instructed? I didn't trust myself to stay sane through Dad's illness. An image of my body flying apart, pieces sailing into the cosmos flashed through my mind.

Would Kind Face help us navigate these rocky emotional waters?

No, I thought. *She won't.*

After all, Kind Face wasn't Harri.

A few months before this, I'd begun group therapy with Harri, short for "Harriet." A tall woman with olive skin and curly, waist-length black hair, she facilitated our group with a firm hand. Her dropped-waist dresses and jumpers with t-shirts demonstrated that a strong woman didn't need her clothes to double as armor. I soon abandoned my business casual attire in favor of her more comfortable style.

The week before, Harri had urged me to tell the group how afraid I was to ask my father how he felt about his illness. When I balked, she encouraged me. When I cried, she handed me a tissue.

Harri only let silence last long enough for it to be effective and usually came armed with handouts and exercises, crayons and pens.

One day shortly after Dad's diagnosis, she gave us papers that had a large spider's web printed on each sheet. She asked us to write the names of supportive family members and friends on the strands of the web, identifying our safety net. I paused before including Dad on the web. Harri asked about my hesitation.

"Won't he need my help more than I need his?" I asked.

"Are you afraid he won't be able to help you while he's sick?"

My pen hovered over the web worksheet before I wrote his name. Harri smiled and tucked a long black curl behind her ear.

The therapy group I attended met in a windowless gray space at the center of a suburban office building. That room enclosed us like a cave, while this room lifted my family as if it were a cloud.

In Dad's cancer support group, I wanted the social worker to press him the way Harri pressed me. With Harri, I'd learned the benefit of putting things on the line. But I wasn't ready to do that with Dad. I wanted the social worker to ask the questions I couldn't, to pull a Harri-style intervention.

But this woman knew none of our family history or my mental health history, and she did none of the things Harri might do. This wasn't therapy. Her job was to support severely-ill patients, people who might die. Harri's mission was to keep her clients alive.

Besides, Kind Face couldn't read my mind.

For now, I had to accept that my father wouldn't answer my unspoken questions and she wouldn't ask them. Tears clogged my throat. When I choked out a small sob, the social worker turned toward me, her face as soft as her voice. I wiped my eyes, took a deep breath, and leaned toward Dad.

"You took care of us growing up. It's our turn, Dad," I said as I pulled a tissue from the box and wiped my nose. I had no idea what taking care of him might mean, but it was what I thought a supportive daughter should say.

Mom, silent and sniffling in her chair next to Dad, pulled a handkerchief from her purse and held it to her nose.

I turned to the window. Now that I was sitting, all I could see was the pale blue sky.

Ed shifted in his chair, faced Dad and said, "We want to do whatever you need." Together, we might get through this.

Dad pulled his handkerchief from his pocket and began to weep openly. Ed pulled out his handkerchief while Mom and I each reached for more tissues from the box on the table. We looked like a synchronized crying team, all blowing our noses and wiping our eyes in unison. *Dark humor*, I thought. That will help us as well.

Once the crying ceased and we composed ourselves, the social worker asked Dad if he could accept our help. As if words had vanished, he closed his eyes then nodded. When he did, something in me relaxed.

Kind Face said that our time was up and reminded us the group met weekly. "Please join us any time."

Dad hugged Ed while Mom hugged me. When I tried to let go, Mom didn't. I tensed. Would she cling to me forever? But a moment later, she released her grip and we switched.

Mom hugged Ed while I reached up to hug Dad. He wrapped his arms around me and gave me a little squeeze while I clung to him. Now I was the one who didn't want to let go. He gave me another squeeze and began to step away so I released him.

Ed and I left Dad and Mom in the room so Dad could meet with yet another doctor. I held Ed's hand tightly as we walked to the elevator. Once the doors closed, safely hiding us, I leaned into his arms.

Chapter 5

The Course that Jack Built

A few days after our visit to Dad's cancer support group, I walked into the family room where Dad pored over the sports section of *The Columbus Dispatch*. A full-page advertisement for the Memorial Tournament adorned the back page of the section he was reading. *Had he seen it?* When my mind registered the Memorial logo above a color photo of the course fairway, my breath caught. *You're not ready for this*, I thought, and considered snatching the paper from his hands.

Unlike my father, I'd taken up golf reluctantly. When I joined a law firm in 1989, my colleagues asked if I golfed. Although I hadn't picked up a club since that college class seven years earlier, I told them I did. With a set of borrowed clubs, I spent my first client outing searching for my ball and repairing divots.

Two of my friends who golfed regularly set out to tutor me. As my friends looked on, I hit the ball twelve times on the first hole. I didn't look at their faces, only at the ball. When one friend suggested we let other foursomes play through, part of me sighed with relief, but my cheeks reddened and my inner scorekeeper bristled. Determined to improve, I continued.

On the next hole, the other friend offered tips: "Keep your head down. Don't bend your elbow." They both helped me find my ball in knee-high shrubbery and ankle-deep water. We groaned together as I missed the ball, stroke after stroke. I only cried once, when I hit the last ball of a sleeve I had just bought at the clubhouse that morning into a pond too deep to wade into. Both friends insisted I walk around the remaining water hazards.

I learned enough to feel comfortable playing with the men at the firm. As the only woman attorney, I did not want to be left out. On the farm, I had baled hay with the men, then played poker and drank Budweiser with them after. I would not be left in the office when it came time to schmooze on the golf course.

As my father told it, he took up golf in his mid-twenties when he started working as a cable splicer for the Ohio Bell Telephone Company. He and a coworker rented clubs and golfed in tennis shoes at the modest Sandusky Municipal Golf Course. When they were invited to play with some Ohio Bell executives at Plum Brook Country Club, they bought used clubs with hickory shafts, old bags, and pull carts for the special occasion. The pair acted as if they knew what they were doing and, after a few beers, they no longer cared if they didn't. But life intervened after a few years, and Dad gave up the game.

When Dad retired, he began to golf again, and our summer visits revolved around it. Although I was now in my mid-twenties, practicing law, and in a relationship, Dad and I were both still getting used to me being an adult. Without electric fence repairs or lawn care to discuss, he and I had little to talk about. Golf filled that void. In the summer, when my parents returned to Ohio, I drove to the farm a few times to see them, clubs in tow.

On one such visit, Dad met me at my car, hefting a five-gallon bucket of "lost balls," i.e. other people's balls Dad had found on various courses.

"Aren't those technically stolen?" I asked.

"Finders keepers," he said, grinning like a schoolboy.

We spent the morning in what used to be the "side pasture," driving the balls into a grove of pine trees and chipping a few around in the grass. My heart filled when I caught him smiling at a shot I chipped right where I aimed it.

At dusk, we made our last sweep of the field with flashlights to gather the balls we'd hit.

"Lookie here!" Dad exclaimed. His light revealed a ball with a cut in it. "Better get rid of this one," he said, his eyes gleaming.

He pulled out his driver, teed up the damaged orb, aimed at the fifteen acres of woods, and pounded that thing. We watched it sail above the trees then listened to the rustling as it descended through the tree canopy. I wondered if one of Dad's white torpedoes ever beaned some unsuspecting indigo bunting, but we heard no complaints.

The firm's senior partner sometimes invited Dad to "round out the foursome" at a work golf outing. The first time I called my father in the middle of the day to pass on the invitation, he sounded worried when he answered. When I explained the reason for my call, his anxiety turned to glee. "I'll meet you there in half an hour." We didn't play together, but it was enough to be on the same course at the same time and talk about it after.

I hadn't realized just how good a golfer my father had become until, during one award ceremony, the secretary of the hosting association called his name for a *third* award. That night after the charity event at Bent Tree, he took home a sleeve of balls, a new glove, and a fancy combination money clip, ball marker, and divot repair tool engraved with the association's name.

Later, when I suggested he leave after the final round the next time he played with our firm, he was nonplussed. "Those guys insisted I stay. It would be rude to refuse." I thought, but did not say, "You could have refused the gifts." If the senior partner noticed, he didn't mention it. Dad continued to receive and accept the senior partner's invitations, stay for the dinner and ceremonies, and gather awards. And I continued to enjoy his presence.

If this had been an ordinary year, Dad and I would have already begun planning our early June trek to the Memorial Tournament at Muirfield Village Golf Club in Dublin, Ohio, a few miles from the offices of the law firm.

The senior partner belonged to The Country Club at Muirfield Village, which hosted the tournament. Sometimes he offered my father and I unused client tickets. While we never had the opportunity to play the gently rolling fairways and exquisitely groomed greens of this exclusive course, he and I attended "the Memorial" as spectators several times.

This year, as I stared at my father and that newspaper ad, the 1995 Memorial Tournament was drawing near. I assumed Dad would want to go again, but that meant I would need to reach out to someone at the firm to ask about extra tickets. The thought made me nauseous.

I'm pretty sure my father thought that my scoring tickets to the Memorial Tournament was the best by-product of my practicing law. Named "the Memorial" because it honors a different golfer each year, the tournament is one of only five given "invitational" status on the PGA tour and is held on the exclusive and extremely challenging Muirfield course. The prospect of watching storied players try their swings on this course made Dad glow.

Usually, we received tickets for a practice round or the first day of the tournament. In 1993, just two years before Dad was diagnosed, Dad and I had struck gold. The senior partner gave us tickets to the final two days of that year's tournament. Dad and I had accepted them gleefully and spent two glorious days together tromping around the course.

And, it rained.

Chief Leatherlips of the Wyandot is alleged to have cursed the outing with torrential downpours because the course disturbed the site of his execution and burial. In truth, the tournament is on the opposite side of the Scioto River from where he is buried, but people, my father and I included, loved to repeat this rumor.

We parked in a flooded cornfield abandoned expressly for the tournament, trekked through ankle-deep mud to the gate, and stood in rain-soaked crowds twenty deep to watch Freddie Couples, "the Shark" Greg Norman, John Daly, and course designer and local celebrity Jack Nicklaus, play "The Course that Jack Built."

We followed Robert Gamez through the drizzle for a few holes. When he hit four balls into the pond on Number Three, Dad analyzed what the pro did wrong. About other players Dad explained what each might do when they hit into a sand trap, and how one had bent an elbow and another hadn't followed through on a swing. I marveled at Dad's knowledge and interest while a hard place inside me relaxed. The pros needed Dad's improvement, too.

As we neared a crowded concession tent, Dad stopped. "You want anything?"

"A hot dog," I said and watched his tall frame recede, easy to spot in the crowd.

When Freddie Couples missed a putt, Dad groaned and twisted his body as if he had been the one to pull a little to the left. When Greg Norman was playing the next hole, Dad bounded ahead then looked back to see if I was following. I waved him on and he took off in a slow trot to watch the Shark drive.

I drank in the rolling green of the course, the incredible tree line, and the hush that came over the crowd as a player was ready to hit. Dad lived for the precision. "Look how tidy that green is," he said, complimenting the groundskeepers. "Those edges are so sharp they could cut you, and that sand glows."

When the downpour forced play to be suspended, we headed into the Muirfield clubhouse. I followed Dad as he looked at photos of young Jack: shocks of blond hair, long limbs, and a shining smile as the "Golden Bear" held a trophy above his head. When Dad leaned forward to get a closer look, the longing in his face tugged at my heart. He could have been a bigger-time champion, a superstar, given different circumstances. Growing up the oldest son of a poor family in rural northwest Ohio hadn't given him that chance. But he had the tenacity, the focus, the will to win. At 65, with a handicap of 12, he regularly shot a respectable score and, as he reminded me earlier in the summer, recently won the club championship at the course where they lived.

My favorite part of the Memorial had nothing to do with the golf. Despite the rain, the traffic, the parking, the long lines, and bad food, we both wanted to go, but for different reasons. He longed to walk the course, watch the players, enjoy the game. I longed to see his face light up when I drew out the words, "I've . . . got . . . tickets." Who was this man I had known all my life? Watching him at the tournament taught me more about what made him happy.

But this year, in my emotionally frail state, I had not mentioned the tournament to Dad. My conflict about this gnawed at me. He had always been thrilled, and I wanted to go if he wanted to go. I just didn't want to contact the law firm. The thought of asking for anything from them now made me shrink, as if I needed to protect myself. And Dad, ever the penny pincher, wouldn't go if we had to pay.

I cleared the anxiety from my throat, pointed to the advertisement in the paper Dad was reading, and said, "It's almost Memorial time. Do you want me to find out about tickets?

Without lifting his eyes from the paper, he said, "Nah."

It took a minute for his words to register, but when they did, they landed hard in my chest. *He didn't want to go?*

"We've got too much going on," he continued. "Let's play together instead."

An alarm sounded in my head. While the honor of him wanting to golf with me instead of watching the pros filled me with warmth, did he have a gut sense about his health? And, was this my last chance to give him the joy that Memorial Tournament tickets brought?

"Maybe next year," I said, choking on the words.

He nodded, already back to reading the paper.

Dad hadn't yet seen the primary oncologist, "the chemo guy," as we called him. There was no official prognosis. Until there was, I chose to imagine Dad being around for the following year's tournament. A sliver of me acknowledged I might be wrong, but there was too much we didn't know.

CHAPTER 6

THE ONLY DAUGHTER YOU CAN BE

When my parents stayed at our house as guests, they knew it meant living with and sometimes caring for our two dogs. Over the years, both of them graciously accepted my menagerie of pets, including their current canine grandchildren: Astro, an American Eskimo Dog and spitfire of white fluff, and Maxine, that gentle giant black Labrador retriever who had accompanied me to the office on weekends. With my parents on dog duty, Ed took a week off and they watched Astro and Maxine so he and I could participate in a silent meditation retreat in Yellow Springs, an hour west of Columbus.

I headed my station wagon toward this retreat longing for the elusive calm that I often found while meditating. On the drive, verdant, lush fields rolled by, inviting and hopeful. As I nosed the car into the narrow entrance of Glen Helen Nature Preserve, Ed touched my arm in a tactile reminder of his support. The wooded lane shaded and cooled the car. My breath deepened.

That first evening, the half-hour sitting periods stretched out endlessly. Although I sat quietly, my body vibrated as if I were still packing or driving. During the walking sessions, I hesitantly lifted one foot then another across the weedy yard, as other forms moved in slow motion near me. My limbs jerked, uncooperative and stiff. My face felt like a mask.

The days proved sticky with slight breezes coming in the open windows of the Ecology Center as we sat on rows of cushions on the concrete floor. Ed and I had taken the retreat vow of "Noble Silence," setting our intention to not speak to each other or anyone except the teacher during the week. We also slept in separate dorms far away from one another. Still, a sort of wifely radar alerted me to Ed's whereabouts. If he stood behind me in the lunch line or walked beneath the maple tree a few feet away, a comforting tingle in my chest alerted me to his presence.

This wifely radar, like my meditation skill, was recently acquired and still being honed. Ed and I had only been married for a year and a half when Dad was diagnosed. Although we dated for more than a year before we married, actually being someone's wife in the eyes of the law was a whole new experience. Plus, I'd only been dating men for a few years.

After several unsatisfying dalliances with high-school boys, and despite being what my sister called "boy crazy," I hadn't found what I was looking for in the arms of teenage males. I wanted to talk and be touched. But in my experience, once a boy knew you would do what he wanted, the sweet talk ended and you were only going to feel the touch of one thing.

When my best high-school girlfriend kissed me on New Year's Eve of our senior year, I melted into her embrace. In contrast to the boys, she wanted what I wanted: deep conversation, hours of touch, and connection. We spent long afternoons lying in each other's arms discussing everything from our high school marching band to poetry. The resulting flood of pleasant emotions quickly convinced me this union would fix the melancholy that had haunted me most of my life.

Since high school, I'd been in several long-term relationships, all with women. Ed knew my history.

When I was growing up, my parents and I never discussed relationships except for one teenage episode involving a boy. We talked about the weather, farming, Mom's creative endeavors, my schooling, then jobs, our respective dogs, and, after they had retired to Arizona, golf, but nothing too touchy or potentially controversial.

I didn't confide in my parents because I feared their judgment and disappointment. Dad had been raised Catholic and

Mom converted to Catholicism when they married. I assumed they both thought homosexuality was a sin. And I convinced myself that my parents believed my domestic partners and I were just close roommates.

Eventually, when I moved in with a different woman in college and then another after law school while not so much as mentioning a male friend, I interpreted my parents' lack of reaction as acceptance.

   ❦ ❦ ❦

Throughout those years I spent in relationships with women, I remained attracted to men. In fact, I remained attracted to anyone who was attracted to me, but my feelings toward men continued to confuse me. I had declared myself lesbian. Most of my friends were lesbians. I thought I needed to repress my attraction to men. But invariably, whether in the classroom or the boardroom, a man would eventually catch my eye.

Still, I stayed in committed relationships with women. When these men knocked at the locked door of my sexual consciousness, I allowed myself a peek, but never more than a passing glance. None of my lesbian friends mentioned anything but revulsion toward male anatomy. If I acted on my attraction to men, I feared losing their friendship. I thought there was something wrong with me because my attractions vacillated. Now, I understand that curiosity and longing are my nature, far beyond the ability of mind to conquer matter.

During the first few years after law school when I worked for the consulting firm, I developed a crush on a male colleague. It began with dangerous flirtation made especially risky by our firm's anti-fraternization clause. But when he reached for my hand in the law library, the desire to be with a man outweighed any fear of losing my job, and my decade of suppression ended.

I hadn't had straight sex since high school. In this man's arms, I was sixteen again.

Predictably, as the affair with my co-worker ripened, my lesbian relationship soured. It would take another two years, however, long after the affair with the co-worker had burned itself out, for me to leave that seven-year partnership. But once I was done, I was done.

On the heels of my decision to date men, I booked a plane to Arizona in an act of quiet rebellion. In all the years my parents lived out west, I had never visited. My partner at that time had insisted we spend our time and money on fine things and destination vacations. "You can see your parents in the summer," she had said. At twenty-nine, I had never been west of the Mississippi River. Now, free from that entanglement, I wanted to travel. And, I wanted to see my parents and their Arizona home.

Mom and Dad picked me up at the airport in Phoenix and we drove north to Sedona. The first morning, we stood on the bank at Red Rock Crossing watching Oak Creek rush past. I was thinking about the seven-year relationship I had ended. As with most major decisions, I hadn't consulted my parents. I was playing "happy camper," pretending I was fine, life with my female roommate was swell, and things back home would go on as they expected. Cottonwood leaves swirled around us on the sandy shore and I looked up at Cathedral Rock. The sun's rays formed diamond patterns on the ground and across my white leather sneakers. Deep green water smoothed the rocks as it had for thousands of years, wearing away the rough edges.

As I struggled to take in the awe-inspiring scenery, my chest began to fill with the familiar feeling of a balloon blowing up inside me. It would burst any moment. Hiding my emotions from my parents across the long distance had been easy. Over the telephone and through the mail I used my job and busy life to shield them from my confusion. But standing next to Mom and Dad before this mountain, I felt small and naked.

I looked to the left toward Dad just as he turned toward me. Our eyes met. Tears filled mine, streamed down my cheeks, and off my jaw. He walked over and pulled me close and I cried as he hugged me. I heard Mom's small feet scuttling through the cottonwood leaves and a moment later her arm was around me as well.

The three of us walked to a picnic table in the crystal-blue morning. A crisp breeze moved the air. When we were seated, I turned to face them.

"I'm leaving my relationship," I said.

Dad nodded but Mom remained silent.

"And . . ." I paused to gather my courage ". . . I'm going to date men."

My father pulled in a deep breath but said nothing. My mother also continued to restrain herself. The only sound was the wind-blown cottonwood leaves rustling at our feet.

For over an hour, we sat at that table and talked about practical things like selling the house my domestic partner and I owned together, and moving to something smaller, closer to work. I told them how scared I was and how excited. They listened.

When I was done, Dad put his arm around me again and squeezed hard.

"Just go for it," he said. "It's okay. Everything will be alright."

I had wanted to believe him, but I felt so shaky inside.

Now, as Dad faced death, I wondered if he would still say everything would be alright.

And, if he said it, would I believe him now?

At the retreat, I headed into the woods during our afternoon break. Down a curved driveway, a house sat surrounded by a group of large, caged enclosures amid trees and underbrush: Glen Helen Raptor Center. Behind a split-rail fence, in boxes that hung along the backside of shaded pens, huddling owls slept. Slits of light showed their unruffled feathers, moving only as they breathed.

The next and largest enclosure sat thirty feet back into the woods and rose fifty feet into the air, more than twice the height of the owl pens. Instead of wooden slats, it was fashioned from woven wire stretched on large wooden frames.

I scanned the enclosure, but didn't see anything. The graying wooden sign on the fence read: "Solo is a male bald eagle of the southern subspecies." The sign explained that, as an immature bird Solo had flown into a power line. His left wing had been severely damaged and had to be amputated.

I slowed my eyes and scanned the pen from left to right, bottom to top. Three quarters of the way up, a flash of white moved from behind the center pole as the huge brown bird hopped from a hidden perch down to one just above my line of sight. Nearly three feet tall, the color of dark chocolate, with yellow claws the size of my hands and a striking yellow beak, Solo stared at me with the intensity of his V-shaped brow. I returned his dark gaze with the curiosity of a child.

He turned away and preened his feathers with the curve of his thick beak. After a few moments, he hopped to yet another perch, this one covered with artificial grass. At first, his back was to me. But then he slowly turned, carefully placing one yellow claw and then another on the perch until he faced me again. He swiveled his head nearly backward to peck at his long white tail feathers then rotated his head back.

Entranced, I bowed.

We watched each other until the bell signaled the afternoon session. A few moments before I had to leave, he hopped to a much higher perch. As he landed, his remaining wing unfolded, extending those brown feathers nearly three feet, offering a glimpse of what had once been his enormous wingspan. Even though he was nearly forty feet away, my cheeks tingled as if his wing had fluttered across my face.

Both Solo and my father stayed on my mind through the afternoon and evening, and as I fell asleep. They remained in my thoughts as I woke in the gray light that filtered through the dorm windows. Will Dad play golf today? What was it like for Solo to live in that cage?

I visited Solo nearly every day. In his presence, my body relaxed. I grew peaceful, curious, and calm. When I returned to the retreat, questions about my father crowded my mind. *Who was I supposed to be? What was I supposed to do?*

During the evening Dharma talks, the teacher reminded us of the basic Buddhist principle: craving and aversion cause suffering. I could not deny that I wanted one particular outcome with regard to my father. I wanted Dad to remain the healthy, happy, golfing man I loved. When I tried to relax, to drop my "wanting," my body tensed with desire. Alongside this lay a deep ache, a kind of hollowness that infused my every breath. The push and pull between wanting and letting go wore me down.

On the fourth day, my mind was busier than before. I couldn't imagine sitting through the morning meditation, but I didn't want to see Solo either. I headed down the trail that led to the yellow mineral spring that gave the town its name. After a few minutes, the insides of my arms and the back of my neck began to tingle: my wifely radar. I turned to see Ed approaching. I smiled and began to walk away in order to keep our vow of silence. When he motioned for me to stop, I looked around to be sure no one was nearby.

Once he reached me, we sat on a granite boulder that jutted out among the mosses and ferns carpeting the forest floor. Unembarrassed he said, "I went into town."

Retreat protocol suggested no one leave the retreat without telling the teacher, but Ed loved to bend rules. Unlike Ed, just skipping that morning's meditation had filled me with shame. I put my finger to my lips and rapped him lightly on the arm to feign disapproval. Usually if he jaunted into town during a retreat, he returned beaming like a kid who'd successfully skipped school. Today, he looked grim.

"I talked to your mom," he said. In these days before cell phones, he'd called our house from a pay phone in town.

I let my gaze fall. I imagined my parents at our house with the two dogs: Dad in the family room watching golf on television with Maxine lying nearby, and Astro pacing while Mom read the newspaper at the kitchen table. What day was it? My sister Amy, through her work at Ohio State, had gotten Dad an appointment with that oncologist who specialized in chemotherapy. Amy and my parents were scheduled to see him while Ed and I were at the retreat.

Ed cleared his throat. "Your Dad saw the doctor," he said.

I looked up, hopeful, but his face was dark. "The doctor told your dad to get his affairs in order."

My mouth filled with tears. I thought Dad was going to have radiation, chemotherapy, and perhaps surgery.

"No chemo?" I mumbled.

The chemo doctor had told Dad not to bother. What kind of treatment plan was that?

"No quality of life with chemo," Ed said, his voice trailing off.

Ed's warm arms enveloped me and the questions temporarily subsided. I leaned into his embrace and surrendered to my shuddering. Tears rose and passed. After taking a few minutes to steady myself, I stood. He kissed me, and then we parted.

That afternoon, Solo had to wait. I was scheduled for a half-hour individual session with the meditation teacher. When Ed and I had talked, he reminded me that the retreat was as good a place as any to receive this kind of news.

I entered the teacher's room carrying this latest update about my father's condition and a thousand unanswerable questions. Was I strong enough to walk through this with my father? How should I behave? What should I think and feel? What would he need? What did he want from me?

How would I cope?

I shared all this with her as I wept.

She listened intently, then spent a few moments telling me about her own journey through loss and grief.

As she spoke, I struggled to focus on the caressing sound of her voice. My body felt limp and my mind hazy.

Finally, she said, "You can only be the daughter that you are. You can't be anyone else."

Her words jarred me.

What if that's not enough? What if I don't know who that is? What if I disappoint him when he needs me most?

Minutes dissolved as I continued to cry.

If I couldn't be anyone but the frail, imperfect daughter I was, what did that leave? Not only did I fear I wasn't enough for my father, I doubted I had what it took to be present for the months ahead—for the journey I had not yet accepted would lead to his death. Facing it head-on seemed impossible.

I looked out the storm door behind the teacher. The shoes of the next student sat on the porch. I wiped away my tears, stood, bowed to thank her, and walked into the filtered light.

The final afternoon, as I headed into the woods to see Solo during our break, I remembered a time Dad had surprised me.

Five years after I graduated from law school and five years before my father was diagnosed with cancer, my parents celebrated their 40th wedding anniversary. Mom planned the party at the Johnstown Recreation Center a few miles from the farm, not leaving it to her children to forget or botch the job. She had summoned our family to appear early so a photographer could document various family configurations and sell us the resulting shots.

I was twenty-nine, working for the law firm, and into my fourth year of a relationship with the woman I'd met during law school. In stark contrast to the easy-going, small-town ways of my high-school girlfriend, this woman—then an undergraduate from an upscale suburb—was a force. I'd found her assertiveness, fine clothes, Camaro Z28, extensive vocabulary, and finishing-school manners alluring. I also found her interest in me irresistible. Maybe this dose of excitement would blast me out of the depression into which I had once again fallen?

Even though Ms. Z28 regularly attended our family events, I remained unsure what my family understood about our relationship. If I didn't ask, they couldn't reject me.

When the photographer began to arrange the entire family for the group photo, Ms. Z28 stayed in the kitchen. The photographer moved us around in front of the fireplace, tall people (Dad, my brother Jim, and my teenage nephew Colby) in the back, and short people (my sister-in-law Deanna and Mom) in the front. Amy and I flanked the sides and he tucked my other younger nieces and nephews Aliceson, Chad, and Jamey, in the various empty spots. As the photographer walked behind the large square camera mounted on a tripod, Dad looked around, then turned to me and asked where my "partner" was.

Ms. Z28 called from her vantage point near the stove, "Right here."

"Get in here," he ordered. My nose scrunched and my face flushed. Everyone stared straight ahead. Once Dad had spoken, no one else dared say a word. I could see the corners of Dad's mouth turned up in his "Let's pretend everything's fine" smile.

I mouthed, "You sure?"

He ignored me and motioned for her to join us. Not moving, she looked at him through the cafeteria pass-through. When he continued to wave, she slowly walked toward my family, maintaining her best poker face and holding Dad's gaze. When she got to the photographer, Dad said, "She's family." My cheeks burned and a glow filled my chest as she walked up and stood behind me. The photographer suggested she put her hand on my shoulder. In an instant he had snapped three proofs of our family, including her.

I still have that photo. In it, my eyes glisten while Mom looks strained. But Dad had declared, "She's family." At that moment, he had accepted me. Now, with everything at stake, I wanted to believe he meant it.

*   *   *

Solo sat on a low perch close to the front of his pen where I could see him more clearly. Light brown outlined the edge of each large feather, giving him a mottled look. He lowered his head and again peered at me across that fierce beak.

I scanned the sign on the fence. At the bottom was a sentence I hadn't noticed before. "He is quite a character, communicating with staff members by whistling and making an 'Ack-Ack' sound."

I looked around. No one. I called, "Solo?" My voice sounded unfamiliar and strained. During the retreat, I had only spoken a few words to Ed and the teacher.

Nothing.

I whistled and he tilted his head.

"Solo," I called again to no response. Our time was up. I needed to return to the meditation hall and prepare to go home to my mother and father—my "dying" father, my mind added, as a lump formed in my throat.

"Goodbye, Solo," I said and turned to leave.

"Ack-Ack!" I heard.

I froze, then slowly faced him. His sharp eyes were deep and solemn.

"Quite a character," I thought as we gazed at one another. *What was he trying to say?*

CHAPTER 7

REALLY CRAPPY ODDS

A few days after Ed and I returned from the retreat, I walked into our kitchen to find Dad frying eggs and hash-browned potatoes. Because he had put himself through college as a short-order cook at that diner, breakfast was his specialty. We expected my brother, sister, and Ed's two adult sons Ken and Paul, to arrive soon for brunch.

"How's it going?" I asked. Nervous energy filled my body, but I tried to act calm. My mind had not yet accepted the facts I had learned at the retreat.

He stood over our stove in his short-sleeved golf shirt and khakis just as he had stood over the stove at the farm in blue jeans and a white work shirt when I was a little girl. *Wasn't he the same man? How could he be in trouble? And what was my role?* His prognosis had changed, but the questions flooding my mind remained.

I might not know my role in Dad's current health crisis, but I knew my role when Dad prepared breakfast: maker of the toast. Just as I had when I was young, I pulled bread from the cupboard and butter from the refrigerator. At his hand, and after many painful corrections, I had learned the "right" way. When the toaster popped, I carefully spread paper-thin curls of butter onto the warm bread. As an adult, I sometimes "cheated" by putting chunks of butter on the bread then setting the slices on top of the still-warm toaster to melt the butter. But not today. I would do it the "right" way in front of my father. And what was the "right" thing to do with him having cancer? Hold his hand? Change the subject? Crack a joke? I didn't know, so I made the toast.

Normally, as a child, when I picked up the knife to spread the butter, Dad reminded me to cut the butter very thin. "Don't tear the toast" he would say. As an adult, I bristled at the thought that he might say that now.

Instead, without looking up from the pan, he said, "They've given me a one percent chance."

One percent. Really crappy odds. Impossible odds.

I thought I should say something, but what? "You'll be fine?" or "What can I do?" The words formed in my head, and stopped there. I knew how to help him on the farm, but I had no idea how to be the daughter of a dying man.

In answer to my silence, he added, "But I intend to beat them."

⚬ ⚬ ⚬

If physical and mental strength were enough to beat the odds, my father had those in droves. Growing up on the farm, I'd been witness and partner to his feats. Our home in rural Licking County northeast of Columbus sat on fifty acres, plenty for Dad to tend while also working full-time as a manager at Ohio Bell in Columbus. It used to remind me of *Green Acres*, a 1960s television comedy in which a New York City attorney and his glamorous wife move to the country. I imagined Dad as the suit-wearing corporate type turned farmer, Mom as the fashionable spouse, with three children as their eager assistants. We all bought into the story. But what's the TV show for watching your father face probable death? There's no lighthearted script for getting his affairs in order.

By the time I was ten, my two siblings—my brother Jim and sister Amy, who are respectively eleven and nine years older than me—had moved away to college and jobs. Their departure turned me and our young beagle, Puppsy, into my father's farm hands.

Unlike my cosmetics salesperson mother, I detested make-up and preferred the out-of-doors. As a result, I spent as much time helping Dad with farm chores as I could, learning the sizes of sockets and wrenches and how to tell tools apart on sight. I was the nurse and he the doctor. Instead of, "Scalpel. Forceps. Clamp," he called, "Quarter inch. Box wrench. Needle-nose."

During the harvest, my job became head beer-carrier. The men who helped Dad bring in the crops were thirsty and they did not drink water. Every two hours, I carted as many long-neck Budweisers from the barn refrigerator to the back field as the side baskets of my gold Schwinn bicycle could carry, while Puppsy chased the tires.

But my primary role was electric-fence repair assistant. The fence spent more time out of commission than working. Puppsy and I learned to listen to the square, metal charger box that electrified the fence and hung in the workshop area Dad had reserved for himself in one corner of the large barn.

One Saturday, in the dead of winter, Puppsy and I stood at the edge of the huge sliding barn doors as Dad walked the fenced acreage. When he yelled, "Unplug it," I ran inside, the eager beagle at my heels, and pulled the thick, black, three-pronged power cord out of the outlet. I then trotted back outside to yell, "Ohhh-Kaay," as loudly as I could. Then I waited while Puppsy ran around me in small circles.

I imagined him tying a bit of loose wire back together or removing the branch (or piece of grass) that had caused the current to arc from one post to the next. After a few minutes, when he yelled, "Plug 'er in!" I returned to the barn to do his bidding. Once the black plug was firmly back in the outlet, my attention turned to the charger. I listened intently, hoping for the solid plunking sound, a thump, thump, thump, like the heartbeat of a living animal, that signaled his success. Instead, the machine merely snap, snap, snapped. My heart fell. This defeat seemed as much mine as his. I ran back to the edge of the barn and yelled, "Nooooo," into the frigid air.

He hadn't heard me and yelled, "Is it fixed?" The hopefulness and yearning in his voice broke me. "Not yet!" I replied, imagining his internal groan. I prayed to whatever God had created the metal and wires from which electric fence chargers were made to help Dad find the problem.

When the charger finally emitted the correct deep pounding, the sound sent me galloping from the barn toward the place from which I'd last heard Dad call. As I ran, I yelled, "You found it! You found it!" My excitement so great I had to stop and jump up and down a few times before I reached him. When I finally saw him striding toward me, he glowed with contentment, happy at having completed his part of the job. As he walked back to the barn, I skipped beside him with Puppsy circling us.

⬤ ⬤ ⬤

Standing in our kitchen watching my father cook, I wanted fiercely to trust Dad when he said he would "beat the odds." I wanted to trust him implicitly, even though I'd seen him fail. The electric fence broke repeatedly. Mice ate the phone line in the barn. Tractor repairs took weeks instead of hours. And other men received promotions he thought he deserved. As a child, I saw these as temporary and fixable setbacks, not failures at all. In my mind, he always eventually solved the problem. At least, that's what I chose to remember. I wanted to trust him the way I had on a different winter day when he asked me to hold fence posts while he pounded them into frozen ground.

The heavy-duty, dark green, cast-iron posts were made to hold woven wire fence. I knelt, doing my best to keep the post straight while Dad drove the sledge into the top of it again and again. I steadied the post with one hand six inches from the top while I ducked my head beneath my bottom hand and rested my cheek against the cold metal. It never occurred to me that Dad might miss, might hit me in the knuckles, or even worse, in the head.

But his aim was true. He pounded the sledge into the top of each post, driving it a foot or more into the icy dirt. I don't know how many posts we did, a full afternoon of them. I cannot remember what we were building, perhaps snow fence or a new pasture. I just remember the cold of that metal seeping through my gloves and the ridges of the post reverberating against my fingers and cheek each time he struck it. My role was to hold it steady. I wanted to do it right, to please him. And I wanted to get the job done so we could go inside for dinner.

Back then, I never questioned whether his plan would work. I just held the post straight. Now, watching him cook in our kitchen, I wanted that certainty back. I still thought certainty meant safety. But I wasn't ten anymore. I knew what "one percent" meant.

I took a deep breath and asked, "What's the plan?" the same way I would have if we'd been setting out to build a fence. *He always has a plan*, I thought.

"Radiation," he said.

"No chemo," I said, not as a question.

"No chemo. No quality of life with chemo," he said, repeating what the chemo doctor had told him when he'd advised Dad to get his affairs in order.

How was he supposed to beat the odds without chemo?

I wanted to believe him when he said he would beat the odds, because I knew how stubborn he was. Everyone in our family had heard Dad recount his college "swimming class" story. You couldn't get out of Bowling Green State University without knowing how to do the crawl. From the first day, my father told the professor he couldn't swim. He dog-paddled in the shallow end while everyone else swam. As he put it, "I floated like a rock."

The final exam required every student to jump off the diving board and swim across the pool. Despite Dad's protests, the exam was mandatory for him as well. When the fateful day came, Dad pulled on his trunks and watched others earn their credits for this "easy" class.

At his turn, he strode to the end of the diving board, took a huge breath, and jumped. My track-star father, all muscle and bone, did not reemerge. When he didn't come up, first a classmate and then the instructor jumped in after him. Dad's head finally popped up at the rope in the middle of the pool, gasping for air.

"Hey Gene," one man yelled. "You can swim underwater!"

Once my father caught his breath, he yelled back, "Nope. I sunk to the bottom and walked out."

For sheer determination, the instructor passed Dad even though he couldn't swim.

       ✾ ✾ ✾

Each time he proudly recounted this story, I'd marveled at his sheer determination and tenacity. But even in my deep denial, some part of me wondered how his ability to walk across the bottom of the pool translated into beating cancer.

I had spent my childhood ignoring the repeatedly broken farm equipment and missed promotions to focus on the times when his hard-headedness worked. I was still trying to be the good daughter who pretended Dad would never miss.

In our kitchen, as Dad plated the food, he repeated, "I intend to beat the odds."

I nodded, finished buttering the last piece of toast, and said, "I bet you will." The words fell flat. So, I repeated them. "Yep. I bet you will." It still sounded hollow. Was I supposed to believe him, prepare for the worst, or keep making toast? Did he need me to be hopeful or realistic? I only knew I was no longer his ten-year-old farm hand and I had no idea what came next.

Chapter 8

Accidental Stepmother

"Hear that?" my stepson Ken said.

Dad looked confused. He cupped his large hand around his ear.

"Elephants," Ken said.

My other stepson, Paul, and I rolled our eyes.

Ken shrugged. "It's possible. The zoo's right over there," he said, pointing toward the Columbus Zoo located less than a quarter mile from where we stood.

Dad chuckled. I shook my head. Paul groaned.

Following Dad's excellent breakfast complete with my perfect toast, my father had driven Ken, Paul, and I to Safari Golf Club fifteen minutes from our house.

I had never wanted children of my own. When anyone asked, I told them, "My biological clock never went off." But when Ed and I married, I became Ken and Paul's stepmother. Due to my lack of maternal instincts for humans, I would never "mother" either of these now grown men. We didn't discuss this, but I considered them family and thought of myself as their friend.

Dad was also new to the "step-grandfather" business, but had plenty of experience with grandchildren. My brother Jim has two sons and a daughter, and my sister Amy had her daughter, but the oldest of those was still in high school. Ken and Paul were in college when Ed and I met. Ken had now graduated and begun his career while Paul had gone from college to law school. Instead of more grand "children," Dad gained two young men nearly old enough to be his sons.

Ed didn't join us because he no longer golfed. In high school, he had been on the golf team. As an adult he had played in chamber of commerce, rotary, and corporate activities when he was chief financial officer of a national corporation, first in California then New Jersey. But ten years before we met, he'd given his Ping clubs to Ken. When I asked him about golf, he said, "Ken beat me." For him, that signaled it was time to quit.

At the time Ken, Paul, Dad, and I played Safari, each of the course's eighteen holes was named after a different animal.

"Not gonna be a cheat-ah," Ken said, riffing off the homophone when he saw that "Cheetah" was the name of the first hole.

An avid golfer like my father, Ken chose to hit from the blue tees, farthest from the hole.

I laughed out loud at Ken's wordsmith joke and he rewarded me with a smile. Of Ed's two sons, I knew Ken the best. After he graduated from college in Indiana, Ken had moved to Ohio to live with Ed and me while he looked for a full-time job. Our large basement became the "Ken-dom" complete with espresso maker and a large library of movies Ken studied like a scientist in his quest to get into film school. I enjoyed our shared interest in writing. He had studied Shakespeare in college and understood plot, character, and many other literary matters I wished I'd pursued instead of the more practical journalism.

While Ken lived with us, he asked me to review a script he'd labored over for months. Honored, I agreed. In an effort to help him secure a seat in one of the top-notch film schools to which he intended to apply, I focused on things he might improve. In my zeal, I failed to note the many gems that shone off the page. I didn't see how my intense critique of Ken's hard work mirrored my father's attempts to "improve" me. It would be years before I recognized how overly critical I'd been of his first serious film script effort.

Ken's film school aspirations didn't pan out, but he inherited his father's tenacity. He pivoted to finance, another area he had studied in college. He found a fast-paced position in the online merchandising division of a large clothing retailer, a business area just developing at that time. After my father's diagnosis, when Mom and Dad came to live with us, Ken had already moved from our basement to a nearby apartment. Within a few years, Ken would earn his MBA and go on to excel in corporate management.

Ed's younger son, Paul, chose the white tees, a few yards closer to the hole. "I've got nothing to prove," he said, forcefully planting his tee and ball into the ground.

I hadn't spent much time with Paul and my natural shyness made me awkward around him. Like Ken, Paul is smart and funny. He's not as off-the-cuff humorous as Ken, for whom one-liners roll out as easily as breathing, but Paul enjoys a laugh and has a good heart.

I wanted both of the young men to like me and for Paul to feel welcome. So, I pretended to be confident—a variant of "happy camper." I asked Paul about his classes, joked about my bad golf, and cheered his hits. When I stayed calm and didn't try to impress either of the young men, we got along fine. It's possible they had no clue of my discomfort.

Paul being in law school increased my normal level of self-consciousness. When he described his courses, many of which I had taken, it was as if he was talking about an entirely different profession from the one I had studied and practiced. He seemed so happy there. As we played around the zoo-themed course with his brother and my father, I watched Paul for the personality traits that might suit him for legal work. I saw confidence, ease of banter, logic, and intensity, all traits I thought I lacked.

I don't know what prompted Paul to attend law school. But the favorable way he spoke about his classes and the prospect of legal work astounded and intimidated me. I imagined him interested in justice and service, and could almost see him in judicial robes. Compared to that type of motivation, my own reasons for going to law school seemed lame. I had applied because I didn't know what else to do.

$\ast\ \ast\ \ast$

In high school and especially during our first year of college at Ohio University in Athens, Ohio, I only left my high-school girlfriend's side when school, classes, or family duties required it. At the end of our first year, we returned to Licking County to our respective family homes. Back at the farm that summer, the ten-mile distance between us might as well have been three oceans. I thought I might suffocate without her when, in fact, I had been smothering her.

In the fall, when she and I returned to college, we moved back in together. But before the end of the year, it was over. Our breakup caused me to lose focus. Convinced I'd done something wrong to lose her love, some days I didn't get out of bed. When I did go to class, I fought tears and once even ran out. A kind professor referred me to the college mental health center. When the therapist couldn't tell me how to get my girlfriend back, I stopped going.

The summer after my sophomore year instead of returning to the farm, I stayed on campus with the "townies" to take classes year-round. I told my parents I was saving money, and I was, but in reality, the newly forming adult me didn't want to return to the childhood status the farm evoked.

To fill the void left by my high-school girlfriend, I began to drink daily with a townie woman. I quickly became a regular at her "home bar" and joined her softball team, for which "practice" meant pitchers of beer before the game. By the time I decided to go to law school, I realized I had no off switch when it came to alcohol, but hadn't yet connected my regular inebriation to a larger problem.

The journalism courses I was taking to finish my bachelor's degree didn't hold my interest. I enjoyed the writing, but balked when pressed to ask sources difficult questions. When I learned that two of my friends were going to law school, I remembered that legal "win" for my sister after her car accident. I set my sights on a legal career, hoping to focus on research and writing.

On my undergraduate campus, in the days before personality tests were the norm, none of the advisers to whom I spoke questioned my plan. I took the LSAT, applied to schools, and earned admission at several. By this time, my parents were out west most of the year. Our communication dwindled to letters and calls. Other than that single conversation with my father during our rainy drive, I did not mention my career decisions to them. I left the townie woman and the hills of Athens behind and headed north to Columbus and The Ohio State University College of Law.

The first morning, as I sat in my alphabetically assigned seat in the front row of Professor Travalio's contracts class, I looked around the auditorium at the other hundred students. Each of them seemed so well put-together, mature, and smart. One after another they recited the facts of the case or answered the professor's questions. They spoke English, but I could not comprehend their words. Despite having read the same cases in preparation for this first class, and forming the same conclusions, I felt lost. Their method of arriving at the results confounded me. A resounding "I don't belong here" echoed in my head.

Dad's voice cut through my trip down memory lane. "Loosen up before you swing." I blinked. We were already on the "Giraffe" hole and Paul was lining up to putt.

Golfing with Paul, Ken, and my father through these holes named Turtle, Ray, Burying Beetle, and Giraffe, I mentioned nothing about my law school struggles a decade earlier, or how I'd arrived there in the first place. I imagined Paul thriving in the legal classroom. I could see him growing to love the logic, conflict, and analysis law school required. While studying law is tough for nearly everyone, I was certain he had easily become an integral part of his class rather than feeling he was in the wrong place, as I had.

But by the time I was in law school, I had already thought of myself as an outsider for years. A pro at swallowing my distress, in this bout of "happy camper" I lectured myself, trying to force a positive attitude. I vowed to act as if I belonged. Depression followed. I struggled through my first year of classes with the help of several friends who generously shared the legal outlines they prepared in anticipation of exams.

My second year, I often showed up late to class, usually in pajamas, and slid into the last row to avoid being called on. When the professor finally found me, if I knew the answer, relief washed over me. When I didn't, my mind attacked: *You're so stupid. You don't belong here.*

I visited the townie in Athens a few times, but I broke it off when that well-dressed woman with the Camaro Z28 showed interest. She introduced me to the owner of Happy's Beverage Center across from the law building where I spent more time drinking than studying.

Alcohol had a markedly different effect on me than it did on Ms. Z28. An evening at a bar with her meant laughter, social interaction, jokes, and fun. An evening out with me was a crap shoot. I might be miserable, jealous, critical, or suspicious, but always unpredictable.

One night she and I visited the home of some lesbian friends to play the card game Euchre. I drank a few beers and sat down at the table to play. The next thing I recall, one of the friends had pinned my arms behind my back. A few feet away, Z28 stood glaring. Her face shone with hatred.

I shook off the friend and regained my composure. Another friend who was also in law school said, "You don't remember, do you?" She guided my wobbly body into one of the bedrooms and explained what had happened. During the game, I had risen from the table and tried to kiss Ms. Z28. She had pushed me away, laughing, but instead of sitting back down, I had punched her in the cheek.

The friend believed I had blacked out while this all happened. She had been a social worker before law school and gently suggested alcohol might not "agree" with me. "There are people you can talk to privately about drinking," she said, then added ". . . and domestic violence. It's all confidential."

I had never hit anyone before. The thought of my having abused someone I cared for made me physically ill.

Luckily, my wimpy punch had bounced off my girlfriend's cheek and not left a physical mark, but the emotional toll could not be denied. When I left that party, I vowed never to drink again.

After the incident, I assumed Ms. Z28 wouldn't want anything to do with me. But a few days later, she left a note in my law school mail box. I forgot my vow and we went back to dating and drinking as if nothing had happened.

By my third and final law school year, between drinking binges, my diet dwindled to oatmeal cream pies and low-calorie root beer. I missed weeks of classes. I tried to only see Z28 when I could be cheerful, the way I saw myself, but my erratic behavior drove her away.

The drinking, mood swings, relationship chaos, and my general insecurity created havoc with my studies. When I missed class, I begged friends for their notes. Despite what felt like daily failure, I received high marks on my legal research and writing project. Most of the exams required essay answers and I absorbed enough to pass. Writing saved me. When asked to put my thoughts on paper, I came through.

The physical distance between me and my parents allowed me to shield them from my bouts of drinking and melancholy. When we did talk, I acted happy. I couldn't bear to submit to Dad "improving" me when I thought I was such a loser. If they asked about my classes, I glossed over the reality, making it sound difficult, but doable.

At the law school hooding ceremony, I mimicked excitement, but felt only relief at having those three exhausting years behind me. For my graduation party, I ordered a cake inscribed with: "Thank God It's Over!"

If only. The Ohio Bar Examination loomed ahead.

* * *

At the hole named "Gibbon," Ken and Paul got to experience Dad's attempts to "improve" each of their games. Dad's instruction included that admonition to loosen up before hitting the ball, complete with a demonstration of his method, direction about how to aim, and a stroke-by-stroke analysis after each hole. I'm not sure if Ken was feigning interest, but the way he tilted his head and nodded at Dad's pointers seemed genuine. Paul also listened, but appeared preoccupied. I imagined him thinking about the cases he should be reading or exams he would soon face. Plus, he's left-handed. Dad's lessons didn't easily translate to his southpaw grip and swing. Still, Paul noted Dad's pointers and smiled at his tales of golfing with the Arizona men.

Each time my turn came up, at the gold tees closest to the hole, that familiar inner cringe arose. My golf game had improved little since my father and I played Wilson Road. And now, Ed's sons got to see first-hand not only how bad I was, but also how intensely my father wished I was better. I focused and refocused, doing my best to enjoy the sunshine and the company, but the scorekeeper in my head chanted and my anxiety rose with each stroke. Much the way I had been when I drank, here with Dad and my "accidental stepsons" I vacillated between tubular numbness and my screeching mind. I tried to follow Dad's instructions, but when Dad said, "Keep your arm straight," my head clamored, "Get your affairs in order" followed quickly by, "I'll never get this right."

My father focused on "improving" all of our golf games as if it was the last thing he would ever do which, since he might be dying, could indeed be the case. My mind screamed, "He's not actively dying," despite the fact that only a week before a doctor had given him that stern prognosis. I reeled from "no chemo" to "I'm going to beat it" while I watched him play golf as if he was going to live forever. Denial? Survival? I found his dogged determination mind-boggling. Why wasn't he curled up in the fetal position or raging at the gods? Why wasn't he talking about his feelings the way I would?

Still in my early thirties, I did not yet understand that people can have different mental and emotional wiring, and as a result react differently in the same situation. Plus, this was *my* father. I wanted him to process out loud. Forget that he never had before. I longed for vulnerability, closeness, and dialogue, while also intending to be the best daughter of a dying man ever in the history of daughters of dying men. This was a lot for me to expect, both of myself, and of this man whom I sometimes still felt I barely knew. And why would I imagine he would be vulnerable in front of Ken and Paul, young men he was only now getting to know?

Worried my spinning thoughts might cause my head to fly off, I took a few slow, deep breaths to keep me from hyperventilating.

* * *

On a June night shortly after I graduated from law school, I sat in a hotel conference room with five hundred other students taking a review course for the Ohio Bar Exam. My limbs began to tingle and the room to tilt. My heart pounded and I had trouble catching my breath.

When I put my head on the desk, the woman next to me asked, "Do you need help?"

My breath grew increasingly shallow. I sat up and tried to say, "Yes." Nothing came out so I put my hands on my chest and patted. The woman yelled, "We need help over here!" Five hundred pairs of eyes turned toward me, so I put my head back down. It felt as if hot liquid were shooting through my arms and legs. I gasped for air.

I don't remember the gurney, the ambulance ride, or who called my parents. When their pale faces appeared at my bedside all I could say was, "I'm so sorry." I was supposed to protect them, not be a bother, and especially not worry my father. Dad reminded my brother and sister when they went out on dates, "I'm a worrier. Don't make me miserable."

Mom held my hand in her small one as Dad towered over us, looming in his Allis-Chalmers ball cap.

Nurses and technicians swarmed. Rather than the heart attack I'd feared, the doctor diagnosed a mild case of "hyperadrenergic syndrome," an increased sensitivity to adrenaline. That's why I was light-headed and my limbs tingled. To my rattled mind, his diagnosis meant "Calm down, lady. Stop panicking."

Afterward, rather than admit the extent of my anxiety, I told anyone who would listen about the medical condition. This wasn't my first panic attack, but it was the first time my parents learned that something real might be amiss.

As I recovered and continued to prepare for the grueling three-day Ohio Bar Exam the last week of July, my depression increased. The morning of The Ohio State University commencement ceremony in "the Horseshoe" (Ohio Stadium), an event few graduates want to miss, fear so paralyzed me that I couldn't get out of bed. I called Mom to tell her I couldn't face it.

"Take care of yourself, honey," she said.

Over the next eight weeks, between study sessions, I called every member of my family and several close friends to ask, "If I don't pass the bar exam, will you still love me?"

Their responses ranged from, "Of course!" to "You're joking, right?"

My father said, "I'm sorry you feel you have to ask."

By mid-July, I could hardly leave my house and was afraid to be alone. As soon as I opened my eyes, depression's feisty twin sisters, panic and anxiety, gripped me. A law student friend kept me company some days. Other days, I sat in my neighbor Betty's kitchen. Without another person nearby, I feared I might spin off the planet.

My high-school girlfriend and I had reunited. On days when I couldn't find someone to stay with me or Betty was busy, I rode with my girlfriend to work and studied at a restaurant until her shift ended. Mom hauled me to a massage therapist, a chiropractor, and the health food store. She never suggested a counselor or psychiatrist.

By the morning of the first day of the bar exam, my daydreams of intentionally hurling my car against a concrete median divider and my nightmares of watching an oncoming semi-trailer tractor veer into my path had whipped me into a heightened mania. I asked my girlfriend to drive me to the test site at Veterans Memorial Hall on her way to work. At noon, Mom and Dad brought lunch and we drove to the back of the large parking lot near the train tracks and sat on a railroad tie wall that was built into the hillside. They followed my sullen lead and we ate our tuna sandwiches in silence.

A few minutes before I had to go back, Mom broke in, "Don't forget, we love you." Dad encircled me with one arm and gave me a hearty squeeze. The rest of that day, I heard Mom's words and sensed the warmth of Dad's arm around me.

By the afternoon of the exam's third and final day, a sense of relief grew inside me. I remembered the bar review course instructor's warning that many people fail the exam by not conserving enough energy for the final run of essay questions on the second half of that third day. I had paced myself.

After I finished, I went home, and slept. When I woke on the Friday after the exam, the worst seemed behind me. On Monday, I began my legal career with vigor as legal research consultant at that labor relations consulting firm. My schedule left no time to worry about the bar exam results.

On an October Friday, nearly three months after the bar exam, a friend who worked in the Attorney General's office called at 7:30 a.m. to tell me that the Ohio Bar results would be released that morning at 8:00 a.m.

When the phone lines to the Ohio Supreme Court opened, I dialed the number. Expecting a busy signal, I was startled when a friendly woman answered on the second ring.

"Please spell your name," she said.

Dripping with dread, I complied.

A moment later, she chirped, "Congratulations. You passed."

I gulped. "Are you sure?"

"You're on the list," she said and quickly hung up.

When I called back, the same cheery woman repeated the good news without even a hint of impatience. And I still didn't believe her.

As soon as I hung up, my friend called again, this time shouting, "We passed! We passed!" She had seen the results posted on the front door of the State Office Tower.

That night, when I came home from work, I opened the envelope from the court with trembling hands. Surely the clerk and my friend had both been mistaken. Surely the letter would say I had failed.

Instead, on official stationery from the Supreme Court of the State of Ohio, the letter confirmed that I had passed. Only then did I believe it. With receipt of that letter, I also believed the depression and anxiety were behind me for good. I threw myself back into my work.

In the years following the positive Bar Review results, my parents barely existed for me. When they came home in the summer, I occasionally visited them at the farm, but I continued to focus primarily on my career.

Spending so much time at work and so little at home took its toll. The relationship with my high-school girlfriend fizzled again and my Camaro-driving lover moved in, beginning our seven years together. Did she have money? I wasn't certain, but that possibility allayed my secret fear of financial insecurity. She traded in her Camaro, first for a Buick, and then a Volvo sedan.

For a while, that relationship, the fancy things we bought, and burying myself in my career staved off my anxiety and depression. But within a few years, the gray moods returned.

To pump myself up for work, I began to listen to motivational books on tape in my car. I woke at 6:00 a.m. on cold mornings, when I would typically roll over for another hour's sleep before finally heeding the voice from the audiobook, "Don't think about it. Just get out of bed."

By this time, Ms. Z28—now Ms. Volvo sedan—and I owned a four-bedroom, two-story house on an acre lot. Three dogs played in the yard and I had bought the Volvo wagon. Things looked so good from the outside.

When the senior partner urged me to take on trial work, Ms. Volvo sedan encouraged it. But the pay increase came at a price. I ignored my gut, agreed to the additional role, and soon found myself involved in conflicts I hated. Instead of questioning the librarian about the location of a legal text in the hushed solitude of the law library, I found myself questioning witnesses before hearing officers in crowded state agency offices.

The senior partner also suggested I take on divorce, dissolution, and child custody cases. Again, litigation. Again, hearings and trials, things to which I was not accustomed. Again, I was not suited for these fights. But the word "No" was not yet part of my vocabulary. I gave myself another pep talk. *I'm smart*, I told myself. *I'll learn it*. I put my head down, did my best, and pretended I would be fine.

                        ⚬ ⚬ ⚬

On Great Blue Heron, I hit the ball well enough that it flew through the air after a satisfying *thunk*. The men cheered. For an instant, I forgot about Dad's illness or the difficult years before I met Ed.

Throughout our game, I pulled myself back into the moment by focusing on the animal name of the current hole. "The boys," as Ed still sometimes called them, had never seen me drink. I wasn't sure they knew that alcohol is what brought their father and I together. But I knew.

When it comes to alcohol, I have a short memory. As the work stress compounded, my desire for booze increased. I could go months without drinking then get drunk on a single glass of wine. Or I'd intend to have one glass and wind up drinking until I threw up.

On New Year's Eve of 1990, I drove Ms. Z28 to a party in my Volvo station wagon. By this time, even she was encouraging me not to drink. When her back was turned, I poured some scotch into my glass of ginger ale. Throughout the evening, I repeated that until I was stumbling and slurring my words. When it was time to drive home, the host suggested my girlfriend take the keys.

I slept most of the next day, but in the afternoon, I dressed and drove to work intending to research cases for an upcoming trial, but the words on the pages of the legal text I was trying to read looked like gibberish. Eventually, I got in my car to drive home. Although it had been more than 24 hours since the party, I still felt drunk.

On the way, I "failed to negotiate a straightaway" and drove my Volvo station wagon off the road and down an embankment.

The car hit a large rock and rolled. As the world turned upside down in slow motion, I thought, "So this is how it ends." But the car landed gently on the driver's side.

A passerby stopped and helped me climb out the passenger door. The state trooper must not have smelled alcohol because he did not test me. He only said, "You're a lucky lady. That Volvo saved you."

I looked back at the battered station wagon. I could have died. I had to quit for good.

Each time I vowed to stop drinking, I hadn't realized I couldn't just stop. In the same way my boot-strap, motivational tape method eventually stopped working on my mental health issues, so did my ability to white-knuckle staying away from alcohol. Despite being scared enough when I rolled my Volvo that I swore not to drink again, I drank a few more times between that accident and the following fall.

On a Tuesday evening in September, I came home from work early with the black cloud of depression heavy in my body. Alone in our large house with our three dogs at my feet, I contemplated my choices for the evening. It had been five months since so much as a sip of alcohol had touched my lips. Ms. Z28, who still drank, was at work. I knew she'd just bought a six pack.

I walked to the refrigerator and opened the door. There they sat. Six glistening bottles. How easy it would be to open one and put it to my lips.

In the past, when I'd negotiated with alcohol, whether standing before an open refrigerator, leaning against a bar, or watching a friend pour drinks, I had no resolve. The booze appeared and I drank it. But this night, I paused. The consequences rolled through my mind. Hitting my girlfriend. Rolling my car. Getting drunk on a single glass of wine. Sometimes nothing bad happened. But when it went south, it wasn't good.

I closed the refrigerator door, slid into my car, and headed to a recovery meeting where for the first time I admitted I had a problem.

My decision to go to recovery meetings didn't sit well with Ms. Z28. She had seen how unreliable I became when I drank, but when she compared our drinking histories, I looked like a teetotaler. Perhaps my choice seemed like an accusation. It was far from it. In truth, I doubt she understood my desperation. Just as I hid nearly everything from everyone else, I never shared the depth of my despair with her. But the people in the recovery rooms understood. And they knew how to do the thing I had tried, but couldn't manage alone. Not only did they know how to stop drinking. They knew how to *stay* stopped. Our relationship unraveled.

That other factor, my attraction to men, ended our union for good. A few months after I admitted my drinking problem, I began to date a man. When I had been with women, it was the late 1970s into the early 1990s. As a result, my partners and I had never displayed affection publicly. Instead of talking about a "girlfriend," I spoke of "my roommate," even to my parents. Now that I was dating a man, I wondered if not having to hide would solve my depression and anxiety.

Like everything else I had tried, it worked for a while.

⬤ ⬤ ⬤

While the course's name "Safari" and the animal moniker on each hole promised adventure, the place was far enough from the zoo that we did not in fact hear an elephant trumpet and saw no more than the occasional blue jay. Dad, Ken, Paul, and I played through Painted Dog, Blue Bird, Rhino, and Tree Kangaroo. Again and again, I quelled my anxiety and set aside my lingering questions. At times, I watched the others intently, hypervigilance in full force until I zoned out again. I came alert in time to hit the ball and follow the men like an automaton, cheering and commiserating as appropriate. A week ago, a doctor told my father he probably had nine months to live. Today, he was correcting my grip. It all seemed absurd.

And yet, golf offered safety. Maybe that's why Dad insisted on it. He could act and feel normal. Could I? On the course, my drinking adventures didn't exist. Neither did my relationship history. Ken and Paul knew nothing about those things and, especially here, there was no need to tell them.

My mind wandered to Ron, the first man I seriously dated in my adult years, the one I told my father about when Dad and I stood on the banks of Oak Creek in Sedona. Ron was quite a golfer. He also bore an unmistakable resemblance to my father. We had our first date at Mill Creek Golf Course under the guise of a lesson. He was certain he could improve my game. Nearly anything could have.

I played my usual round of very bad golf while he drove the ball further and further each hole. After the third hole, he suggested that I pick up my ball and drop it where his landed. I had been eager for his approval and his disappointment in my lack of skill stung.

As my infatuation continued, letters to Mom and Dad included references to my golfing "friend." Dad responded with inquiries about our golf adventures and "Can't wait to meet Ron. Tell him I said to hit 'em long and straight."

But winter and my intense neediness killed our relationship. After a lackluster New Year's Eve, he called me at work to announce that he needed "space."

A few weeks later, I saw Ed for the first time at a recovery meeting. He had just moved to Ohio from New Jersey. I hadn't noticed him until a few of us gathered in the kitchen around a plate of cookies, discussing different group formats.

From directly behind me, a man spoke.

"Where I come from . . ." he said, then continued, explaining that group's procedures.

His voice sounded familiar. I turned, expecting to see a face I knew.

Instead, there was Ed, a total stranger with blond hair, piercing blue eyes, a square jaw, and a shy smile. I stared.

He was a few inches taller than me and wore a suit. I guessed him to be forty-five, fifteen years my senior. I caught glimpses of his blond head and sharp blue eyes at a few more meetings before I mustered the nerve to introduce myself. Soon we were seeing each other regularly. By the time I learned that he was actually twenty years older, it was too late. I was in love.

Because he was new in town, Ed claimed to need a tour guide. But his natural curiosity made him more adept at finding interesting things in central Ohio than me, even though I had lived there most of my adult life. We spent the spring learning about the state's landmarks and each other. I loved his voice, the thing that had first drawn my attention. I soon learned that he also had the most delicious touch.

As our romance flourished, I barely noticed the absence of the little white ball.

Mom and Dad, due for their regular spring return from Arizona, would meet Ed for the first time at a fourth of July party. Nervous as a mouse in a cat shelter, I felt conspicuous in a sun dress with no bra and a very exposed back. But Ed kept complimenting me and putting his warm hand on my shoulder blade.

Ed and I had been at the party about half an hour when Amy, also at the party, found me. "Mom and Dad just pulled up!"

A blend of excitement and raw fear formed a fist-sized knot in my stomach.

What if Ed didn't like Dad? Worse yet, *What if Dad didn't like Ed?*

Dad stepped through the door, followed closely by Mom, and we embraced.

"Welcome home!" Amy, the family cheerleader, yelled from behind us. Frozen, I stared. Their return always left me a little discombobulated. Then, I sensed Ed behind me.

"Mom, Dad. I want you to meet Ed. Ed, this is Mom and Dad. Um, Gene and Ellen," I blurted.

Dad stuck out his hand. As Ed grabbed it, Dad quickly said, "Nice to meet you. I hear you're quite a golfer." My face burned.

Ed never took his eyes off Dad. He smiled, firmly shook Dad's hand and said, "That was Ron. I'm Ed. Nice to meet you, too."

Dad turned crimson and bent over laughing. When he straightened up, he turned to me and said, "How's that for a first impression?" We all began to laugh, especially Ed.

Dad said, "Could I have put my foot any further into my mouth?"

Amy stopped laughing long enough to say, "Nope. Toes are permanently embedded in your tonsils."

Dad recovered, turned back to Ed and said, "Nice to meet you too, Ed."

Now, here I was on this golf course with Ed's two sons, neither of whom knew any of this background, and my father who had recently been told he was dying. I had blinked and the world had transformed with overwhelming complexity and startling reality. Yet there was nothing else to do but finish our game. So on we played around the Safari course, through Monarch Butterfly, Gorilla, Bear, and Bald Eagle.

Ken laughed at something Dad said about the Gorilla hole. I'd missed it entirely, once again lost in my head.

As we approached the final hole, Ken shouted, "Hellbender!" emphasizing the "Hell."

"What a name," Paul said.

"Indeed," Dad said, and shrugged.

I shivered. The word sounded dark and terrifying.

"What's a hellbender?" Paul wondered. In these days before smartphones, we couldn't look it up. We finished the round in near silence.

Until now, with the exception of Ken's wordplay on "Cheetah," the hole names had seemed inconsequential. But "Hellbender"?

As we packed our clubs into Mom and Dad's green station wagon for the short drive home, Ken, always trying to lighten the mood, quipped, "So disappointing. I hoped we'd at least hear a zebra."

At home, my research revealed that a hellbender was a giant, but harmless salamander. Still, I couldn't shake the jarring I'd felt when Ken had yelled "Hellbender!" I was just coming out of my own bend of hell. Were we in for another?

CHAPTER 9

TRIP OF A LIFETIME

The Sunday after the "Safari" golf outing, I walked into our kitchen to find Mom and Dad leaning over a set of TripTik plan maps from the American Automobile Association. Their TripTik laid out a route from their house in Bullhead City, Arizona, heading north through Nevada, Utah, Montana, and Wyoming, to Yellowstone National Park and the Grand Tetons.

"It's the trip of a lifetime," my father beamed.

I didn't respond, but my mind shot back, *It's the trip of your death.* I vacillated between wanting to keep everyone happy and wanting to scream at our collective denial. When Dr. Grecula, Dad's chemotherapy oncologist, told my father to get his affairs in order, he also said, "If there's anything you want to do, now's the time." In addition to playing golf, this trip was what Dad wanted.

Seeing my parents review the maps reminded me of trips they had planned from the kitchen table at the farm, trips that eventually led them to leave Ohio every year, move to Arizona, and only return to the farm during the warm summer months.

But the maps they looked over today differed vastly from the well-worn maps of the past. The edges of these maps were sharp and the pages still crisp. The whiteness stood in stark contrast to the marked and refolded maps and dog-eared AAA tour books Mom and Dad had used over and over on their annual treks to Arizona and back. None of us had traveled this route before.

"Why don't you come with us?" my father asked.

Until he posed the question, I hadn't realized I wanted to go. And, ironically, I had the time.

My depression had peaked the year before. When it hit, I could no longer summon the willpower of earlier days. I had sat in my law firm office with the door shut, performing only the simplest tasks and farming out any complex work. It was as if someone had filled my limbs with lead.

With my mood already declining, the senior partner unknowingly added a weight I feared might crush me. He and I had started the firm together. We invited the other attorney "partners" to join us over a period of years. But only the senior partner had a financial stake in the firm. Now, he wanted each of us "partners" to contribute financially on the chance we would benefit from the firm's continued growth. This meant negotiating a formal partnership agreement and buying into the firm. It also meant getting a second mortgage on our house.

While I understood the senior partner's dilemma, that financial responsibility terrified me. When anyone mentioned the partnership agreement, my insides shouted "ABSOLUTELY NOT!" But I'd never developed a tolerance for saying "No." Thinking I needed to keep the senior partner happy and convinced I would never find a different job, I stayed quiet and stalled.

Now that the motivational-tape, pull-yourself-up-by-your-bootstraps, think-positive tools had stopped working, I doubled down on recovery and meditation.

Before Ed and I met, I had investigated alternatives to the Catholicism of my childhood. He, a lapsed Catholic like me, had turned to Buddhism. I'd heard of Zen, the form of Buddhism he practiced, but had not tried to meditate myself.

One night while we were still dating, as we sat in my straight-backed dining room chairs relaxing after dinner, Ed asked if I wanted to "sit."

"Wanna what?"

"Meditate," he said.

"I don't know how."

"Focus on your breath and try not to fidget," he instructed. He set the microwave timer for five minutes so the buzzer would be our "bell."

Five minutes felt like an hour. My mind raced. I stole glances at the clock. And, I fidgeted.

Over the next three years, I progressed to a meditation mat and cushion of my own. At first, a mental tape loop chattered from somewhere behind my right ear: *you're lazy, ugly, not any too smart.* The messages affirmed what I'd always believed about myself: I didn't measure up. Eventually, I learned to notice those thoughts without believing them.

By May of 1995, when Mom and Dad began temporarily staying with us, Ed and I "sat" every evening. I could sit nearly motionless for half an hour. After learning how truly ill Dad was, however, meditation no longer quieted my mind. Instead, my head filled with terrifying scenarios. I sat anyway.

Before Dad's diagnosis, when I was still practicing law, meditation also revealed that I had lied to myself about who I was and what I was built to do. Over time, my sitting practice and the tools I learned in sobriety began to teach me to see myself as I was, not as I wished or hoped or prayed to be.

I could no longer pretend to love litigation. I could no longer pretend I wasn't terrified in court or that I didn't detest family law. And I could no longer pretend I wanted to be a financial partner. Meditation and sobriety made it impossible to hide from myself.

And I couldn't lie to Ed. He had fallen in love with the real me, not the lawyer in the expensive suit, but the sensitive woman who read his every facial expression. When someone loves you for who you are, it becomes impossible to keep lying to yourself.

During this continuing decline in my mood, an article appeared in the *American Bar Association Journal* about the Myers-Briggs personality typing system. It gave a small self-test, listed the sixteen personality types, and ranked the most common among lawyers. I walked up as several of the attorneys and staff were comparing their results. One of the interns handed me the magazine. I scored my answers and handed it back.

"Wow!" she said. "You're the only one in the office so far with that type." I asked what she meant. She pointed to a graph at the bottom of the page. When I saw that fewer than .01% of all attorneys had the ISFP personality type, the one my results indicated, my throat filled with bile.

Before I could excuse myself, one of my partners joked, "You're just special." The room swayed.

As I walked down the long hall back to my office, I wanted to keep walking right out the front door. Comparing my test results to those of the other attorneys brought to awareness a truth I'd been trying to dodge since that first day in Professor Travalio's contracts class in law school when I felt so out of place.

Over the next few weeks, I checked out several library books on the Myers-Briggs and took a more extensive test. It hadn't been my imagination. I *was* different.

I tried to get help understanding what was wrong with me. When an attorney friend changed professions with the help of a career counselor, I made an appointment. Perhaps she could use the Myers-Briggs test results to steer me toward a career better suited to my skills. After two months of weekly visits, the career counselor said my psychological problems prevented further progress. I needed to see a therapist. Part of me knew she was right, but I wasn't ready.

Then one morning, nine years into my legal career, I sat at my law office desk staring in disbelief at an order from an administrative agency. Two words glared off the page: Appeal Denied.

The agency had ruled that I had missed the deadline to file an appeal.

Stunned, I read and reread the document. The voice of Professor Whaley from law school rang in my ears. "Miss a filing deadline? No matter. Your client still has a cause of action: Malpractice, *against you!*"

The appeal had been due within fourteen days after my client received the agency's order. When I learned from our client that the agency had ruled against them, I asked what day they had received the order. From that date, I counted off fourteen business days and marked the calendar with the appeal deadline. By my calculations, the appeal was due by 5:00 p.m. on a Monday.

The Friday before the Monday appeal deadline, I had stayed home in bed suffering from the black cloud of depression. Despite my attempts to look, feel, and act like a lawyer, interior mental health battles plagued me. In my mind, what seemed to outsiders like a well-oiled machine in an expensive women's suit had been built with shoddy parts, or maybe the wrong parts, or in some places no parts at all. I chided myself for what I saw as laziness, but simply could not get up.

The following Monday, believing with full confidence I was meeting the deadline, I hand-delivered the appeal to the agency.

What my client at the home office hadn't known, and shouldn't have mattered, was that a satellite office had received a duplicate copy of the order a day before my client did. The opponent had argued that the appeal window ran from the date the satellite office received the order and not from when the home office did. They argued that I had filed the appeal one day too late. The agency agreed with our opponent.

"Appeal Denied."

The edges of my vision blurred and my heart pounded in my head.

I believed the agency was wrong. But to those who don't understand administrative procedure, this looked like I had missed the filing deadline. And that looked like malpractice.

Worse yet, unless I could convince a hearing officer to overturn the order, the Ohio Bar Association, Ohio Ethics Commission, and Ohio Supreme Court might consider it malpractice as well!

I bent over and put my head in my hands. Had the carpet always been that shade of green, the color of money?

In my already frail state, it took half an hour to compose myself enough to call the other partners into the conference room. Shaking, I handed the senior partner the document.

"I'll make it right," I promised, intent on finding legal opinions to support my understanding of the law.

The senior partner put his arm around me. I didn't think I deserved comfort, so I pulled away.

Another partner agreed to handle the challenge. The others reassured me that the decision would be reversed.

"You're a good lawyer," one said. Another joked, "Shit happens!" which only made me cry harder.

They meant well, but I was already on a slow slide toward a major mental health breakdown. This ruling shattered my remaining confidence. I lacked the resilience to shake it off as the cost of doing business or a lesson to leave more room around filing deadlines. It felt like a failing of the first order. The biggest failure of my life.

When we finished, the senior partner called the client, who promptly fired our firm. Then, he called the malpractice insurers.

❀ ❀ ❀

In the ensuing weeks, my mood continued its downward spiral and my body's sensitivity to adrenaline increased.

One spring evening, I headed around the Columbus outer belt to meet some women friends. As I approached the bridge across the Scioto River, my heart rate increased and the blood rushed from my head to my limbs. A vision of the bridge collapsing beneath me flashed in my mind. I turned up the radio, willed myself to keep driving, and held my breath until I was on the other side. When I saw the short overpass across Smokey Row Road ahead, my heart rate soared again. Crossing the previous bridge had depleted my willpower. I involuntarily slowed and cars sped by. When a delivery truck swerved and honked, I gave in to the wave of adrenaline and pulled to the berm.

Parked on the edge of the highway with cars and semis flying past, I rolled down the window to catch my breath. I didn't yet know that more oxygen exacerbated my symptoms. I'm not sure how long I sat there with my heart pounding in my head before, in the rear-view mirror, I saw the familiar sedan of one of the other partners pull up behind me. By the time he was able to get out of his car in the heavy traffic and reach my passenger door, I was crying so hard I couldn't speak. He crawled in, sat quietly beside me, and handed me his handkerchief.

After I stopped crying long enough to tell him what had happened, he shared that his wife also suffered from panic attacks and agreed to keep my ailment in confidence. Still terrified to drive, I got in his car and he dropped me off at my destination. Later that night, Ed picked me up and drove us to where my car had been, but it was gone—towed to the impound lot.

I felt defeated, but in a different way from the filing deadline debacle. My car being impounded disturbed me, but having one of my partners appear out of nowhere and learning that his wife also suffered from panic attacks made me want to get help. My body and mind surrendered, similar to the comfort I felt when I joined the recovery community to stop drinking.

Hoping for a simple solution, I saw a psychiatrist. He prescribed medication, but it exacerbated my depression, so I stopped taking it.

One Sunday a few months before we married, Ed and I drove from Columbus to Indianapolis to visit Paul at college in Indiana. As Ed's car sped down the highway, my heart began to pound in my ears.

"Stop the car!" I screamed and grabbed at the door handle, intending to jump from the moving vehicle.

Ed pulled me toward him and guided the car to the berm. When I heard the click of the emergency flasher button and the rhythmic snapping, my body relaxed. As his arms encircled me and he clutched me to his chest, I could hear his heart pounding. I wrestled free, found the door handle, and got out. The rush of air burned my lungs. I put my head between my knees and leaned against the car until the spell subsided.

A few days later, when I saw an ad for a thirteen-week panic and anxiety group, I signed up. These professionals offered skills, not drugs, and promised to help me manage my fear. At the end of the thirteen weeks, my anxiety was not gone, but it had lessened considerably.

❧ ❧ ❧

One night a few months after I'd nearly jumped out of a car he was driving, Ed came home from work and asked me to join him in the kitchen. On the table sat a small, square box.

He pushed it toward me.

Inside was a finely detailed, ceramic turtle figurine. I must have looked confused because he immediately explained.

In his office at work hung a monthly calendar of "Sacred Spaces." When Ed turned the 1993 calendar from May to June, the image for the month was of "Turtle Island" in Japan. It showed a pond with hundreds of turtles sunning themselves on rocks in the water and along the surrounding banks. The caption told how the long-lived turtle symbolizes longevity. It also explained that guests at wedding ceremonies present the bride and groom with ceramic turtles to show their wish for a long, happy marriage.

"I wasn't sure I wanted to get married again," he said. "But when I turned the calendar, I had my answer." He'd purchased the turtle in lieu of a ring because he wanted me to choose my own.

He didn't ask, "Will you marry me?" He just sat there looking down at the turtle.

So, I wrapped my arms around him and said, "Yes!"

A year-and-a-half before I watched Mom and Dad show off their shiny, new maps, Ed and I married in the Japanese garden at Dawes Arboretum, twenty miles from the farm. With my parents at my sides, I walked the curved pathway from the tea house to the arched bridge that leads to two tiny islands. On one island, a pair of flutists played Japanese music to signal our approach. On the other, Ed, his two sons, my sister, two of my friends, and the officiant waited. After the service, in the receiving line, my parents beamed.

My favorite wedding photo, taken after the ceremony ended, shows Ed helping me back across the little bridge to meet our guests. I'm wearing a floor-length black dress with pastel pink, aqua, and olive-green flowers. A white floral headband holds back my curly, chin-length hair. I have gathered my dress in my right hand, which also holds a white bouquet. Ed, in his gray suit and tie, holds my left hand as we both look down at the bridge. His smile is kind, but determined. My eyes are trusting. He will make sure we cross to safety. He will make certain we are okay.

Like all the other things I had tried, I hoped marriage might heal my depression and anxiety, but it didn't. I continued to be miserable, especially at work. Although I did my best to hide my increasing depression from Ed, as my mood worsened, I couldn't keep it from him any longer. Unlike my mother, who was famous for giving my father ultimatums instead of sharing her emotions, I began to tell Ed about my desperation. I told him I needed a break. I wanted to go to Arizona and intended to ask my parents if I could stay in their house for a week. Ed asked, "Are you sure a vacation will help?" but was otherwise supportive.

With my parents in Arizona during the winter months, 1,700 miles away, I easily kept them from seeing how miserable I had become. I only talked to them on days when I could sound perky.

When I called to ask if I could use their Arizona house for a getaway, something in my voice must have alarmed my mother because she immediately called Dad to the phone.

"You going alone?" he asked.

"Yes."

"Is your marriage in trouble?"

It hadn't occurred to me he might jump to that incorrect conclusion, but given my relationship history, it was a reasonable question.

"No!" I said. "We're fine."

And we were. My marriage was one of the few areas holding together.

I explained that Ed didn't have any vacation right now. But I couldn't say why I needed a break. I didn't understand it myself.

"I'm stressed," I said. "I just need to get away."

Relieved, Dad agreed I could use their house.

I traveled to Arizona, but the temperature in Bullhead City where Mom and Dad's house was located soared to 120°F and held. Instead of facing that heat, I drove to Sedona. I spent long days in the shadow of Cathedral Rock. The books I read on "finding your passion" and "following your destiny" only made me more depressed. I spent most of the plane ride back to Columbus crying.

Eight months before my parents invited me to join them on Dad's bucket-list trip, a crucial part of my mind felt broken. A decade of untreated chronic depression took its toll. I lost the ability to play "happy camper" at work. The facade collapsed and with it my ability to think, write, plan, and sometimes even speak.

I could no longer walk directly into my office without first going to the bathroom to throw up. I didn't intend to vomit, but no matter what I tried, each morning began the same way.

At night, I came home exhausted. Previously, Ed, Ken, and I took turns cooking. As my mental health declined, recipes confused me. I became irritable when I tried to prepare a meal and often burned the food. Ed and Ken took over.

When I complained of lethargy, Ed listened. I knew him to be a man of action and sensed his frustration. We didn't speak of it directly, but I could feel the strain of him waiting for me to get better or for something to change. He wanted to be empathetic, but he also carried worries of his own.

Ed specialized in helping companies in financial crisis. I pictured him galloping in on a white horse to rescue companies in need, as much knight as executive. Unfortunately, he had recently discovered that his employer was committing fraud. Ed wouldn't perpetuate it and told the auditor, who reported it. Later, Ed testified before the grand jury. He didn't need any more pressure.

But one day shortly after I returned from Sedona, I sat at our long oval conference table in my usual place to the right of the senior partner for the monthly partners' meeting. His words about billable hours, client development, and the possible partnership agreement sounded garbled, as if they were coming through cheap, ancient speakers.

I looked around the room at the four men I admired and respected, each clad in a well-tailored suit. A ball formed in the pit of my stomach, so I looked out the window. A white Lincoln Continental pulled into the parking lot. The chrome shone. A man got out, walked to the back, and pulled a box kite from the trunk. The kite fluttered in the slight wind as he closed the trunk lid.

It had been over a decade since I had flown a kite. I wondered if I still knew how. Instead, I had spent the last ten years perfecting the art of volleying the opposing counsel's shots like tennis balls. I wanted to be that kite: free, sailing across the breezes as they came.

The senior partner's voice faded to a distant beat against the drums pounding in my head. I imagined ripping off my pearls and my natural-fiber suit jacket, tossing my navy pumps in the trash as I ran for the door. I feared the ball in my stomach was a time bomb that would explode, leaving only a pair of pantyhose as evidence I ever existed. I closed my eyes and the kite became a deer, white-tail high as it ran through the open field next to our office. It jumped into the sky and flew away. When the meeting was over, I returned to my office and called a psychologist.

A few days after that partners' meeting, I slipped out of our building and drove to the offices of a behavioral health clinic. The woman who greeted me in the lobby wore her brown hair long and straight with bangs. My hair was also long, but curly. We both wore suits. Mine was gray Glenn plaid with a long jacket and a calf-length skirt. Her brown skirt had pleats.

When I saw her, I thought, "She'll understand." Her suit, like mine, seemed hard, armored. But her eyes were soft. In their brown depths I saw hope. Maybe she knew a way out of the pain.

She extended her hand. I shook it firmly.

In her office, I sat in a side chair facing the door with my back to the wall.

"How can I help you?"

I wasn't sure.

Eventually, she would tell me that mine was the worst case of "poor job fit," she had encountered in several decades of psychology practice. Eventually, I would call her Joan. I would learn that choosing work that didn't suit me compounded my natural propensity for depression. And I learned that in part, I chose work that didn't suit me to prove my father wrong.

As a principal in the firm, an executive disability policy covered any severe illnesses or injuries. The provisions included mental illness. At my next therapy session, I asked Joan about taking time off. As I spoke, a vicious voice that sounded very much like my father screamed: *You're lazy. You don't want to work.*

But I wasn't really working. The billable hours on my weekly time sheets had dwindled. I only needed Joan to tell me that time off might help. And she did.

Then, I told the senior partner.

"I think I'm having a nervous breakdown," I said and asked for time off.

He didn't seem surprised. We had been colleagues for nearly a decade. Only once, after I rolled my car, had he asked about my erratic behavior. As long as I was turning in high hours, he hadn't acted concerned. But he knew me well enough to suspect that the decline in those billable numbers meant something serious. Now, when I explained how depressed I was, he said he was relieved I was getting help and supported me.

I turned my clients over to other attorneys in the firm and left for a brief leave of absence.

The healthiest suggestion about how to spend my time off came from Ken. He prescribed long, slow walks by the river, strolling around town with the dogs, and not worrying about anything. But I couldn't follow his sage advice. Instead, I enrolled in writing and psychology courses at the community college. I also pitched my first major publication—that *Dog World* magazine article I was looking over when, six months later, my father called to tell me the cancer was in his bones.

I also tried to write a book. The working title was *Divorce with Dignity: A Lawyer's Perspective on the Cruel End to Marriage.* But I was neither a divorce specialist nor a therapist. More importantly, I'd never written a book. It was as if I'd decided to take up dentistry and wondered why I didn't have the first clue how to drill a tooth.

I kept trying to *do* something, to *fix* something, when what I needed was to simply *be*.

As the close of my imagined month of leave neared, I grew desperate. My mind filled with vivid daydreams of ending my life. On September 29, 1994, I arrived late to Joan's office in the same clothes I'd had on for a week. In the past, I'd dressed carefully for my appointments.

When Joan saw me, she did a double take. I slumped into the chair with my hair uncombed, face unwashed, three-day-old blue jeans and ratty, gray sweatshirt. I'd been playing "happy camper" even with her.

She calmly asked what I'd been up to. I forgot to act nonchalant. Bottled inside were fears of the entire month: worry about getting a job, fears about not being able to write a book, general anxiety, and an inability to tell anyone how much pain I was in.

I told her about feeling like a clock was ticking down and my "If I have to go back to work, I think I will die" thoughts. I told her about oversleeping all the time and not wanting to get up. I thought everything was hopeless, especially me.

Without feeling the gravity of my words, I said, "I've been thinking about suicide."

Her eyes narrowed and flashed. She leaned forward.

"When?"

"This morning," I said as flatly as if I'd told her I had taken up knitting.

Her long hair swirled as she sat up very straight then leaned in again. "I'm going to explore this further with you."

I nodded. I wanted her to help me find the cause of the depression and vanquish it. Hope rose in me like a tiny flame.

"Would you be willing to take a cab to the Riverside Hospital Emergency Room if you felt that way again?"

Suddenly alert, I said, "That seems extreme. I'd rather just call the suicide prevention hotline again."

"Again?"

I looked out the window at the parking lot. Where was the man with the kite? Oh. That was a different building, a different day.

I looked back at the carpet. "I taped the number to all the phones."

From the corner of my eye, I could see her teetering on the edge of her chair, "How many times have you called?"

"I don't remember. Maybe six."

"But you didn't call this morning?"

Feeling the intensity of her gaze, I said, "I came here instead."

"I need you to wait here."

She was gone for what seemed like a very long time. When she returned, the staff psychiatrist walked in behind her. He asked me about that morning and any other times I'd thought about, "taking my life."

"The thoughts drift like clouds," I explained. "They seem matter-of-fact, as if I were thinking about taking out the trash or doing the laundry."

His reply startled me.

"What do you think about going to the hospital now, for a short period of time? Just until we're sure you're through this current crisis."

My eyes felt like saucers.

"I'm concerned about your safety," he said.

I hadn't realized what I'd been saying and ratted on myself without knowing it. Some part of me wanted their help. I didn't mean for things to get so intense, but I was exhausted. I imagined a quiet place where I could rest. Maybe even nap. A room where no one could get in. No phone. Someone would bring me three meals a day and leave me alone.

"Maybe," I said.

Both Joan and the psychiatrist insisted I was unfit to drive myself to the hospital. They continued to talk about how my mind was turning on me and how much danger they thought I might be in. Eventually, they suggested I call Ed at work, so I did.

On the phone, I explained their concerns and suggestions to him.

Because Ed had no idea how badly the terrain of my mind had deteriorated, he was confused and unconvinced. "Is hospitalization really necessary?" he asked. When I said that's what Joan and the psychiatrist recommended, he asked why I couldn't drive myself.

I had to come clean.

I hadn't cried during the entire session, but I choked back tears as I told Ed about the number of times I had called the suicide hotline and my thoughts of ending my life.

He went silent. He'd no doubt seen the numbers taped to the phones. But I'd never told him I had actually called. Through the line, I sensed his initial shock followed by a shift as the reality settled in.

When Ed spoke again, his demeanor had changed. He would come right away. With him at my side, I signed myself into the hospital that afternoon.

After a few days in the psych ward, I didn't feel like killing myself anymore. They released me, but I wasn't sure I wanted to live. The single screw holding me together had popped out. The springs had blown away. I feared they would never go back together.

Seven weeks in a highly structured outpatient "partial hospital" program followed my hospital stay, then group therapy of three half-day sessions per week as well as individual counseling.

Seven months later, my father called to tell me he had cancer in his bones.

⚬ ⚬ ⚬

After Dad's diagnosis, when my parents returned to Ohio, I was still in group therapy and individual counseling. I wasn't ready for them to come home, but I was willing to be present and awake for the experience, whatever it entailed.

I had believed that if I followed the rules, prepared thoroughly, and worked hard enough, I would be safe. Now, with my career in question and my father planning his last great drive, I saw that certainty could fail. Maps, deadlines, and good intentions all assumed that time would behave and the road would wait. None of that was true.

Earlier in the month, when my father had said that all he wanted to do—even before seeing a doctor—was play golf, I wasn't ready, but I was available, even on a Thursday. If he also wanted to take an extended road trip, I could do that, too.

When Dad looked up from the "trip of a lifetime" map and asked me to join them, I didn't hesitate.

"I'm in," I said.

Dad beamed and I watched his mental wheels kick into high gear.

I hadn't asked Ed. I hadn't considered being away from my mental health providers. And I hadn't thought about what the trip might cost. In that moment, with Dad smiling at me, none of that mattered.

"Here's the plan," he said. "You and I play as much golf as we can through August. Then, your mother and I will drive home to Arizona. In September, you fly to Vegas. We'll meet you there and head north."

"Let's do it!" I said. I was all in.

THE FRONT NINE
JUNE 1995 TO SEPTEMBER 1995

Success depends almost entirely on how effectively you learn to manage the game's two ultimate adversaries: the course and yourself.

—Jack Nicklaus

Chapter 10

Repairing Divots

The yellow sticky note on the dashboard of my car read "BROADVIEW." For the past seven months since I'd been in the psych ward, each time I drove, I put a note on the dash bearing the name of my destination in big magic marker letters. Today's note reminded me to drive to a nine-hole course in Pataskala a few miles from the farm. In those days before GPS, I sometimes forgot where I was headed before I reached the end of the driveway. Without the sticky note, I had to check my date book or go back in the house and call Ed to figure out my destination. On days when I didn't have any activities, I stayed close to home, exhausted by the swings between depression and anxiety.

Now that Mom and Dad's rental trailer was ready and they had moved out of our house, we followed Dad's plan. Yellowstone would wait until the end of the summer after Mom and Dad drove back out west in August. It was still June and those dimpled white balls weren't going to hit themselves.

Dad and I decided to golf weekly on Thursdays, the same day we had originally played at Wilson Road. I didn't have group, individual therapy, or class on Thursdays. Dad didn't have doctor's appointments and Mom was occupied watching my niece, Jamey. But golfing with him meant driving to the inexpensive Licking County golf courses he favored. My anxiety would make these trips a challenge, but I would face it, to get to spend the time with Dad. So, off I headed to Broadview.

❧ ❧ ❧

The narrow country road to Broadview with its deep ditches triggered a dark childhood memory. My heart raced and I shook my head as if I could rid it of the agonizing images. They kept surfacing, so I pulled over. From the glove box, I grabbed the paper bag I'd stashed long ago after the panic and anxiety course. I breathed into it. Once my heart stopped beating in my throat, I continued toward the course.

I had recently traded the Volvo for a high-mileage Toyota wagon and chided myself for my ambivalence about my lowered automotive status. My concern over what type of car I drove seemed ridiculous in light of Dad's plight. That familiar, berating, inner voice arose in my head, so I channeled the group therapy leader, Harri, and reframed things. I was driving! I only missed one turn. Arriving less than ten minutes late was a victory.

When I pulled up, Dad, for whom "prompt" meant "early," stood leaning against his Honda. He didn't ask why I was late and I didn't offer an excuse. We hugged and pulled our clubs out of our respective wagons.

❧ ❧ ❧

Awkward and painfully shy during my grade school years, I had trouble making and keeping friends. Beyond the two girls at the neighboring farm, my closest school pals lived miles away. Between school years, when the long summers stretched our farm into fifty acres of loneliness, I rarely saw them. As a result, my little beagle Puppsy was also my best friend.

During those lonely summer months, I sat with Puppsy on the dirt floor of the barn and told her my secrets: the new boy I hoped would still be at school in the fall, my fear of my horse

Baylady after she threw me, and how I didn't know why the other kids didn't like me.

On the third hole, after a few of Dad's strokes and many more of mine, we walked our pushcarts across a quaint covered bridge over the south fork of the Licking River. Dad pointed out the craftsmanship. The way he noticed these details reminded me that he was a skilled woodworker, a hobby he seemed to have abandoned when he took up golf.

After I putted out and we headed toward four, the memory I'd tried to stuff into the back of my mind during my car drive to the course pushed through.

In fourth grade, at the end of each day when I got off the bus, Puppsy trotted to the end of our gravel drive to meet me. One March afternoon, following the sweet smell of boiling maple syrup, Puppsy, Sally—one of the girls from the neighboring farm—and I headed down the road toward the sugar shack, hoping for a sample.

We walked along the edge of the woods on the opposite side of the ditch from the road. I turned my head to see Puppsy trotting behind us. Just as a car was cresting the top of the hill, Puppsy zipped across the road in a black-and-white blur. I tensed, and then relaxed when I saw her wiry form safely on the other side. "Puppsy! You silly dog," I yelled, smiling at her brown eyes. But our line of sight was cut off by a second car speeding past. Puppsy's black-and-white shape flew through the air followed by a sickening thump.

I ran into the road where Puppsy lay on the pavement. My best friend was on her side, blood streaming from her panting mouth, her open eye looking toward the sky.

Sally pulled me out of the road, then ran toward her own house. I tore off after her toward our house, yelling for Mom and Dad. As I ran into the yard, Mom came out the front door. When she reached me, she wrapped me in her arms to calm me.

I pointed down the road, "Puppsy. A car. She's bleeding." Over Mom's shoulder I saw Dad look out through the storm door then disappear into the house. Over my protests, Mom ushered me in after him. "We've got to get her to the vet," I cried.

"Dad will take care of her," Mom said. I imagined Dad folding Puppsy into his arms and whisking her off to the vet. Perhaps she would return as good as new. I wanted to go with Dad, but Mom kept her arm firmly around me. My legs wobbled, so I leaned against her.

The front screen slammed and Mom tightened her grip, trying to turn me away from the door. I pulled back enough to see Dad's figure disappear down the tree-lined road. From his right hand swung the stock end of his .22. I broke away, shoved through the door, and ran after him. I could hear Mom's feet scuttling through the grass as she ran behind me.

Dad was almost to the spot where Puppsy lay. I screamed "No!" Dad stopped, turned, pointed at me, and yelled, "Go back to the house with your mother right now."

Mom caught me, grabbed my shoulder, and pulled me back down the road toward the house. "She's still breathing," I wailed in a long, deep howl.

In the yard, Mom pulled me closer. "Honey, her brain is probably dead. She'd be a vegetable."

When the shot cracked in the air I sank to the ground. The sound echoed through the valley as Mom sat down next to me in the stiff grass.

On six, Dad pulled a club from his bag and let it hang from his hand as he walked to the tee. It dangled casually, swaying the same way Dad's .22 had when he carried it down the tree-lined road so many years before.

As Dad walked towards the tee, oblivious to the sad memories crowding my thoughts, he looked strong and vibrant with that ball cap perched on his handsome blond head. I found it hard to believe this was the same man I'd been so angry with as a child, and harder still to accept that both versions of him were true.

When he placed his ball on the tee, it fell off. We both laughed, but I thought I detected a slight tremor in his hands. I decided I had imagined it.

The night of Puppsy's death, I'd lain in bed feigning sleep when my parents came to check on me.

"Why's she so upset?" Dad whispered.

"She just didn't understand," Mom answered.

After a few moments, Dad muttered, "It was just a dog. We can get another dog."

I squeezed my eyes shut as hard as I could and waited for the door to click. When it did, an emotional door inside me swung shut with it.

Puppsy's death was the first time I'd lost something I couldn't imagine living without. It was also the first time my father disappointed me by simply being human. Despite his stoicism, when I was a child I'd thought of him as all-powerful and benevolent. I'd run to him to heal her. Instead, he'd picked up his rifle. I thought he hadn't given her a chance. For a few weeks, I refused to speak to him and he did the chores without me.

For months after, I had nightmares. For decades, I repeatedly checked the backyard gate before leaving the house, despite knowing the dogs were asleep inside. To this day, I will only walk dogs on a leash.

*   *   *

Dad and I finished an enjoyable and otherwise uneventful round. He did not ask about my mental health or my writing. I did not ask about his doctor's appointments or his symptoms. Instead, he regaled me with another of his seemingly endless supply of tales about golfing with his buddies in Arizona.

I wanted to ask: Did you know what Puppsy meant to me? Did you understand I had no one else? But his face was open and relaxed. He had no clue that I was still angry about a beagle from 1970.

Or maybe I wasn't angry anymore. Maybe I was scared of losing him the way I'd lost her.

On nine, when I missed a putt, Dad didn't correct me. He simply waited while I hit again.

At the car, I asked, "Same time next Thursday?"

"You bet," he said.

As I stood in the Broadview parking lot, I acknowledged to myself that I'd misinterpreted his actions all these years. He had thought Puppsy was beyond saving and he may have been right. It had been kind of him to end her suffering. He hadn't failed me. He'd done what he thought was merciful. At thirty-three, I could see that. At nine, I couldn't. We might have all summer, but it was already the end of June, time to start letting things go.

*   *   *

The following Thursday, Dad and I headed to another course near the farm, Nomis, which got its name by spelling the owner's name, "Simon," backwards. On the third hole, Dad spotted gouges and nicked bits of sod. "Somebody chopped the hell out of this course," Dad said, surveying a fairway filled with holes from other players' clubs. "Don't people know you're supposed to clean up after yourself?"

Dad believed other players should notice these divots as well as the dents in the crew-cut grass on the greens. They should repair them by replacing each sod chunk in the fairway and stomping on it. To fill the bare spots, players should sprinkle the grass seed that many courses provided. And each green should be tapped flat with a putter. "It's common courtesy," Dad said. To my father, tending the course was an obsession.

Dad relished the tidiness of golf. It was like the Latin Mass he had memorized when he was a child. The chalice sat in the same place on the altar every Sunday and, as an altar boy, he would ring the bells at the precise moment the liturgy demanded. On the golf course, people also had responsibilities. He thought his job was to help them live up to that. Every course could look like the immaculate Pebble Beach Golf Links if people just did their duty. Then his world could be the precise, orderly place of which he dreamed.

Dad reached into his pants pocket, pulled out a handful of grass seed and began broadcasting it across the fairway with long strokes of his right arm, the same practiced motion he used to spread seed by hand across the acres of lawn on the farm.

While my father enjoyed farming, his true passion, arguably his primary reason for having land at all, was to manicure the grass. He tended it with the care I showed the dogs, cats, and horses I loved. When my brother learned to drive, he dared not veer off the gravel driveway lest my usually stoic father run out of the house and bellow, "Stay off the grass!" The rest of us had animals, but that lawn was Dad's pet. Hours spent seeding, fertilizing, and weeding engaged Dad's primary characteristics:

a tendency toward perfectionism and a penchant for growing things, especially lawns.

When I was six or seven, I sat on Dad's lap as he drove the riding mower. When my legs grew long enough to reach the pedals, pushing them became my job. I rode the mower for hours, craving his approval with every turn of the wheel.

Once I was tall enough, Dad trained me to trim the borders of our ten-acre "lawn" with a twenty-one-inch push Lawn-Boy. I longed to hear him say, "You're getting the hang of it!" as he showed me how to pivot the mower around the row of pines at our property line. He and I were groundskeepers of our "green acres."

As the years passed and my body matured, my desire to please Dad waned and along with it my willingness to mow the lawn. If he mentioned the length of the grass, I snapped, "I know!" and stomped toward the barn before he could complete his sentence. Meanwhile, after a decade of childhood spent relatively unaware of my body, I started crossing my arms over my chest when I walked into a room. At dinner, I hunched forward, shoulders curved inward. When Dad asked me to pass the salt, I kept my arms pressed tight to my sides. I thought everyone was watching my changing body and it made my skin crawl.

The insatiable hormonal longing for connection with a boy my own age further complicated my relationship with my father. I spent hours writing in little red journals I tucked between the mattress and box springs: *He smiled at me in math class. He winked at me in the hallway.* I walked alone in the woods, sauntering up to a tree and leaning against it for a few moments before wrapping my arms around it and placing my lips upon the bark. The sturdy tree became the boy who had held my fingers in his warm hand in the dark backseat of his parents' car as we rode home from a school event. I didn't think of sex so much as romance and physical closeness. I also didn't think about the thump of the electric fence charger except in the way it mimicked my heart when that boy was around.

When Dad tried to ruffle my hair or "steal my nose" the way he always did when I was younger, I jerked away. He would reach for his coffee cup and act like nothing had happened.

On eight at Nomis, I hit my ball into the rough. Dad searched, moving methodically through the grass, determined to find it.

"Let me drop another," I said, holding up the ball I'd already pulled out of my bag.

"It's got to be here," he said, eyes to the grass. "I'll find it."

The way he insisted on finding that one lost ball, needing to remedy the situation, reminded me of a time when I created a different, more awkward mess, one he couldn't fix.

Boys had been on my radar since second grade when I'd carefully written a boy's full name in my tiny journal. By seventh grade I had allowed the first boy who had ever held my hand to kiss me amid the hay bales in our barn. During the summer between my eighth grade and freshman year, I let that same boy take my virginity on a hay wagon at the county fairgrounds. We had "wandered" away from the shelter house where the marching band was holding a fundraiser. My father had brought me to the event and when I was gone a little too long, he came looking. A friend interrupted our tryst before Dad found us. The boy fled while I composed myself.

"Where'd you go?" my scowling father asked when he found me walking around the empty fairground.

"For a walk," I lied, still tingling from the encounter and the terror at such a close call. I could not meet his eyes.

Shortly after I turned fifteen, physical distance compounded our emotional separation. Ohio Bell transferred Dad to Cleveland for a short-term assignment. He never questioned the decision or thought about looking for another job. He'd been with the company more than twenty years and hoped to retire from it in twenty more. He also expected to be back in Columbus again within a year. I'd just begun my junior year of high school and didn't want to leave the friends I had finally made. Likewise, Dad couldn't bear the idea of giving up the farm. He and Mom decided that he would commute three hours from Columbus to Cleveland on Sundays and back again on Friday evenings. Dad packed his black-and-red plaid, zippered suitcase, got in his car, and left.

Dad's "year" in Cleveland turned into more than two and ended what was left of our evenings in the barn together. When he was home on weekends, I groaned at his requests to mow or mend fences, tasks I used to beg for. My focus had shifted entirely to my horse, my flute, or that boy.

In September of my senior year of high school, while Dad was home from Cleveland on vacation, the boy's father called him. The two men knew each other from our school activities. When Dad got off the phone he asked if any of my classmates were in any kind of trouble. I did not know. The boy's father had asked to meet Dad at our elementary school playground.

"He sounds secretive," Dad said.

I left for all-day band practice before Dad came back from their meeting.

When I returned at dinner time, company filled the back yard. My brother Jim, my sister-in-law, Deanna, their three young children, and Deanna's parents, Carol and Carl, sat in lawn chairs with Mom and Dad. They had been talking quietly, but stopped when they saw me. I felt uneasy, but told myself I was imagining things.

My brother and his family stayed until late in the evening. As we all talked, I thought about the boy and his father, but pushed aside my worry. After the company left, Dad said, "I need to talk to you." My mother hurriedly dried her hands on a kitchen towel and scurried down the hall. Their bedroom door closed behind her.

At the end of the dining table, Dad turned a chair sideways and placed another chair facing it. He sat in one chair and pointed to the other. I sat. Already my face had flushed and I didn't even know what I'd done.

"You know that phone call?" he said, referring to his call with the boy's father.

I nodded, barely able to breathe.

"His son may be in a little bit of trouble."

"Oh?" I tried to act mildly curious, but not too interested.

Dad continued, "He's a robbery suspect."

"What?" Now I was truly shocked. The boy was fast for his age, but I didn't peg him as a thief.

Dad shifted in his chair. "And guess whose house he might have robbed?"

I shrugged. Dad was playing cat and mouse. I honestly didn't know what he was talking about.

"Have you ever met a woman named Mrs. Wilford?"

One of my classmates had that last name, but I'd never met her family. "I don't think so," I said, trying to be honest while sweat poured down my back.

"Well, she's a friend of Carol's." Carol was my brother's mother-in-law.

I nodded, still puzzled, and Dad, perhaps needing to end the agony himself, began to fill in the details.

Carol and Mrs. Wilford, both teachers, had taught together years before and stayed in touch. When Carol came to visit us at the farm, she would call her friend to save long-distance phone charges. Tonight, when the two former colleagues chatted, Mrs. Wilford had told Carol that her home had been robbed and her television stolen.

She had added, "I felt awful reporting that girl."

As Dad, continued, I still wasn't sure if or how I might be involved.

Finally, Dad shouted, "Don't you remember parking in Mrs. Wilford's driveway! That girl is YOU!"

I stared at the brown swirled kitchen carpet as I remembered.

A few months before, during our tiny town's summer festival, the boy had persuaded me to drive to his house and meet him for a tryst in his basement bedroom. "My parents will be asleep. I'll turn off the alarm." My desire to be touched and held outweighed my common sense and he easily convinced me to park in his neighbor, Mrs. Wilford's, driveway.

But his sense of danger was high and he had called her not once, but twice, to ask permission. This raised Mrs. Wilford's suspicions and she had jotted down my license plate number. A week later, when, in an unrelated event, her home was robbed, she gave my license plate number to the police. When the boy's father called that morning, it was to warn Dad that I too might be a suspect.

"Carol told us all!" Dad said. No one had needed to tell any of them what the boy and I had been doing. They had all been teenagers themselves.

By the time Dad finished, I was sobbing, my head in my hands. Emotions flooded my body. I was relatively certain that the boy hadn't been involved in the robbery, and, as it turned out, he wasn't. But I was angry at him for tipping off Mrs. Wilford, furious at Carol for telling everyone, and outraged at Mrs. Wilford for being a nosy old lady.

Deeper than any of that was my shame. I pictured the family sitting in their lawn chairs as Carol told them. Dad's face reddening. Mom and Carl looking off into the distance. Deanna nodding. Jim shifting in his chair.

In my version of teenage invincibility, I believed we had gotten away with it. And, it never occurred to me how my behavior might affect Mom and Dad.

"Are you pregnant?" Dad asked, jarring me from the swirl in my head.

"No!" I said, surprised at my sudden incredulity.

"How do you know?" he insisted.

A knot rose in my throat. Dad and I never broached the subject of periods or sex. On the farm, we sometimes talked about equine, bovine, canine, and feline reproduction, but never where human babies came from.

"That was a month ago. I've had my period since."

He nodded.

We sat for a few more minutes. As I continued to look down at the carpet, I sensed a change. His body relaxed. Had he only been worried about that? Or, perhaps he didn't know what to say next.

Finally, he muttered "I'm so disappointed. I expected better of you."

Disappointing my father was the worst. I tasted salt as tears again streamed down my face.

He grounded me for a month and forbade me to see or speak to the boy ever again.

"You know he's trouble," he said.

Of course, I knew. That had been the attraction.

Still, I promised.

Avoiding the boy would be simple. In six years, he'd never even called me once. We barely spoke except to make plans. I knew from hearing other girls whisper about their encounters with him that I wasn't his only lover. His touch meant the world to me, but if I meant anything to him, he didn't show it. It didn't break my heart to think of never seeing him again. What did break my heart was to have so badly disappointed and embarrassed my father.

I did see the boy again twice, by accident, once on the street in town, and the final time at a high-school concert. Both times, it seemed as if my father's eyes were burning into my back. Otherwise, I kept my promise. I have not seen the boy since.

❦ ❦ ❦

"Here it is!" Dad cried triumphantly.

My father had found my ball. Of course he had.

Standing there on Nomis watching him restore order to this tiny chaos, I realized what I'd missed all those years ago when he'd interrogated me about the boy. Dad hadn't meant to be cruel. Of course, he was embarrassed, but that wasn't what caused his fury. He'd been terrified. He thought I had derailed my life and that he had failed to protect me. That was his job in our family. And now, on this golf course, his job was to protect me from losing more golf balls.

As it turned out, my father didn't need to protect me from boys much longer. In December of my senior year, when my best friend kissed me, I kissed her back. After years of chasing the boy who didn't want me, I found a partner who genuinely cared. My heart bloomed.

Despite our attempts to keep our love secret at our homes and school, others suspected. Two girls falling in love in a small, rural high school in the late 1970s created a stir. I turned toward her strength and away from everything else, including my family.

Whispers followed us through the school hallways and slurs appeared on our lockers. On more than one occasion, we were summoned separately to the principal's office and questioned by the principal, guidance counselor, and superintendent about what went on while we were spending so much time with a teacher in whom we'd confided. We never divulged our relationship to the administrators. If we had, it might have made it clear that the teacher was trying to keep me from harming myself while preventing my girlfriend from hurting the people who taunted us. My teenage mood swings and inherent sensitivity morphed into a Tilt-A-Whirl. I was jubilant if my girlfriend and I got along. When we fought, I grew desperate. She maintained a tough exterior, but we shared the same pain and confusion. Meanwhile, we marked time until college, where we hoped attitudes would be more tolerant.

As my longing to spend time with my girlfriend blossomed, the farm that had once been fifty acres of peace became fifty acres of sadness. My father still worked in Cleveland and my mother kept busy with numerous church and other volunteer activities. I stayed at my girlfriend's house whenever I could. Dad noticed my absence.

One weekend when I was at our house and Dad was home from Cleveland, he asked where I'd been spending all my time. I mumbled something about studying at a friend's house. He nodded slowly. If he suspected, he didn't ask.

Then he said, "Grass is getting long."

I glared at him. After a few moments I spat, "When I grow up, I'm going to have my entire yard paved! I never want to see a blade of grass again!" I stomped out to mow and cursed him with every roll of the tires.

All these years later, my father was still tending lawns. Once he retired and took up golf, the grass at the courses became his. Stepping onto the tee box turned him into the divot king. He took care of them as if he owned them. Now, as a grown woman watching Dad kneel to pat down the seeds, his fingers tenderly working them into a bare spot at Nomis, my throat tightened. *His need to restore order is a form of love.* I looked at the tree line and tried to swallow the emotion: regret.

Throughout the afternoon, Dad stopped to repair any nick, any bump, any bare spot. I watched, content to let him tend the courses himself. It was his obsession, not mine, I told myself. But that memory of my angry teenage self, the one yelling at him that I was going to pave my lawn, nagged.

On sixteen, he again pulled a handful of seed out of his pocket and began to sprinkle it onto one of many small bare spots on the green. "It just takes a second to keep a course in shape," he said patting the spot down with his putter. "Most people are just lazy."

Despite my teenage protestations, I had grown into a lawn-tending adult who spent hours every week mowing and trimming my own front and back lawns. Only the driveway was paved. I too admired the tidiness of a freshly mowed yard and edged beds filled with flowers. When I was in my own yard pushing my own mower, I heard his voice in my head. *You're getting the hang of it.*

I took a sharp breath then slowly let it out. When the pang of regret didn't pass, I held out my hand and asked "Got anymore?"

He grinned and handed me a palm full of the tan slivers. A glow filled my heart as we spent several minutes patting seed into the bare places before we moved to the next tee.

CHAPTER 11

MIND IF I HAVE A BEER?

Reminiscent of our snacks at the Memorial Tournament, after nine holes on any course we played, Dad and I would stop at the clubhouse for a snack: root beer for him, coffee for me, and hot dogs for both of us.

But today, at the turn, Dad asked, "Mind if I have a beer?"

In high school, the distance between Dad and me had eventually grown wide enough that I defied him outright. On a Sunday afternoon, as Dad packed his plaid suitcase to leave early for Cleveland, he said, "Don't know about that concert. If it starts to snow, stay home."

My friends and I had tickets to see the band Heart at St. John Arena on the university campus in Columbus. The weather forecasters predicted strong snowstorms. Flakes began to fall shortly after he departed.

I left anyway.

I wanted to prove to my friends how mature I was by drinking openly. I'd already paid for the liquor my friend's older boyfriend was buying. And, I'd agreed to drive. In embroidered bell-bottoms and a polyester shirt, I strutted past my worried mother and got behind the wheel of my royal blue Plymouth Valiant.

At that time, both of my parents still drank. A bottle of cheap Mattingly & Moore whiskey, which Dad called his "M&M's," lived beneath the kitchen sink. Stacks of long-necked Budweiser bottles lined the bottom drawers of our refrigerator.

Dad rarely slurred his speech or appeared outwardly drunk. Usually, drinking mellowed him. But one evening, after he'd had a few beers, he erupted over Mom's spending. He threw the checkbook at her, yelled, "I give up!" then stomped out the back door, which slammed behind him. With my gut reeling and my body shuddering, I watched and listened as he hurled sawhorses at the house, wood against wood crashing against our white siding. I turned away and cowered, waiting for one of them to smash through the kitchen window, but it didn't.

Eventually it grew quiet. When I looked again, the security light illuminated Dad trudging down the long driveway toward the barn. My mother, who had also been in the kitchen, disappeared down the hall. He never hit Mom or me, but those sawhorses and other farm equipment sometimes took a beating.

Mom and Dad believed that children who drank at home wouldn't abuse alcohol elsewhere. Dad offered me sips from his drinks as early as I can remember. In my teens, when my sister and brother-in-law came to visit, our first outing was always to the liquor store. "Get what you want," my sister would say. The small bottle of sloe gin or Johnny Walker I chose didn't last the week as I steadily decreased the amount of soda I mixed with it.

Mother tried not to drink and we preferred that she didn't. As soon as a bottle touched her lips, she was drunk. One beer led from giggling to bawling to wailing. After I left for college, her drinking escalated. I came home on break to find an open handle and several empties of Dad's "M&M's" hidden in the back of what had been my bedroom closet.

After I graduated from law school and they began traveling out west, Mom joined the ranks of former problem drinkers who'd found a way out of their addiction. With their help, she quit for good.

On the forty-five-minute drive to Columbus for the Heart concert, I drank straight from a fifth of Seagram's. When we stopped at a party on the university campus, I took hits off the joint they passed. I vaguely recall swigging from a bottle as we walked to the entrance. I have a dim memory of throwing up in the women's bathroom and of a friend yelling at me because we couldn't find the car. Snow had fallen steadily during the concert. The vehicles were covered and I could not remember where I had parked. My next clear memory was of lying on the floor of my bedroom. The night had passed and the inside of my head sounded like the machinery of a bowling alley.

Mom banged the pots and pans in the kitchen, but was otherwise silent. I remained quiet. My friend had been forced not only to find my car, but to drive us home. The friend's mother had called my mother to complain. Mom barely spoke to me that week. I gritted my way through school awaiting Dad's weekly return. But there were no fireworks. Like Mom, he was also too angry with me to talk.

I fear they were both shocked speechless that their National Honor Society daughter had come home drunk. There had been the incident with the boy, but this drunken daughter business was new to them. When Dad left again on Sunday, he only said, "I'm so disappointed in you." He was the last person on Earth I had wanted to hurt.

Folks in the recovery groups I now attended emphasized that we couldn't control anyone else's behavior, but I still grew awkward around people who drank. It was kind of Dad to ask whether I minded if he had a beer. I assumed he was concerned for my welfare. But who was I to say whether he could drink?

I'd spent the years between that Heart concert in high school and my late twenties trying to quit and failing. Finally, a few years before Dad's diagnosis, at twenty-nine I had gotten help and quit, following my mother's example into that same club of former problem drinkers.

Because I'd stopped drinking and still attended meetings, my life had improved. Even so, when someone ordered a beer at dinner, my hands started to sweat. *Was I being ridiculous? If someone near me drank, would I drink too?*

And, despite my father's typically calm demeanor, I'd seen his anger flare when he drank. Now that my mother had quit, I wished he would, too. For a while I thought he had.

But two summers before his diagnosis, only months after I'd stopped and begun to attend recovery meetings, he and Mom had stayed with me for a few weeks. During their visit, I discovered a handle of whiskey wrapped in a big grocery sack tucked behind the cookie sheets. Mom hadn't had a drop of alcohol since 1988, so I knew it was his. "Please lock it in your car," I'd asked. Dad had apologized. "I didn't think you'd find it." He locked the bottle in their car while I acted as if I didn't know where to find the keys.

Dad even attended one of my recovery meetings along with my mother, sister, and some recovery friends where I shared about my drinking and recovery. As I spoke, he squirmed in the folding chair. What parent wants to hear the details of their child's misconduct and distress? Not my father. But I couldn't empathize with him then. I had hoped for support and compassion which, if I'd let him, he might have given. Instead, I saw judgment. He and I never spoke of that meeting again.

At this golf course clubhouse, with him staring down probable death, and me still crawling out of an emotional black hole while facing losing him for good, when he asked if I minded if he had a beer, I lied.

"Course not," I said, my throat tight.

He smiled, ordered two hot dogs, a coffee, and a long-neck Budweiser. As I watched him lift the familiar brown bottle to his lips, his shoulders relaxed. Mine did too.

CHAPTER 12

CERTIFIABLE

Dad and I continued our golf outings, this week back to Broadview. It had rained all night and I'd successfully driven to the course through splattering raindrops without needing to death-grip the wheel. And I'd forgotten the dashboard sticky note, but didn't get lost. Dad and I waited in the clubhouse while sprinkles turned to drizzle and drizzle to clouds. We needed a motorized cart because I'd turned my ankle a few days before and couldn't push my usual cart. The groundskeeper gave us the go-ahead, but asked us to stick to the paths so the cart didn't tear up the turf.

We played steadily until the fifth hole. Dad hit a long drive straight up the fairway. I hacked my usual three strokes to every one of his. He waited patiently, driving the cart along as I hit. As he drove toward where he had sighted his ball, a groundhog waddled across the fairway in front of us and disappeared into the rough, slipping through the thicket of thigh-high weeds that bordered a narrow creek at the edge of the course. Although the creek was shallow, its banks were steep. A row of vinyl-clad suburban houses was visible beyond.

Dad slowed the cart, pretending to point a rifle at the robust rodent. "Pow!" he said, firing an imaginary round complete with kickback. For a moment, I remembered Puppsy, grimaced, then relaxed. We got out to look for his ball.

"It landed over there," Dad said, pointing to a spot on the fairway about six feet to the right of a large tree.

I had used the same tree to spot his ball and saw it drop there before we got in the cart, but neither of us could find it.

"You don't think . . ." he said.

"Impossible!"

My words met empty air. Dad had already hurled himself into the cart and was barreling toward the place in the thicket where we'd seen the groundhog disappear.

"You're supposed to stay on the path!" I yelled as I limped toward him. If he'd brought his .22 that groundhog might have ended up on the supper table in Mom and Dad's rented travel trailer. When I was growing up, Dad sometimes threatened to feed us groundhog, squirrel, possum, and chipmunk, but he never brought anything home that he shot. I never hunted with him or anyone, but I watched him murder many a beer bottle in the name of target practice. He'd even given me my older brother's BB gun, shown me how to compensate for its crooked barrel, and set me to work scaring away the sparrows that tore the insulation out of our barn roof. I didn't have the heart to kill any of them, but I practiced enough that I could scare the bejesus out of them and make my father proud.

Dad misjudged the cart's braking distance and the cart skidded toward the thicket, nearly plunging into the creek. Unfazed, he hopped out, stepped through thigh-high weeds and hiked toward a place where a man was trimming shrubbery in one of the back yards across the creek.

"Did a groundhog come through here?" Dad yelled at the bewildered gardener.

The man nodded. "One wandered down the bank a few minutes ago."

I reached the cart in time to hear Dad ask, "Was he carrying a golf ball?" The gardener slowly began to back toward his house.

"That damned rodent stole my ball!" Dad yelled. The gardener turned and ran.

My laughter reached Dad's ears and he turned. "You're no help," he yelled as he strode past me toward the thicket.

He surveyed the mangled undergrowth, began to laugh, then looked down at me. I was still holding my sides and wiping away tears. "Don't just stand there. Get over here and help me fix this mess."

He backed the cart away and began fluffing up the weeds with his hands the way he might have tried to remedy a patch of wheat a sleeping deer had flattened in our back field.

"Will that really help?" I asked.

"You got any better ideas?"

We did our best to erase the cart's tracks into the thicket, righting the tall green spines of the few plants that remained unbroken.

"Not exactly good as new," he said.

"What about these?" I asked. The cart's fat tires had worn a fresh set of foot-wide tracks leading up to the thicket.

"Damn," he said. "I left my seed in the car." He grimaced as he took in the deep grooves. "They'll never let us play here again."

"That's probably in their best interest," I said, rolling my eyes.

"Enough out of you, smarty-pants. Mr. Groundhog didn't take *your* ball."

When we were both back in the cart and settled, I quietly said, "I just have one question."

He waited.

"Which one of us is certifiable?" I asked, stifling a giggle.

By "certifiable" I meant that at one point I had presented symptoms dangerous enough that my mental health care providers felt I needed to be locked away for my own protection. While I was grateful the hospital stay had saved my life, I was also now able to laugh about it. But this was the first time I'd joked about it with Dad.

Six months earlier, I wouldn't have dared make that joke. Back then, in group, Harri had given us more paper and asked us each to make a list of ten things we would do before we attempted suicide. When my turn came, I read several items including, "Call my husband. Walk the dogs. Make a peanut butter and jelly sandwich. Eat it." I stopped, realized I only had nine items, then added, "Call my husband again."

When I had finished, Harri said, "Wouldn't you call your parents?"

"No."

I hadn't even called my parents when I admitted myself to the psych ward. Instead, from a tiny, windowless room with a phone that did not accept incoming calls, I phoned my older sister, Amy, and begged her not to tell them.

I wanted to protect Dad, to shield him from being hurt. But I also didn't want to let him down. I could see his big eyes, sad and disappointed, and his long face saying, "I'm a worrier."

With Mom, I feared she would charge in and take over my treatment. I could see her ordering the doctors to find alternative healing methods. She might smother me, or make herself sick so we'd have to take care of her instead.

Amy's silence at the other end of the line opened like a cavern.

"Amy, promise," I pleaded.

With a deep sigh, she agreed. "It's okay, Sis. I promise."

I waited to tell my parents I'd been hospitalized until after I got out of the locked ward and was well into the seven weeks of partial hospitalization. When I did call, I didn't explain how I wound up there and neither of them asked. I assured them I was getting help. They didn't ask for details.

A few weeks later, Mom called again and told me that she and Dad had gone to an information session on depression at their local community college out in Arizona. After a few minutes she put Dad on the phone.

"Are you doing what the doctors tell you to do?" he asked.

"Yes, Dad."

"And you're taking your medicine?"

"Yes, Dad."

He was silent for a beat, then he said, "Well, good then," and that was that.

But here, on this golf course, so many months after my hospitalization, I could hazard a joke about it.

"Which one of us is certifiable?" I repeated. "I mean, I have papers. What about you?" I'd said the words before I was sure I should and they came out lighter than I intended.

When he punched me softly in the arm before pushing the accelerator, I relaxed. I hadn't realized I was holding my breath. It was refreshing not to hide my mental illness from him anymore. More than that, I'd risked joking about it even though I wasn't sure he'd see the humor.

A little louder than necessary, I asked, "And just how many strokes do you lose for a groundhog hazard?"

He punched me harder, fighting the laughter that had consumed us both earlier. Stifling more giggles, I said, "And tell me, oh keeper of the official rule book, how many strokes for scaring the neighbors?"

He stopped the cart to take out his cloth handkerchief and wipe his eyes. I hung over the edge and howled, "Fore! Groundhog! Fore!"

Dad was still chuckling as he drove us to the next hole, blades of green disappearing behind us. All those months spent trying to hide my mental illness from him, afraid of his judgment, also disappeared under the wheels. This time together, in this cart with our respective bad jokes, was what it meant to shine light into the closets and let the skeletons dance.

In the weeks after the groundhog incident, Dad and I continued to play golf on Thursdays at the less expensive courses near the farm. As spring turned to the heat of summer, we kept to the "goat pastures," as some might call the cheaper courses. Dad admired well-tended spaces, but his pocketbook—and Mom's watchful eye over their joint accounts—kept him from playing the finer courses.

"I've got just enough mad money to cover this," he said, his eyes shining with a boyish glee as he pulled bills from the secret compartment in his wallet. When I was younger, I thought he called it "mad money" because he stashed it to use if he got mad at Mom. But he corrected me. "She holds the purse strings. It's for when she's mad at me."

We played steadily for seven holes. On number eight I sliced the drive badly and my ball flew deep into the tree line at the edge of the fairway. As we looked for it, I pulled a diet root beer from my bag's side compartment and sipped it as we walked.

The day before, Mom had called me to complain about the cost of grave markers and to express misgivings about the funeral plots our family owned in a cemetery near the farm.

After making the "certifiable" joke during our groundhog game a few weeks before, I'd grown braver. When Mom mentioned the headstone, I decided to ask him directly.

"Has Mom told you she's looking into a double headstone for you two?" I asked.

Dad narrowed his eyes and spoke softly. "I told her I don't want a headstone."

The tree line was impenetrable and after making a few circles in the tall grass, I said, "Let's give that one up for lost. I'll drop a ball next to yours."

We walked in silence to that spot. When we stopped, I put my hand on his arm and asked, "Why don't you want one?"

"It's a waste of money." He pushed his Ohio State golf cap back on his head. When he did, the sight of sweat on his brow sent a shiver through me. *Was it the heat or something else?*

"I'd rather have a new set of custom clubs," he said.

My father was born in rural northwestern Ohio just before the Great Depression, into a family that had little and expected less. You didn't buy anything you weren't going to use.

Dad's Depression-era tightness around money stung me a few times. The September after I graduated from high school, the same week I left for college, Ohio Bell transferred Dad back to Columbus. The morning before I left, Dad and I walked to the barn so I could say goodbye to the cats and the dog. I took in the smell of newly mowed lawn and the green sway of the trees as we walked.

"Can I move back some day?" I asked.

"Sure," he said. "But you're grown now. You'll have to pay rent."

Rent? I thought, but knew better than to say anything. His own father had dropped him at the gates of Bowling Green State University and told him that was all the help he could give him. Why wouldn't my father do the same? Still, his comment hurt. I took it personally, as if he were throwing me out. I packed that emotion away with my belongings.

They drove me to Athens. Other than that one summer between my freshman and sophomore year of college, I never moved back.

On the golf course with Dad, I stared at the flat green acreage of fields that bordered the course beyond the trees.

He continued, "I don't want to pay perfectly good money for some headstone I wouldn't get to appreciate after I was gone."

"What'd Mom say?"

"Nothing."

I laughed, internally imagining their conversation. Mom and Dad at the kitchen table. Mom's face drawn, serious, concerned. Dad responding by joking about custom clubs—half serious, half not—stirring three spoonfuls of sugar into his instant coffee.

His deflection and denial mirrored my own. We both used humor to soften the pain, and sometimes avoided topics we didn't want to face. If Dad bought a headstone, he'd have to use it. If I knew he'd bought a headstone, I'd have to admit he was dying.

Some part of Dad knew he was going to die. But that little boy who loved to carom around golf courses refused to accept that the fun was going to end. Perhaps he clung to that little boy in order to retain his last shred of sanity. Part of me clung there with him, wanting him to hang on tighter, to tie a knot when the rope frayed. I too was holding that rope, that hope, that the little boy inside him would save the little girl inside me.

Chapter 13

Sprinkle Me on the Back Forty

The following Thursday as my father and I left the clubhouse headed for the first hole, Dad said, "Father Ron thinks it's okay for me to be cremated."

Earlier in the summer, he would have said, "Beautiful day," or asked about our dogs, anything but this. I would have nodded and asked if he had any sunscreen. No more "happy camper." He had come out and said it.

"What exactly did Father Ron say?"

I wondered how Father Ron, their rather progressive Catholic priest, would justify my father's preference for cremation in light of the general Catholic stance against it at that time. Without looking at Dad, I pulled my club from my bag.

⛳ ⛳ ⛳

After Dad took early retirement from Ohio Bell, he didn't know what to do with himself. He hadn't expected to retire, but during my last quarter of undergraduate school, when Ohio Bell asked for volunteers to take early retirement, he put his name in. Two weeks later, they told him to pack his things.

Mom told me that, after Dad's last day at a job he'd held more than thirty years, she watched him sit in his leather recliner in the living room for hours at a time. Busy volunteering as a church organist, she let him sit, hands folded in his lap, staring at the wall. Dad later admitted he secretly hoped Ohio Bell would realize their mistake, call him back, and offer him a large raise. But they did not.

A solution to Dad's retirement boredom and grief came from the local priest, Father Ron. The building next to Johnstown's Catholic church was a rundown house. From my days of catechism, I remembered tripping on the crooked floors and gagging on the smell of mold. We referred to it as the "CCD building," short for "Confraternity of Christian Doctrine," the basic teachings of the Catholic Church. Dad took the house on as his personal renovation project.

Mother had been a farm widow and a phone company widow before Dad retired. Now she'd become a CCD building widow. From college, I'd call home and Mom would say, "Your father's busy at the CCD building pissing off the church guys again."

"Pissing them off how?" I asked, rearranging a picture on the wall of our dorm room. Other college students had posters. I had a girlfriend majoring in interior design. Matted pictures decorated our cinder-block, dorm-room walls.

"Last Tuesday, he arrived at 7 a.m. with the level and saw cuts marked. By 7:30, no one else had showed. When they finally made it, one guy showed up drunk."

She named three or four men, most of whom were also retired, who had since refused to work with him.

"Didn't he have this problem at Ohio Bell?"

"He was a real bear to work for."

I imagined these retired men intent on a good time, drinking a few beers while fixing up the old building. Here comes my father with a level and a circular saw and they scatter.

The project got more complicated when Dad and Pete, a carpenter friend of his, agreed to work on the interior of the church as well. Now, instead of other parishioners, Dad was pissing off the priest.

"I think Father Ron likes Dad's work," Mom said in a later call. "But your father's such a perfectionist."

Mom always called him "your father" when he was in trouble.

"He was so obsessed about getting the wall colors right that he made six trips to the Sherwin-Williams store before he was satisfied."

"Good lord," I said.

The project expanded: new lectern, altar, confessionals. Dad drew up the plans. He and his carpenter friend, Pete, built the structures in our barn. They hauled the completed pieces to the church in our Ford pickup.

By this time, I was in law school. When I came home for a visit, my job was to admire his work. As he told me about the latest phase of the project, he rolled out plans for the new altar onto the kitchen table.

"It's supposed to look like a butcher's table," he said excitedly. I don't know if this was his idea or Father Ron's, two Catholic literalists trying to replicate the butchering of Christ.

Dad pointed to the arches at the bottom of the page. "We'll veneer curved wood onto them to look like they've been cut out of a single piece of wood." The end result was a gorgeous monstrosity. Heavy and solid and amazingly beautiful.

The parishioners didn't appreciate Dad's craftsmanship in the way he thought they should.

"They don't understand how much work that took," he said later when the altar table had been installed in the front of the church.

The same was true of the lectern. Another masterpiece, matching the altar, but with inlaid wood, and so heavy they had to put wheels on it so the priest could move it. Function interested Dad, but design captivated him. Was it pretty? Yes. Did it work? Yes. Was it expensive and a pain in the butt? Also, yes.

At the same time, Dad rejoined the Knights of Columbus, attending the local meetings he'd had to miss during his years of travel for his job. When the local K of C group sent Dad into the state echelon as a director, Mom's mood soared. She could add to her collection of fancy dresses, with purses and shoes to match. Mom didn't buy clothes; she bought outfits. A peek into her top dresser drawer revealed a rainbow of costume jewelry in deep tones and boxes with pearls, sequins, and chains, while her closet held boxes of shoes and rows of matching purses.

Dad felt like a local yokel around these men, many of whom were from the three largest Ohio cities: Columbus, Cincinnati, and Cleveland. One weekend, when I joined him and Mom at a K of C event, I watched my father hold his drink while a Knight from Cleveland discussed his construction company expanding into three states. When the man asked what Dad did, Dad said, "I retired from Ohio Bell and have a farm near Johnstown." The man's eyes glazed and he moved on to chat with someone else. Dad introduced me by saying, "She's studying to pass the bar." After a comedic beat, he added "I've never passed a bar in my life!" I had to restrain myself from covering my eyes, but his attempts to impress them pained me.

I didn't have to worry about what they thought of him for long. In February while I was in law school, Mom's brother, Johnny, convinced Mom to visit California, where he lived. A six-week bout of bronchitis during a long Ohio winter had fueled her discontent. She booked two tickets and gave my father one of her famous ultimatums. "I'm going. Stay here or come along."

A few months later, Mom and Dad drove to Kansas City for Mother's Day to visit Amy, her then husband, Jo, and Jamey, their infant daughter. On the drive back to Ohio, Mom spotted the first sign for Tom Raper's RV dealership.

As she told it, Mom mustered all her courage and said, "Let's stop at Tom Raper's and just take a look." Dad, who did most of the driving, was not one to stop the car for three or four hours at a stretch. But instead of the groan Mom expected, Dad said, "Alright."

In our family, stopping to "take a look" was tantamount to saying, "Let's buy." On the farm, the several tractors, a combine, a corn picker, a grain drill, a grain and hay elevator, all temperamental at best, had each arrived when Mom or Dad "swung by" a farm auction or a dealership to "take a look." In fact, we'd ended up with the farm itself after Mom drove me from Columbus to Johnstown to "take a look" at a small house on fifty acres.

Mom and Dad left Tom Raper's with a fifth-wheel RV trailer and a truck to haul it.

In the fall, they drove it to California planning to stay for a month. In California, Uncle Johnny and Aunt Ruby house-sat and took part-time jobs to supplement their retirement incomes. Mom and Dad hoped to do the same. Once, when I visited my aunt and uncle in Palm Desert, they were working in a business that ran a crematorium and a car wash on the same lot. I cannot recall what they did there, but when I learned that Mom and Dad planned to find odd jobs, I pictured Dad pushing bodies into the oven while Mom wiped spots off the windows of the widows' Mercedes coupes.

This was not to be their fate. They rented a space in an RV park near Oceanside, California, where Mom worked in the office and Dad did maintenance. A month turned into nine. Each night as they sat around their hibachis, the couple renting the space next to them regaled Dad with tales of avid golf on the sweet nine-hole course nearby. Dad shrugged off the man's invitation because he didn't own clubs.

On one of Mom's daily walks, she met a woman whose husband used to golf, but was ill. When she mentioned that Dad wanted to take up the expensive golf habit, but "luckily" didn't have clubs, the woman cheerily responded, "I'll sell you my husband's, cheap." That was the first of many sets.

I imagine Dad's face the night he came home from his first day back on the links: sparkling, shiny, and tan with a wonderful sense of exhaustion from using muscles he'd forgotten he had. I envision an exuberance similar to my mother's fervor when she'd announced, when I was in eighth grade, that she'd found Christ. Dad, a born-again golfer, had a new purpose in retirement, something else to worship, a god he could manage if he only practiced enough. A god who would love him if only he moved that little white ball around the course. Mom's religious zeal had faded with the years, but Dad's passion for golf never would.

After a few years at the California RV park, my parents gave up the fifth-wheel for a second home in Bullhead City, Arizona, near Laughlin, Nevada, where the Colorado River marks the Arizona-Nevada border. Mom would have preferred a larger city such as Palm Springs or Oceanside, but they both preferred the cost of living in Bullhead. Mom also found the clear air there soothing to her lungs since a breeze blew nearly every day. Dad found his solace on a nine-hole golf course called Chaparral. They bought a triple-wide modular home on the fourth tee.

Once Dad got out on the golf course, felt the wind in his hair, his arms swinging that club, and the camaraderie of men laughing under the blue sky, he was gone. Dad had never been a social man and Mom had hoped golf would improve his social skills. Instead, he disappeared into golf completely, the way he had into the CCD building, and his job and the farm before that. He found men who wanted to play the way he did, seriously. Mom joined the women a few times, but she didn't like to practice and since she wasn't as good as many of these women who had been playing for years, she dropped out. Mom would go out for nine holes once in a while, but she never took to it.

I believe Dad's connection to golf had as much to do with spending time outdoors as the game itself. I don't know if the men at Dad's golf club—men not raised in the country—understood the spiritual connection between the heart and the land the way I believe Dad felt it. I don't think you have to grow up on a farm to love the land, but if you didn't, the beauty would be easy to miss.

The way Dad walked the length of a fairway paralleled the way he loved walking to the back field at the farm. He loved riding across a course in a golf cart the same way he loved riding across a pasture on his Allis-Chalmers tractor. The wind in his hair, fresh air in his lungs, sun on his skin, and the way his muscles ached after a day of hard work. For more than a decade, I had watched my father worship the soil with a shovel and a hoe, tilling his holy garden with the rototiller and plowing the sacred back field on his tractor, serious as a prayer. But he wasn't going to spend his retirement years in hard labor. He was done mowing pastures with a brush hog and felling trees with a log chain, so he found another way to pay homage to the soil. The golf course became his cathedral.

On the golf course now, having another of the few direct conversations with my father about the real probability of his death, a sense of comfort came over me. My heart rate dropped and my breathing eased. Whereas a fearful and deeply superstitious part of me thought we shouldn't be talking about it, I was curious. We were finally speaking of "real" things and I felt safe enough to ask the questions I hadn't been brave enough to ask during our earlier outings: the kinds of things we talked about when I was little.

During my childhood, Dad and I spent countless evenings staring at the cosmos. He taught me about the moon and the stars. One cloudless night when I was in junior high, as we craned our necks toward the North Star and the dippers, I asked: "How can God have created the heavens and Earth if man evolved from apes?" In my young mind, catechism collided with Mr. Sebastian's science class the way I imagined neutrons striking heavy atomic nuclei in a nuclear reactor.

"I think it's both," he said.

"What?"

"Who created the apes?" he asked. Then he pointed to the stars. "Who created the stars?"

I shrugged.

"God did."

"But . . ."

"But that doesn't mean we didn't evolve. God created the stuff from which we evolve and the process by which we evolve. It's all God."

"You don't see any conflict?"

"Nope."

"But what about that stuff in the Bible, 'on the seventh day' and all that?"

"Those are just stories," he said. "We don't know for certain. Our job is just to wonder."

* * *

This summer, playing golf with him, I had tried to resurrect that sense of wonder. Some days, I managed. Other days, I failed to see the wonder in any of it and only wondered what the heck I was supposed to do.

Dad brought me back to reality. "If anyone tries to bury me, you tell them I want to be cremated, okay?" he said.

I knew what to do with that. My voice shifted into "full-grown woman attorney" mode, the tone I had used with clients.

"Tell Mom. Put it in writing. Set it up in advance with Crouse." Although Mr. Crouse, the Johnstown undertaker, had been dead for years and the funeral home now bore the new owner's name, we still referred to it by the name of its previous owner.

"I told your mother. You guys can handle the details."

Dad pushed his cart up to the tee and stopped. He turned toward me and said, "I told Father that I thought the idea that you had to have all your parts to get into heaven was hogwash. I mean, if God is all-powerful, can't he put you all back together anyway?"

"Makes sense to me," I said.

As an agnostic, I was not only uncertain whether there was a God to do these things, but even less convinced there was a Heaven to go to anyway. I omitted to mention this. Why confuse the issue with technicalities? He seemed content to talk about it. The old urge to reassure him arose. I longed to say the correct father-daughter thing. Instead, I listened. That was my job now. It was surprisingly easy.

I started to walk toward the women's tee box, but Dad kept talking.

"I asked him about people who have lost a leg in the war or a foot to diabetes. Do they get barred from heaven because they don't have all the parts?"

The skeptic in me wondered if the Catholics got kickbacks from the funeral directors for every person they deterred from cremation.

"Of course not," I said.

"Father Ron said it sounded reasonable to him."

I nodded and looked around at the green grass and the green trees and thought about how someday, not so far away, Dad's cremains might be under the ground fertilizing plants.

"It's not legal to bury me at the farm like I wanted," he continued.

On more than one evening during my childhood, as he, Mom, and we three kids sat under the pine trees near the barn, he told us, "When I die. Just bury me in the back field. Steal my body from the hospital if you have to." But none of us, him included, wanted to go through the legal wrangling necessary to turn the back field into a cemetery. Now that his death seemed imminent, he faced the sad reality that Mom might need to sell the place to stay afloat financially. He was willing to compromise.

"Just make sure some of me gets sprinkled across the back forty," he said.

"Will do," I said, looking at my shoes.

I felt a guilty relief that Dad was talking about the inevitable. Some days it seemed as if he had forgotten he might be dying. And while this might have seemed like a preferable way to spend the summer while he was still looking and acting fine most days, I worried about what would happen to him when his health started to decline.

And, what would happen to me when those days came?

I could talk about cremation all day long, but the thought of a future where I could no longer walk beside him turned my gut cold. It was easier to talk about what would happen to him than what would be left of me once he was no longer here.

"How do you feel about being cremated?" I asked. "I mean, how are you doing with this whole thing?"

Now it was his turn to look at his shoes.

"Most days I try not to think about it," he said. "I keep putting one foot in front of another, hitting one golf ball after another, playing one hole at a time. What the hell else can I do?"

A wave of sadness swept through me so strong it buckled my knees. I righted myself then glanced at him. His eyes still pointed toward the ground. When he began to tilt his head up, I expected his face to be grim.

Instead, he shone with that big goofy smile. I shook my head, smiled back, and pulled my driver from my bag.

Our family at my law school graduation party in 1985: (left to right) my sister, Amy, holding her daughter, Jamey, me in my law school hood and gown, Dad, Mom, my brother, Jim, and my sister-in-law, Deanna.

Me playing ball with Maxine (left) and Astro (right).

Ed and I on our wedding day, September 25, 1993.

Dad on his beloved mower with the woods in the background. This John Deere was an upgrade from the Huffy mower we had during my teen years.

Men winners

Daily News photo by Richard "Robbie" Robertson

Men winners in the Chaparral Country Club Tourney are from left Gil Carter, Low Gross, Dick Harmon, Presidents Cup (250), John Little, Vice Presidents Cup (251), Gene Buddlemeyer, Treasurers Cup and Mack McCalister, Secretaries Cup.

Dad, second from right, with the other winners of the Chaparral Country Club golf tournament.

Family golf outing in Bullhead City, AZ, during Mom's March 1995 birthday celebration: (left to right) Nita, Dad, Mom, Jim, and, Amy.

Me, Mom, and Dad in the Grand Tetons on Dad's "Trip of a Lifetime" in September, 1995.

 SCAN to see more photos.

CHAPTER 14

SINGING

This Thursday, Dad and I played The Knolls. Ken had nicknamed the course "Death Knolls" because the long, narrow greens improved your odds of death by an errant ball.

Despite 100-degree heat, sprinklers kept the golf course fairways and greens verdant. That gorgeous turf comes with a price tag our grandchildren will pay due to how scarce water is in many parts of the world. I did not broach this with my conservative father. This might be our last year together. I wanted nothing to disrupt the peace and comfort I had begun to feel in his presence.

By now, my panic attacks were manageable. I still kept paper bags in the car, but the antidepressants combined with desensitizing myself by driving to meet my father for golf once a week, continued to curb my anxiety. I still slept through most days when I wasn't with my parents, in therapy, group, or class, but I no longer needed the yellow dashboard sticky notes and could travel the forty-five minutes without losing my way.

My father had only seen glimpses of my anxiety. Six years earlier, I sat in our darkened living room with my parents watching the movie *Murder in Texas*.

Whether it was the antihistamine my mother had given me to combat one of my chronic headaches or watching a trusted husband secretly poison his wife, my breath shortened, my heart pounded, and my fingertips began to tingle.

I waited for a commercial break when Dad had stepped outside to smoke a cigarette.

"Mom?" I said quietly. "I can't breathe."

She jumped up.

"I can't feel my fingers and toes. My head feels weird."

"Put your head between your knees. Just breathe slowly. You'll be alright."

The door opened and, with my eyes closed, I listened to my father enter the room.

"What's wrong with her?" he said.

Mom told him about the cold pill. "She's probably having a reaction."

The movie was back on and Dad sat down in his chair to continue watching.

"Gene. Can you turn off the movie? It's making her worse."

"What?" he said.

"The movie's bothering her."

Determined not to interrupt my father's evening television ritual, I forced myself to stand. Mom and I walked hand-in-hand down the hallway. By the time I got to my room, the uncomfortable sensations had passed.

* * *

At "Death Knolls," Dad and I putted out on the first hole as a mower roared in the distance.

"Do you miss mowing?" I asked while we walked to the second tee.

"Naw," he shrugged. "While we're gone, the neighbor boy does it with the brush hog. It's not as pretty, but I don't have to see it."

Dad pulled out his driver and, as if reading my mind, said, "You used to do a good job, even though you hated it."

"I didn't exactly hate it," I lied. "I was just, well, a teenager."

"You hated it," he insisted.

"But I always did it," I retorted. Then added, "I loved singing while I mowed."

"You sure did!" he said, grinning.

Twenty summers before, on another blistering day, my father had been the one suffering from anxiety.

After Dad once again gave me the "Grass is getting long" cue, I stomped to the barn, hopped on the mower, and began to mow at full speed. Dad waved me down the first time I passed the barn. Once again, I had let the farm grass get too high and the front mower tires mashed the long blades before the mower deck could cut them off.

"Slow it down!" he yelled as I shifted. "It'll clog."

I scowled. I loved driving the mower in the highest gear. It made the job go faster and I relished the wildness of the wind in my hair. I imagined I was on a galloping horse instead of a green and yellow John Deere.

But I didn't say anything directly to him for fear he would backhand me. He'd never hit me, but he had once hit my brother, nearly a decade before. So I downshifted, and rolled away. I'd have to fantasize in low gear.

When I drove past the house, I went inside for a portable radio. I bungee-corded it to the mower seat and cranked up the volume so I could hear above the engine's roar.

I found singing therapeutic. To curb anxiety, boredom, and loneliness, I would sing to myself as I walked through the woods. In school and church choirs I sang tenor because there weren't enough boys. My voice wasn't strong or on key, but I enjoyed learning the words and tried to match the pitch and rhythm of singers I loved. On the ten acres, I belted out the lyrics as I mowed.

Minnie Riperton, with her rare five-octave vocal range, began rolling through *Lovin' You*. My alto voice strained, but I sang along anyway, blissfully screeching the coloratura soprano notes. I imagined myself in a recording studio holding the headphones to my ears as an enthusiastic man—who looked very much like the high-school football player I fancied—mixed the tune.

When a firm hand gripped my shoulder, I slammed the clutch and brake to the floor and spun in the seat to see Dad, red-faced and panting.

"What's wrong?" I yelled over the engine. I assumed I'd been mowing too fast, but his face was soft, his mouth open, and his chest heaving. I rarely saw Dad out of breath. Were the cattle loose? Was something wrong with Mom? Had another dog been hit by a car? I shut down the mower and braced myself for bad news. The absence of sound created a stillness between us.

"I was about to ask you the same thing," he said. We stared at each other. Then, he said, "It sounded like you were screaming."

I turned my face toward the grass as heat flooded my cheeks. Keeping my eyes on the green blades, I said, "I was singing."

"Singing?" he asked.

I didn't look up.

"I thought you were in trouble."

I shook my head without speaking. He patted me on the shoulder, turned and strode away. I distinctly heard him snicker under his breath. I put the tractor in gear, dropped the deck and engaged the mower. When I was out of sight of the barn, I allowed myself to cry, gasping big gulps of air as I wept.

⬤ ⬤ ⬤

On the golf course together now, Dad had begun to giggle as soon as I said the word, "sing." I did my best to recreate my teenage scowl, but his laughter caught me.

"You thought I was screaming," I howled.

"It sounded like you were being killed!"

Moaning with glee, I swayed back and forth, held my face, and wiped at my eyes.

"I thought you were under the mower!" he groaned.

"It was a high note!"

As my father and I roared at my teenage singing and his past worry, something else dawned on me. The grass seemed greener and the sun brighter than I had noticed in any of our prior golfing days. It was as if someone had pulled back a veil that had been blocking the sun. And I wasn't playing "happy camper." I wasn't faking this joy. I could see the world's colors, smell the fresh grass, and truly hear my father's splendid laughter for the first time in what seemed like forever. Today, on the "Death Knolls" with my father, someone had turned the lights back on.

As we walked toward the next tee, I caught myself holding my breath. I knew how easily the lights could flicker. But, for now, this was enough.

A movement to our right caught my attention. We both turned to see a foursome approaching.

"They're on us," he said in his best chase-scene voice. "Sing something so they'll slow down."

I hit him hard on the arm and tried to regain my composure as I trotted toward the tee. But I was still laughing so hard that I couldn't swing.

"Stop! I can't hit the ball!"

He turned his back, but kept laughing. The men stopped a respectful few yards away from us. Dad motioned to them and yelled, "You'd better play through."

Chapter 15

Go Home and Live Your Dreams

A few days after my father and I had joked about my singing, the office manager from the law firm called. The senior partner wanted to have lunch. A year had passed since I left, intending to return in thirty days. Over this time, I had tried to forget I needed to resolve things there.

The senior partner and I had always been friendly. Hours spent together, first at the consulting firm then forming and running the law firm, grew our closeness. I knew his wife and children well. My various domestic partners and I had socialized with his family. When the senior partner had needed to round out a foursome at a client event, he had asked me to call my father. And he generously gave Dad and I those tickets to several Memorial Tournaments.

Earlier in the summer when the Memorial had rolled around again, I considered contacting the senior partner for tickets because I assumed Dad would be eager to go. The firm usually had extras, and Dad and I always had a great time. Since my departure, the few "conversations" I'd had with the senior partner had been through the office manager. Instead of calling him directly to ask about tickets, I had intended to call her. But Dad hadn't been interested and that let me off the hook for a while.

The thought of seeing the senior partner's face and hearing his voice made my insides quake. I worried he was angry that I had left the firm in the lurch. I'd referred my clients to other attorneys, but I wasn't there to bill all those hours. Plus, while I understood that my job was waiting for me if I wanted it, I hadn't decided whether to return. What would I do if he asked me to come back? I'd never been able to tell him "No."

During my time away from the law office, I had only tried to visit once: six weeks after I'd been released from the hospital. Late one evening, hoping no one would be there, I drove Ed's car to the office. If anyone was there, I didn't want them to recognize my own car. I had planned to sit at my desk and cry. Even though I hadn't decided anything, it seemed right to grieve the firm and possibly the practice of law.

But the light of an office window revealed the newest attorney bent over his desk, still hard at work at that late hour with no sign of stopping. The time of day and the angle of his body showed determination and a drive to succeed at all costs. His presence stymied my plan and the recognition of my own tendencies made me queasy. I quickly drove home to the safety of Ed's arms.

After that failed attempt to visit my office, I could not drive past the building for fear of being sucked in by some invisible vortex and dying. For a year, I would drive ten minutes out of my way to avoid the place.

Much had changed over those twelve months and I could no longer dodge this conversation. The story my mind had created about some mythical force dragging me back into the firm against my will was beginning to evaporate.

One thing that hadn't changed was me not telling my parents about important decisions. I didn't want to burden them and still feared their judgment. Even as Dad and I grew closer on the golf course, I kept my imminent lunch meeting with the senior partner to myself. I wasn't ready to test whether the intimacy we were developing would survive my choosing myself over the life he'd watched me build. Plus, if I told him, the decision would feel final. Some part of me had needed the illusion that I could go back.

But playing golf with Dad had helped me feel stronger. I began to imagine leaving the firm, not necessarily with my head held high, but without the sting of shame I'd felt before.

Plus, I had Ed. After nearly two years of marriage, complete with my trip to the psych ward, I trusted his love in a more solid way. I also knew he would help financially. He wasn't the Camaro-driving former partner I'd allowed to steer me toward trial work for the pay increase.

At the upscale restaurant, the senior partner and I sat at a corner table, him in his well-tailored suit and me in my casual jumper and t-shirt. The upholstered chair felt too soft and the white linen napkins too crisp.

He asked about my treatment. I gave him an overview.

When I met his eyes, he said, "I'm so glad you're recovering."

I thought about the "appeal denied" case. Shame still burned in my throat when it came to mind. Two months before my leave of absence began, I'd attended the final hearing. The opposing side didn't show. I presented the cases I'd found that proved the agency's error. In under ten minutes, the hearing officer ruled in our former client's favor. "I guess they knew the agency was wrong," she said of the other party's absence.

I'd won.

On paper, I'd been redeemed and what seemed like the greatest failure of my life reversed. But it held no relief. The victory hadn't repaired the emotional damage.

Fortunately, as the senior partner and I dined, he did not bring up the case. Instead, he repeated exactly what he had said the day I left. "I'm so glad you got help."

After a pause, he added, "I never thought about depression when we signed those disability policies."

I agreed. I too had thought of disability as the result of an auto accident or a physical illness, not emotional infirmity. But months of hearing my psychologist Joan say, "Your illness is real," was teaching me otherwise.

Joan also assured me that my disability leave would continue. I wasn't ready for any job, let alone this one. The only thing I'd accomplished in a year was hospitalization, therapy, a few community college classes, one magazine article, and golfing badly with my father. When I told Joan I thought I was a slacker, she urged me to reframe that. "You deserve to heal," she said.

The senior partner told me he missed our talks, of which there had been many. I had missed them too.

Then, he asked about my father, whom he remembered fondly from the golf outings.

"That must be tough," he said about Dad's diagnosis, but he smiled when I told him we were ignoring the bad parts by playing golf.

Finally, he asked if I had contemplated my future with the firm.

The word "contemplated" hung in the air. Even while I'd tried to avoid it, I'd contemplated it for a year.

After my inpatient hospital stay, I'd spent seven weeks in outpatient, "partial" hospitalization. In group sessions, I kept saying, "My job is making me sick, but I can't quit. What else am I going to do?" When the partial hospitalization counselors pressed me to explore options beyond law, I'd felt trapped. I shut down or lashed out like a writhing animal, a far cry from the refined law firm partner I imagined myself to be.

On my last day, a counselor handed me two bright orange pins that read, "Nita. You did good. You have permission to go home and live your dreams." I cried, but not from relief. The buttons made me think I would never know how to "go home" or "live my dreams." I still thought I was responsible for everything, as if the very spinning of the Earth on its axis depended on my staying "on guard." Surely the world would fall apart if I relaxed?

From another partner at the firm, I learned that the senior partner had not filled the office I'd previously occupied. For nearly a year, even as new attorneys were added, the physical space that had been mine remained untouched. When that other attorney told me this, my cheeks flushed and tears filled my eyes. *He guarded my place. I should go back.*

But in the year since I walked out, I'd come to realize that in a law office, a person who can't say "No" to doing things that are beyond their ability is a danger to their clients and themselves. Legal research, writing, advising clients, and public speaking fitted my personality. Trial work or anything that required me to defend someone face-to-face or go on the attack did not. Litigation hadn't just been a horrible idea. For someone wired the way I was, it was nearly lethal. My gut had known this, but I ignored it because the senior partner believed in me. I didn't blame him. But I finally understood: I'd been good at my job. At times, great. And I tolerated it for a while. But my frail mental state couldn't take it any longer.

"I'm not coming back," I said, my voice quavering. The words tasted thick and medicinal, difficult to swallow, but necessary.

I'd expected to be relieved. Instead, I felt numb, as if a door had closed, but not quite latched.

A childish part of me watched his face, hoping he might argue, insist I stay. I thought of my father and how, after thirty years, he had waited to no avail for them to call him back. That little girl inside me wanted that, too. Instead, the senior partner looked down at his plate.

And I thought about the silk blouses and natural-fiber suits that still hung in my closet, attire that had once made me feel competent and protected. I'd worn that armor instead of seeking health and peace.

The shame I'd anticipated didn't come. Instead, recognition rose like rays of sun shining through a fog: I had already left long before I spoke the words.

When he said, "I understand," I shifted uncomfortably, certain he was angry, though he didn't show it.

In the months since I'd walked out, I'd worried about the mess I must have left behind. *Do I owe him amends?* Other than failing to get help until it was nearly too late, I had done my best. He did not mention my shortcomings. I'd been bracing for a verdict that didn't come.

We had never formalized the partnership agreement, my health insurance with the firm had ended, my disability insurance would continue, and I'd been paid for my outstanding client work. To dissolve my relationship with the firm, I only needed to pack my things and give the office manager my key. It seemed too simple. Shouldn't it be harder to end a decade-long career that at one time had been your entire identity? The Volvo wagon was long gone, but my body held the powerful memory of chatting on the speakerphone while flying down the highway. Apparently, when your life is on the line, it's not that tough to let it go.

When we finished talking and eating, I waited. Over the years and our many dinners together, he and I often fake-fought over the bill. The only time I remember him being genuinely angry at me was once when I secretly told the waiter to give me the check. After that, I always "let" him win. Today, I was through fighting. He put down his credit card and we were done.

CHAPTER 16

LAZY

The Thursday following my meeting with the senior partner, I woke to the sound of rain against the window, a strong summer storm not likely to pass anytime soon. I called my parents. Mom answered.

"Looks like golf is off today," I said.

"I'm going to see if your father will go shopping. He's pouting."

I laughed. "Maybe golf is his therapy. Writing is mine. I don't know what to do with myself when I don't write."

"Yep. In Arizona, he pouts when he can't play every single day! I'll get him."

I imagined Dad sitting in the lawn chair under the Airstream's awning staring into the rain.

"No golf today," he said like a warning when he picked up the phone.

"Mom says you two are going shopping."

"That's news to me."

"Maybe I'll tag along."

"Suit yourself," he said flatly.

I had half a mind to tell him to stop it or I'd give him something to pout about, or say, "Birdie gonna shit on your lip!" the way he did when I was little. Instead, I tried another of his favorite things. "We could go to Newlon's and have baked steak."

"Now there's an idea," he said, his voice suddenly animated.

"I'll be out in an hour."

When I got to the RV park, Dad was sitting in the booth that served as their living room reading *Golf Digest*. "Doesn't seem to be letting up," Dad said, not looking up from the magazine.

"Anything good in there?"

"An article about O. J. Simpson's golf game the morning his wife was murdered."

"In *Golf Digest*?"

"Rabbi Marc Gellman says, 'People who cheat in golf always cheat in life.'" Dad looked up. "What do you think?"

I wasn't sure what he was asking and didn't want to talk about OJ. "I think you play an honest game," I said.

"That's not the point," Dad said. "OJ's toast."

"How can you be so sure?"

"The husband is always guilty until proven otherwise."

I looked out at the rain. "Sorry about the weather."

"It's not your fault."

I turned back toward him. "I know, but I wanted to play, too."

The edges of his mouth turned sharply downward. "Won't you be able to play next week?" He looked like a very small boy.

"Of course!"

Mom emerged and we drove the fifteen miles to the Meijer store in Newark. Dad and I browsed the sporting goods section while Mom picked up groceries and checked out the craft supplies. When we rejoined Mom, she said, "Did you find anything?"

"Tees." He'd found a brightly colored set that he held up for her inspection.

"Don't you have enough tees?" She spoke to him as if he were a child asking for an action figure he already had.

"I don't have *these* tees," he said.

She shrugged and he put them in her cart. I smiled knowingly at her when his back was turned. Dad's golf spending bordered on legendary. The Christmas after they moved to Arizona, my parents had driven three hours to Palm Desert for a cream-colored Yamaha Sun Classic, the "Cadillac" of golf carts, complete with windshields, a radio/cassette, and turn signals. Mom turned around and sold their old jalopy cart for a profit.

I couldn't criticize him. I'd bought a set of teal-blue graphite, made-to-order clubs and a matching bag so I would look good on the course. We both thought spending proved something.

"Anything new, he's got to have," Mom said. I wondered whether she was jealous of Dad's game the way she might have been if he'd taken a mistress. Or maybe she worried about the money. When it came to finances, Mom was the worrier.

Newlon's restaurant, a hole-in-the-wall adventure in down-home cookin', complete with surly waitresses and huge portions, didn't disappoint. We each ate a generous serving of cubed steak, mashed potatoes, and creamed lima beans slathered in thick gravy off of plastic divided plates like the ones in a grade-school cafeteria. The chairs were the wooden school version as well. Dad leaned back and rubbed his stomach. "Now that was some food." Although, as an adult, I'd grown accustomed to finer fare and a more sophisticated atmosphere, I'd been raised on country meals and eating at Newlon's turned back time. Watching my father enjoy it enhanced the pleasure.

I don't want this to end, the little girl in me thought. The adult knew it would.

On the drive home, I pointed to a golf course on Route 161.

"We haven't played Raccoon Valley yet," I said.

Dad replied, "The green fees are astronomical."

"Time's a wasting," I said, using a phrase Dad often said. "I'll treat," I added.

All summer, Dad had insisted on paying my green fees even though I could afford them.

"There's plenty of reasonable places to play," he said.

Mom kept her silence. I couldn't see her face, but imagined her studying the landscape out the backseat window.

Remembering the same argument I'd had with the senior partner, I asked, "Why won't you let me pay?" in a tone sharper than I intended. "I'm not a charity case," I added softly.

He tightened his jaw. "Just let me pay. I want to and I can."

I never argued after that, but the question lodged in my chest and tugged at me any time he pulled out his wallet.

            ✺ ✺ ✺

By mid-July, our Thursday pattern had become familiar. I'd watch the morning vapor rise off the rolling green hills as I drove from Columbus to a Licking County golf course. I reveled in the fact that, for the first time in years, I had Thursdays entirely free. No client emergencies or court dates. Just me and Dad and eighteen holes. It was also one of the first entirely uneventful trips I'd made. Not even a blip of panic.

But as I parked the car, the pleasant sensations quickly gave way to mild anxiety. Across the lawn I could see Dad packing his bag into a little white electric cart. Dad and I usually pushed our carts. It was a point of pride with him.

As I approached, he said sheepishly, "I thought we'd be lazy today and ride." The week before, I hadn't noticed the dark circles that were beneath his eyes today. And he seemed more stooped than I remembered. *It's the beginning of the end*, I thought, then pushed the idea away.

The word "lazy" had also made me flinch. I remembered a Sunday in high school when Dad needed help packing for Cleveland. I'd come home tired from a girlfriend's house and collapsed on the couch while trying to fold his clothes. My arms were heavy and my head throbbed. I leaned against the back of the sofa.

I must have fallen asleep because I woke to Dad yelling "You didn't sleep all weekend, so now you're sleeping when I need your help!"

"I don't feel good."

"I have no time for your laziness," he said, gathering the clothes with a grand sweeping gesture and carrying them away.

Glued to the sofa, I watched out the living room window as he drove off.

The following morning, I got up and began to make instant coffee. The next thing I remembered was waking on the floor to a sharp metallic smell. I'd passed out and the kettle had boiled dry. My temperature was 104 degrees. Telltale spots signaling measles appeared later that day and I spent the rest of the week in bed.

I don't know if Dad ever made the connection between my illness and my inability to fold his clothes. I only remember thinking, over and over as I lay in my fevered slumber, "I wasn't lazy, Dad. I was sick. I was really really sick."

I sometimes wondered if my father thought my trip to the psych ward had been "lazy." Notwithstanding my memories of *One Flew Over the Cuckoo's Nest*, I had hoped the psychiatric hospital would be peaceful. As Ed, a nurse, and I rode the elevator up from the emergency room, I imagined a little room all by myself where everyone left me alone to rest.

Reality sunk in once we arrived on the floor and the door locked electronically behind us. Ed sat with me while the nurse rifled through my bag. She confiscated any of my cosmetics that were in glass bottles, my pointed metal nail file, even my dental floss. Then she asked questions. Who is the President of the United States? What day is it? What year? Do you ever hear voices? Do inanimate objects talk to you? Do you believe someone is following you? I did my best to answer with a straight face since her stern expression let me know she was serious.

After the interview, the nurse led Ed and me to a yellow cinder-block room with two twin beds. Except for the bars on the windows and the bare walls, it reminded me of my first college dorm room. Every fifteen minutes a tall male nurse poked his head in.

Ed stayed until dinner. We didn't talk much. I don't think he knew what to say. We'd been married just one week over a year and this had all come as a shock to him. When I had called him from Joan's office to ask him to take me to the emergency room, he'd asked, "Can't I just meet you there?" That's when I knew how much I'd hidden. I'd been keeping it from everyone, shielding them and myself, for most of my life.

After Ed left, I pushed the institutional mystery meat around my plate then stretched out on the bed. A few minutes later, I opened my eyes to see the male nurse standing in the middle of the room. Under ordinary circumstances, I might have sat up, but it seemed someone had swapped lead for the blood that ordinarily ran through my veins.

"It's okay," he said. "I'm Rick, one of the nurses."

"Hi," I said. Now, even I noticed how flat my voice had grown.

"We don't encourage sleeping until bedtime." His eyes were kind.

"I'm just so tired."

"I understand. You can sit on the bed if you like, but it's not good to sleep during the day." I heard echoes of my father. "Anyone worth their salt would stay up." I wasn't in the mood to argue, especially not with a man taller than my father. I swung my legs over the side of the bed, stood, and slowly walked out into the hallway. Following the staff's suggestions was the beginning of the treatment to save my life.

            ❦ ❦ ❦

In response to Dad's claim that he'd be "lazy" today, I patted my stomach, which had grown flatter from walking the courses with him.

"Damn good thing. I couldn't stand much more fitness!" I lifted my bag onto the holder. He slid the little cooler between the bags.

Today, Dad wore a scarlet and gray golf shirt—the colors of The Ohio State University—I had bought for him. Before he began to play golf again, Dad had been impossible to shop for. His return to the game ended my agonizing quest for gifts for a man who, when he wanted something, simply bought it. Everything golf pleased him and he lost interest in nearly anything else.

I still spent hours choosing golf shirts with one pocket in the front. Now, I winced at the fact that this pocket had originally been for the cigarettes that would kill him. But as we rode, the July sun poked from behind a layer of low clouds, caught the colors of his shirt, and they shone.

We played around to the fourth hole. When Dad got out of the cart, I noticed sweat darkening the underarms of his shirt. It was still early in the morning and the sun was not yet hot. I studied him. Was he in pain? His face revealed nothing.

The cooler at the back of the cart carried cans of generic "Big K" root beer: regular for him, diet for me. It also held a bargain-sized bottle of ibuprofen, the only pain medication any doctor had yet prescribed. Today, when I opened the lid to pull out a diet root beer for myself, I noticed something new, two cans of a high-calorie nutritional drink. I held up one of the cans, "Want one of these?"

"Nah."

"Some drugs?"

"Next hole maybe." He carried his driver toward the tee.

I shuddered at his refusal. Why wouldn't he accept my help? Was he preparing for the inevitable?

The fairway was freshly mowed and I pulled the scent into my lungs, trying to calm myself, as Dad set his ball on the tee. He took a practice swing, then another, and stepped forward to put his driver against the ball. He pulled the club back then whipped it around to smack the white orb across the fairway. The ball flew a little to the left and he muttered, "Dummy. You pulled it," as if I wasn't there.

I couldn't watch him do this to himself. I made up a little song on the spot and began to sing:

It's closer to the hole than it was when you hit it.
It's closer to the hole than it was when you hit it.
It's closer to the hole than it was when you hit it.
And that's a great big deal!

He glared at me then rolled his eyes, slammed his driver back into his bag, and headed the cart toward the women's tees in silence.

I took a practice swing and he yelled, "Keep that arm straight." I set my driver up for the shot, hit the ball solid, but it flew to the left toward the rough areas beyond the fairway. I shook my head and turned back toward him, my face screwed up in a quizzical look.

He shrugged. "You hit it right where you aimed it."

"You're supposed to tell me where to hit!"

"I can't do everything!"

Thunder rolled across the hills, interrupting our exchange. I looked around. There was no lightning, just the low rumble in the distance, but dark clouds had gathered behind us. When we reached the next tee, lightning flashed. Neither one of us was afraid of the weather. In addition to watching the stars, we'd spent many nights standing beneath the aluminum awning over the side porch watching lightning illuminate the night sky.

Dad began to count, "One thousand one, one thousand two . . ." the way he taught me in my first science lesson as a little girl. "Light travels faster than sound," he had explained. "Every second you count means the lightning struck a mile further away."

Today, thunder boomed before my father got to "one thousand four" and he cranked the wheel to point the golf cart toward the clubhouse. He hit the gas pedal hard and I gripped the side as we sped back. The wind picked up as the approaching storm chased us. We made it to the clubhouse just before it began to pour.

From under the clubhouse awning, we again watched the rain as we had at the farm so many times before. Dad pulled out his scorecard.

"We'll have to finish this round later," he said.

I looked again at the stains under his arms, then glanced at the unopened cooler that held the nutritional drinks he had refused.

"Of course," I said.

But a part of me knew there wouldn't be many more Thursdays.

Chapter 17

Dummy

The Friday following my Thursday outing with Dad, Harri came to our group therapy session armed with lists of cognitive distortions, an article on negative self-talk, and sheets of lined paper, which she handed out. The group she led had shifted over the months. Now, only Kelly, a former dental assistant, and I remained as regulars in the windowless, gray room.

Harri reviewed the handouts then asked us to list our negative self-talk. "What kinds of things do you say to yourself?"

I stared at the paper and only began to write once I heard the scratching of pens. I listed, "You're stupid. You don't know what you're doing. You're lazy." The others continued to write after I had recorded my three sentences, but I couldn't think of anything to add.

We went around the room and read our sentences aloud. A small woman with long, curly blonde hair cried when she read, "You're a terrible mother and your children hate you." The middle-aged woman next to her handed her a box of tissues.

Harri looked at the mother and said, "Tell me one good thing you did for your children today."

The woman stared at the carpet.

"Did you make them breakfast?"

"Uh huh."

"Did you wash the clothes they're wearing?"

"Uh huh."

"How about school supplies? Did you make sure they had those?"

"Yeah."

Harri looked at the rest of us. "Whatdya think gang? Terrible mother?"

All of us, including the blonde mother, laughed.

"What makes you think your children hate you?"

The woman shrugged.

"Did you hate your mother?"

We all knew she did. She'd spent weeks in this room talking about it. Harri didn't wait for her to answer.

"Did your mother do terrible things that led you to hate her?"

When the woman again began to cry, my vision blurred and the room tilted. Harri's tone stayed soft, almost soothing, but she pressed forward like a prosecutor closing in. I shifted forward in my chair, longing to leave. But Harri caught my eye and I froze. No matter how tough it got, we all stayed in the room.

"I was a terrible child," the mother said.

"What did you ever do to deserve the way she treated you?"

Now, Harri was the judge and we were the jury. The room swayed and I began to taste metal. Saliva flooded my mouth.

Harri picked up the wastebasket and handed it to me a second before I vomited.

She moved to the chair next to me, clapped her hands, and said, "Five-minute break." The middle-aged woman handed me the box of tissues, then she and the others left.

"You're okay, Nita. It's not court." Court had been the perfect environment for me to keep score of my failures. Thinking of it left me weak.

"Look around the room," Harri continued. "See where you are." I did as she instructed, trying to focus on the gray speckled walls, the blue stackable chairs, and the blue multicolored carpet.

"Why don't you go to the bathroom and wash up. I'll get you some water." She reached into her purse and handed me a pack of gum. "Keep reminding yourself that you're safe here. It's not court."

After the break, she covered everyone else's lists except mine.

The following week, Harri returned to the negative self-talk theme. She spent the first part of group reiterating what she'd said earlier. At the break, she handed me my self-talk list from the week before.

"Review it and we'll talk about it after."

When we returned, she asked me, "What's the worst thing on your list."

"I'm lazy."

"Did you get out of bed today?"

I laughed. "I'm here, aren't I?"

"Did you put on clean underwear?"

"None of that counts!"

"You want us to experience you in dirty underwear?" Harri said.

"I just don't get how this is going to help me figure out what to do with my life."

"What do you want to do with your life?"

"Write, but . . ."

"And are you writing?"

"Not enough." My voice sounded faint and far away.

"Where have we heard that before?"

The blonde woman who'd been cross-examined the week before cut in, "'Never enough' was on the cognitive distortion sheet," and gestured with air quotes.

"Right! Never enough," Harri echoed.

I examined the Velcro strap of my brown sandals and words came out before I could stop them.

"Nothing I've written matters! The *Dog World* article won't come out until next year. I was stupid to think it would make a difference."

The editor had loved the piece. When she said they would buy it, I'd imagined Dad holding the magazine in his hands, smiling and nodding at me. I hoped he might finally recognize and really see me. But instead of the article being published this fall while he was still alive and golfing, it had been pushed back to March or after.

"Dad might not . . ."

Harri cut me off. "It's possible he won't."

She continued, "But why do you think it's stupid to want him to see your work?"

I looked at my hands.

"Do you think he'll love you more if you're published?"

My vision blurred and I blinked hard. I had spent so much time on that piece, going over the sentences again and again. I longed to show him the glossy pages, point out my byline, watch him glow with pride. Now, he probably wouldn't even see it in print.

"It's not black and white, Nita. I doubt his love is conditional. Just because the article won't come out as promised doesn't make it any less valuable. And just because you're not working at a job today doesn't mean you're lazy."

I nodded, eyes down, hoping she would move on. I wanted to believe her, to know Dad loved me regardless, but understanding my cognitive distortions didn't change the cruel, scorekeeping mechanism inside me.

My mind began to chant, "Lazy. Stupid. Don't know anything." The more Harri talked, the louder my mind grew until I couldn't hear Harri at all. It was easier to disappear than risk hearing something that might undo me.

"Are you with me?" Harri touched my hand and suddenly I could hear her and see the others again. "You left us for a minute. It's okay. Just stay with us. We'll move on."

A few weeks later, when Harri asked me how things were going, I told the group, "I'm not sure what to do with my father." It was early August. Dad and I had been playing golf for more than two months. "His negative self-talk is awful."

"Hmm," Harri said. "Remind you of anything?"

I thought she meant something from my childhood.

Before I could say anything else, a woman in a floral shirt chimed in. "I got my inner critic from my parents. That's probably where you got yours."

"Of course it is," I said. "But his is different. He says it out loud, in front of me."

"What does he say?" Harri asked.

"If he misses a golf shot, he calls himself, 'Dummy.' He shakes his head and scowls and curses at himself."

I told them about my little song, but Harri ignored that.

"Sounds unpleasant. Have you told him how it feels to hear him criticize himself?"

"When I say anything, it's as if I'm not even there. He's gone somewhere else."

Harri shook her head. "Uh huh. Sound familiar?"

The others laughed.

It had occurred to me that Dad might be zoning out in the same way I did, but I didn't think I did it that often. Plus, it didn't feel the same. His self-deprecation was brutal.

"I know you're all here when I disassociate. I just can't talk to you."

Harri held my gaze. "So, when he's checked out you can't fix his self-talk any more than we can fix yours."

Sure. But that didn't mean I was ready to stop trying.

No one spoke. In the quiet, I let her meaning settle within me. Dad's scorekeeping voice had played in my mind for so long that I'd mistaken it for my own. Meanwhile, I'd been trying to earn the love of someone who couldn't even give it to himself. Knowing that seemed important, but it didn't ease the pain.

CHAPTER 18

RUNNING AGAINST TIME

By the end of August, my father and I had played nearly every week. Labor Day weekend, we met at St. Albans, the most expensive course we had played all summer. It would be our last round before he and Mom drove back to Arizona.

At the time, number eleven was a 375-yard dogleg right. The fairway stretched along a tree-lined creek for 150 yards then took a sharp right turn and headed up a steep hill, with the green tucked beyond where the land leveled out.

Dad teed up, intending to cut yards off his drive by hitting the ball across the dogleg. He would aim for that shortcut while I played it safe, hitting straight down the fairway, around the turn, and up the hill toward the green.

But Dad's ball sliced and landed on the left side of the fairway near the creek. He shook his head and muttered, "Dummy. You pulled it."

I muttered, "Stop it, Dad." He ignored me.

I hit a solid drive that landed halfway down the fairway. "Not bad," he said and I felt a little glow. We got in the cart and drove to my ball. Dad stayed in the cart. I got out and hit my ball further down the fairway, just to the bottom of the steep hill. "Have you been practicing behind my back?" Dad asked with a smile.

"I'm not telling," I said as I got back in the cart. I hadn't been practicing. I'd only had enough energy that summer to play golf with him, but my golf was getting better and I enjoyed his positive attention.

Dad's ball sat directly across the fairway from a farm bell that hung atop a heavy post at the crook of the dogleg. Before you hit, you pulled a rope to ring the bell and alert other players. When the metal clapper hit the cast iron, the sound would reverberate for miles. It was a rural Ohio way of yelling, "Fore!"

Dad pulled an iron out of his bag and walked to his ball. I drove the cart to the post where the bell hung. Dad signaled for me to ring it. When I did, its sound pulled history from me: the farm bell at his parents' house, the one at my Great Aunt Mary's, and the bell just two miles up the road at the farm where I grew up. I wondered if the bells heard each other, their iron voices bellowing across the green waves of land.

Once the bell had sent its song up the hill to alert the golfers ahead of us, Dad squared his feet with the ball and bent forward to place his club against it.

This was the warmest summer in twenty-five years. We'd begun to play earlier every week because the temps were hitting the 100's by mid-afternoon, and by this time Dad was weakening—not noticeably to anyone but the closest of us, but two or three hours in those temperatures would put him in bed for a few days.

I watched Dad from across the width of the fairway. I had taken the list of cognitive distortions home and Harri gave me the homework of staying awake to all the flavors of these disruptive thoughts throughout my day. As I stood in the warming August morning, watching my father stand at the tee, the thought arose: *You don't even know how to play this game.* The weight of it made me stoop. I shook my head as if I could dodge it the way I might a fly.

Dad pulled the club back to begin his swing. He was trying too hard. When the club swung down against the ball, his elbow bent. The club face turned, hit the ball crooked and it sliced, flying deep into the rough beyond the right edge of the fairway.

"Take a mulligan," I yelled.

He didn't hear me. His lips were pursed in a critical scowl. He shook his head as he tromped toward the cart.

As he grew closer, I could hear him repeating, "You dummy," and "Stupid," under his breath.

"Dad!" I cried. "This is the toughest hole on this course."

He was right beside the cart now, and still didn't hear me. He slid his driver into his bag and sat down heavily on the seat without swinging his legs in. He put his head in his hands and said, "You don't even know how to play this game."

I stopped, frozen by the echo.

I thought back to all those mornings before the psych ward, all those days when I would wake, swing my legs over the edge of the bed, and sit there, while a voice in my head yelled, "You dummy. Don't be lazy. Just get up. Get dressed and get your ass to work." I recognized my father's determination, his unwillingness to give up even when things were stacked against him.

I'd inherited his method.

At the law firm, for my career to grow, I needed to bring in clients. The senior partner pushed me toward those divorce and child custody cases because plenty of people I knew were getting divorced. But I was neither trained for it nor emotionally equipped. Divorce court wasn't labor negotiation, mediation, or arbitration. It was open warfare complete with crying and screaming spouses, vicious lawyers, and useless motions. Litigation was a full-fledged brawl. I was wholly unprepared.

One morning as I argued a motion in Domestic Relations Court, my eyes brimmed with tears. As the opposing attorney and I walked from the chambers into the hallway he turned to me and in a sharp tone said, "You're just not cut out for this, are you?"

I shook my finger at him and spat, "You have no idea what I'm made of," but I couldn't stop the tears from streaming down my face. I turned on my high-heeled pumps and clomped down the hallway to the women's room, where I sat on the toilet and held my hand over my mouth to stifle my sobs. By the time I came out, he was gone.

But I am my father's daughter. We do not give in or give up. We regroup. We reform. We make a new and better plan and attack again. And like my father, the thing I knew and trusted was work. I chanted, "I am a strong and healthy person," for the entire twenty-minute drive to work. At lunch, I drove to a nearby park and ate in my car while I listened to a New Age guru profess that I was more than a human body and meant for more than a human life. I cried in recovery groups and cried alone, but mostly I steeled myself and kept plugging away.

And I thought about all the days since I'd left the law firm, days when I tried to write, putting words to feelings I barely understood. "You dummy. You don't even know how to do this. Why don't you give up?"

In therapy, when I closed my eyes and listened for the critical voice, I saw a tall man in a suit telling me the rules for living. Of course, he looked a lot like my father. I knew they were the same, but I'd never realized that it was literally his voice I was hearing—the same words, in the same tone—his actual voice. My chest tightened and for a moment I couldn't breathe.

Dad had never said these things directly to me. He never called me "dummy," or told me I didn't know how to do anything. He said I could do or be whatever or whoever I wanted, if I put my mind to it and made the effort. He told me to take action, tempering his advice with, "If wishes were horses, poor men would ride."

Instead of listening to what he said, I watched how he treated himself. Instead of becoming the "anything" he said I could become, I had become the person he displayed. How many times as I handed him a wrench while he lay on the barn floor beneath a piece of farm equipment had I heard him mutter to himself something along the lines of, "You idiot. You never should have bought this damned combine anyway"? It had become my mantra, and here it was before me on St. Albans in the unbearable glare of an Ohio summer.

I wanted to give my father everything I had learned, to help him get off his own back. Perhaps if I could fix his inner critic, I wouldn't have to face how permanent my own might be.

I put my hand on his shoulder and shook him hard, "Dad, stop it." His head snapped toward me and he focused as if I had just woken him from one of his rare naps.

Like the farm bells I imagined reverberating with each other, his eyes began to well up in sympathy with the tears already in my eyes.

"Take a friggin' mulligan or let's just drive up the hill," I said softly. "It doesn't matter."

He looked past me and glared. I turned around to see a foursome coming up behind us, driving their cart toward the tee.

Dad swung his legs back into the cart, gunned the engine, and tore up the hill. We rode in silence to the top, the place where Dad thought he'd lost his ball. The rough was thick with Queen Anne's lace and horsetail. We swung our clubs around in it for a few minutes until we heard the bell ring. The foursome that had been at the tee was now at the bottom of the hill.

"Can't we let them play through?" I begged.

"No," he said fiercely. "Go hit your ball onto the green and I'll drop a ball next to yours."

There are rules in golf, rules my father taught me. If your putter digs into the green, you fix the mark it made. If someone else's ball is closer to the hole than yours, you either let them mark their ball or you let them hit out of turn. And if a faster foursome comes up behind you, you let them play through.

Normally a gracious player, Dad wasn't in a rule-following mood. Could he feel time ticking away, the road ahead growing shorter? He couldn't stop the cancer cells from gobbling up his rib bones as they multiplied. He couldn't unsmoke the cigarettes or unbreathe the varnish fumes or uninhale the dust off the barn floor, but he could refuse to let these men play through.

We walked briskly to where my ball lay just off the backside of the green. I could feel the foursome's eyes on my back. My hands shook. I swung twice and missed so I picked up the ball and threw it at the green where it landed at the lip closest to us.

Dad dropped a ball and chipped a shot right past the flag and we watched it roll over the hill and back down the slope from where we'd come. "Dummy," he said again.

I tugged his arm. "Listen, you," I said in my sternest big girl voice. "It's a good thing you're not in group. Harri would never let you get away with that."

"It was a stupid shot. I pulled it."

"We're not playing for thousand-dollar bills."

When Dad was fourteen, his parents sent him to live with his grandmother miles away from his home with only a bike for transportation. His grandmother was ill, "loony," Dad said when he told me about this. The doctor gave her a cough syrup, which sedated her, and told him to tie her in a chair. Some days, Dad had to leave her tied in that chair while he went to school and work. He had to make enough money to buy his own food because she existed entirely on fried baloney which she cooked on a coal stove, the old kind that smells up the entire house.

He wasn't old enough to be hired by a business, so he mowed lawns with a rotary push mower, collecting pennies a yard. When he turned fifteen, he convinced the local grocer that he was sixteen and began to work bagging groceries. The grocer called him in one day and accused him of stealing meat. Dad denied it, but the grocer stuck by his decision and Dad had to tell his folks he'd been fired. Even if he was hungry and there was all that meat just lying around, I cannot imagine him silently stuffing a steak into his coat, walking out with it, and pedaling off to his grandmother's to cook it up on her stove. He would not do that. That was the only time he got fired and he repeated the tale often.

On St. Albans golf course that day, it seemed as if Dad was still that boy, still trying to prove he wasn't guilty of the crime of which he was accused. "You dummy," he swore with every bad swing. I could not console him or even reach him. And this boy was running with the man, running against time.

His face crumpled. I walked back to the cart, not ready to give up yet.

The foursome was gaining on us. As he walked back to the cart, he saw them too and tensed. I thought about asking him again if we should let them play through, but clamped my mouth shut.

That foursome had become something else. He was on this golf course with me every day we could manage it, trying to prove to himself that he wasn't sick. He was trying to play faster than the tumors in his lungs and ribs could grow. If he let the men play through, the cancer would have won. Plus, this was the last time he would play in Ohio, and one of the last times we would play together.

So, I let him run and let them chase us. I stopped trying to make it better and I stopped berating him for yelling at himself. Me trying to fix his self-talk made about as much sense as me trying to cure his cancer. For that day, I would admit defeat in the face of several foes.

We played the rest of the back nine on the run. The foursome behind us were better players: men in their mid-forties, well-practiced, and feeling energetic on a Thursday afternoon. The faster Dad tried to play, the worse he hit. He grimaced with pain each time he swung the club. Each time he hit, I dropped my ball near where his landed and hit from there. We forgave any bad shot by picking up the ball or leaving it in the rough.

We might as well have been on a racecourse. The strokes meant nothing, so we stopped keeping score. Hole after hole, the only thing that mattered to Dad was to outrun those men. The only thing that mattered to me was to stay alongside Dad.

At the end of eighteen, we pulled up to the clubhouse. Sweat ran down the sides of my face and soaked my underarms. Dad's face glowed red beneath his visor and the chest of his shirt was ringing wet.

We sat at a table by the window that faces the cart sheds, but neither of us looked out. Dad eyed the beer on the menu, but ordered a root beer and a hot dog. I sipped a scalding coffee and ate tasteless nacho chips from their little bag.

"How'd you play?" asked Mr. Price, the owner.

"Like shit," Dad said.

I opened my mouth, intending to put a positive spin on our game. But anything I might say would be dishonest. I closed it. Lifted my head, squared my shoulders, and turned to look out the window.

THE TURN
SEPTEMBER AND OCTOBER 1995

In the big picture what truly matters is the lives we touch.

—Tiger Woods

Chapter 19

End of the Season

"You won't believe this place," Dad said as he pulled onto the highway heading for The Palms golf course in Mesquite, Nevada, on the Utah state line. "The front's really flat, but the back! Whoa!"

In September, after Dad and I had played golf all summer in central Ohio, my parents drove back to Arizona. The next week, they headed to Las Vegas and I flew in to meet them. From there, Dad, Mom and I would drive north toward Yellowstone National Park and the Tetons. This was it. We were on Dad's "trip of a lifetime."

My father set the itinerary so we could play The Palms on the way. He and I headed out early, leaving my sleeping mother in the room. She planned to spend the morning bronzing herself by the pool and the afternoon gathering gifts at the hotel shop. After all that activity, she would certainly need a nap.

Dad had played The Palms often enough to memorize the course layout, but within a few minutes after he drove away from the hotel, he began to shake his head. "I thought it was a left back there." I stayed quiet, but felt disoriented. I had inherited his excellent sense of direction and alarms rang when he didn't seem to know where he was. *Maybe they had changed the signs.* To calm myself, I focused on the map, but it didn't have a close-up of the area. Dad pushed his golf cap further down on his head and squinted at the road. After a few extra turns, we arrived.

Dad went to the clubhouse, got a cart, pulled it up to the station wagon, and opened the hatch. I pulled my golf shoes out of my bag.

"What an idiot!" Dad said, pulling off his cap and slapping it against the top of the car. "How could I forget my shoes?"

I opened my mouth to urge him to take it easy on himself, but quickly closed it. I'd fought this battle with him all summer. I would never win.

He frowned at his Velcro sneakers. "Damn, I'm stupid." We packed up the cart and he pointed it toward the first hole.

Number one was a slight dogleg which I happily double-bogeyed. I'd never be a pro, I thought, but perhaps the days of completely embarrassing myself were over. Nope. The second hole included my nemesis—water—as did the next seven. I smiled despite my disappointment.

"These greens are so smooth and the fairways, wow!" I said even as my mood slipped. The best antidepressants on the market couldn't counteract losing three balls in five holes. Dad ignored my sullenness and we rode in silence for a few moments.

"The cart seems noisy," I said. Most of the carts we'd driven in Ohio made a smooth hum while this one sputtered like a mower.

"Gasoline cart," Dad said. "You're used to electric." I thought I heard him chuckle, but when I looked, his grin gave way to pursed lips. We finished nine and he drove to the clubhouse for lunch.

We reveled in poor food choices: deep-fried mozzarella, zucchini sticks, and deep-fried mushrooms dipped in marinara sauce. Dad drank his nutrition beverage and I sipped a diet cola. We sat at the bar not talking, but several times I caught him watching me in the mirror with the look of a little boy who's up to something. He poured some ibuprofen pills into his hand, tossed them in his mouth, then chased them with a few sips of my cola before we walked back to the cart.

As he drove us toward number ten, the deceptively flat front gave way to a landscape reminiscent of those calendars with computer-generated images of a fairway superimposed onto the side of the Swiss Alps. Above the engine's roar, I yelled, "This isn't a golf course; it's a roller coaster!"

Dad's smile bloomed into a full-blown grin as we climbed the first steep hill. "Wheee!" he yelled as we flew down, "See why they need gas carts!" I clung to the side as we climbed the next rise.

Chocolate-colored mountains surrounded us on three sides. I turned around in the cart and watched light and dark stone patches sparkle on the deep rust plateau behind us. The emerald carpet of the front nine lay below and a herd of cattle grazed in a field along the river that wound around the edge of the course and mountains. Arnold Palmer and his team had built the back nine of The Palms across a gorge. Our hearty gasoline cart stalled on one of the hills. In a role reversal from the days of Dad pushing me on the lawn mower at the farm, I pushed the cart while Dad floored it. He was too weak to push.

One tee box was 144 vertical yards above and 555 horizontal yards away from the green. It would have been a long hole if it had been flat, but you were also fighting gravity. A sign warned us to yell before we teed off to alert golfers who'd be impossible to see on the fairway below.

"They should have installed a farm bell," I said. When Dad drove, it looked as if he'd hit the ball up into the air, but it was actually flying straight away from us. We watched as it sailed out then dropped seemingly into nowhere. The only way to tell if he'd even hit the fairway was to get back in the cart and drive down the hill. The word "rough" doesn't come close to capturing the terrain: creosote bushes, cactus, tumbleweed, sagebrush, rocks, and sand. Not a blade of grass anywhere off the fairway.

Just when I thought Dad couldn't smile any brighter, his grin widened revealing more teeth. Even the pounding heat didn't dampen our spirits: 102 degrees of hot dust. The wind blew the chocolate dirt back into our mouths and eyes. I only attempted three of the back nine holes. Dad hit on all of them, but didn't bother keeping score. He focused on the scenery while I took in his delight.

But on sixteen, he began to grimace every time he swung the club. Like a wind-up toy that goes and goes then grinds to a stop, his gestures became awkward and his pace slowed. Forcing a smile, I pulled the bargain-sized bottle of ibuprofen out of his bag and handed him a nutrition drink from the cooler. He poured six more of the brown pills into his palm and chased them with the drink. I turned away so he couldn't see my eyes fill.

On the way back to the hotel, I offered to drive and he let me. This was the first time I remember driving with him as a passenger since my high-school days when he helped teach me how to operate the car. He fell asleep before I pulled onto the main road. At the motel, he barely woke long enough to walk from the car to the room. He changed to his pajamas in the bathroom and fell back to sleep as soon as he lay down. Mom and I ate dinner together. Dad slept through the night.

In the morning, Dad was rejuvenated. We three headed north from Mesquite to St. George, Utah, through the Virgin River Gorge. The highway wound through the mountain range and thousands of feet of rocky cliffs and mountain peaks jutted up toward the huge blue sky.

We stopped at Shoney's for breakfast and got a booth where we could see the red hills surrounding the little strip of town that stretches gracefully through the canyon.

Dad told the waitress, "We'll all have the breakfast bar."

She screwed up her face. "I'm sorry, sir. We're serving lunch."

"What time is it?" Dad asked.

"Eleven fifteen."

"Darn! Mountain time," Mom said, looking at her watch. We had all forgotten the time change from Nevada to Utah.

Mom frowned at her menu. Dad stared longingly at the bar that should have held his breakfast. I looked at the wall, the floor, anywhere but their pouting faces. Now that we were actually on my father's "trip of a lifetime," it was as if a countdown timer toward his death had flipped on inside me.

When the waitress told us breakfast had ended, my heart backslid into my childhood role. I imagined storming the kitchen and forcing the chef to cook sunny-side-up eggs, hash browns, link sausage, and lightly buttered toast for my parents. The manager walked past and I could almost see myself standing on the table and yelling to the other patrons, "Help! My father is dying. My parents must have the breakfast bar. Now!" Instead, I sat very still, gripped my thighs, and willed myself to stay in my seat until the compulsion passed.

Dad set his menu aside and said, "Guess we'll have the soup and salad buffet." Mom nodded. When they both slid out of the vinyl booth, I exhaled.

Back in the car after brunch with Dad behind the wheel, I relaxed into the scenery. The red mountains of St. George yielded to a relief of open land. Cattle grazed serenely. Bales of alfalfa were stacked at the edges of newly planted and irrigated fields. Jagged mountain ridges streaked with blood-red soil framed the peaceful farm scene. Stubborn olive-green clumps dotted the hillsides and the long flat expanse of hopeful golden fields formed the basin floor. Ignorant of my family's plight, farm life continued.

Dad drove all day, covering 400 miles of Utah in one stretch.

That night, we shared a room at the Comfort Inn. Dad was watching *NYPD Blue* and the sound of gunfire and yelling disturbed me.

"That back nine yesterday was amazing!" I nearly shouted over the TV.

"Yep," he said, eyes glued to the show.

"I'm going to the lobby for a bit," I said.

"I'll join you," Mom said and stood.

"I was going to write."

Mom frowned and sat back down.

As I made my way to the elevator, I held back tears. I didn't feel consciously sad, but my body was tight, knotted up, signaling that I'd been playing "happy camper," pushing away the feelings to hide them from my parents. We had the bad habit of absorbing each other's emotions and I was struggling just to sort out my own. Despite knowing better, I still didn't want them to see my fear and sadness about Dad's declining health. I didn't think I was strong enough to handle them being upset about me on top of everything else. I had learned young to hide my emotions with a smile or a blank expression and resorted to it under extreme stress. We'd spent nearly three days straight together. I needed this break to recalibrate and be my real self for a while without having to fake resilience.

In the restroom near the lobby, I wept into wads of toilet paper. After I washed my face and examined my eyes for telltale redness, I walked to the lobby, poured a cup of coffee from the sideboard, and opened my notebook. As Dad's illness progressed, I'd shifted my writing goals away from publication and toward taking thorough notes. I hoped to record the details I knew I might forget once the crisis was over. More often, my conflicting emotions filled the pages.

I wrote about my irritation at Mom. With Dad sick, she had become clingier. If I headed to a coffee shop, she wanted to tag along. If I went for a walk, she wanted to come. I tried to emotionally distance myself from her, the way I was learning in therapy, group, and recovery, but when I was this tired, I couldn't access these newly acquired skills. I sensed her yearning, her wanting, especially when she and I were together for more than a few hours.

Sometimes she was trying to protect me, to keep me from feeling too sad. More often she was trying to protect herself. Part of me knew how much pain she must be in, but I had difficulty mustering empathy. All of my emotional support was used up on Dad.

From Dad, I felt nothing. He was receding into himself, escaping into those cops-and-robbers shows, and hiding in silence, the way he had all the years I had known him. Over our summer of golf, we'd developed a bond. Without that connection, I struggled to reach him. With him, I was the one straining, yearning once again for a tidbit of emotion while he grew more and more absent. I hoped this would change when we arrived in West Yellowstone.

After twenty minutes, Mom joined me in the lobby. When I saw her, I closed my notebook, a reflex from thirty years before when, as a second-grader, I had caught her reading my journal. She sat on the floral sofa beside me.

"Did you get some writing done?"

"A little."

She looked at my cup of coffee then searched the room. When she saw the pot on a sideboard, she said "I should get a cup," but did not get up. This was my cue to get it for her. I stayed where I was. A few minutes passed in silence.

"Your father seems more tired and confused."

I nodded. *Was my face red?* Talking to Mom about my father seemed disloyal, as if Dad and I were the children and I was tattling on him to a parent.

"He told me that he forgot his golf shoes at The Palms."

I nodded again, choosing not to tell her that he also got lost on the way.

I had noticed his decline, but the "happy camper" part of me tried to ignore it. The reality of Dad's illness lived in a little compartment at the edge of my consciousness. The section of my body that experienced sadness at his illness sat side-by-side with another part that acted as if his new exhaustion were nothing unusual.

With a sigh, Mom said, "I think it's hitting him at a new level."

It was hitting us all at a new level.

I set my notebook on the cocktail table and picked up my coffee.

"He doesn't want to do anything except play golf and watch television," she added.

Dad had only wanted to play golf and watch television ever since they moved to Arizona in the mid-1980s, but she was actually trying to say something else.

"Do you talk about his cancer?" I asked.

She looked away. "He doesn't want to talk about it."

I imagined her asking once, being rebuffed, and never asking again. My mother had many years of learning the hard way not to push my father.

"Can't they do anything about his pain?" My mind flashed to the handful of pills Dad took every morning and the palm-full of ibuprofen he needed to get through a few holes of golf. He grimaced all the time. I knew she too must be seeing his agony.

"I don't know." She bent over and put her head in her hands. She looked small and frail, like a child sent out on an impossible mission. I set down my coffee, touched her arm for a moment, then picked up my coffee again.

"He doesn't want to see a doctor," she said. My father's last medical visit had been in July in Ohio when he finished radiation. He hadn't seen a physician since, even after they returned to Arizona. As a result, we had no idea where he was on the cancer trajectory or how much time he had left. Did he think being in Arizona or on this trip made him immune from the Ohio diagnosis?

Did I believe if he just kept playing golf, it would all be okay?

Throughout the six months between his inability to swallow that smoked sausage sample at Albertsons and now, beginning our journey through the western states on Dad's "trip of a lifetime," my father did his best to "try not to worry us," in effect, to keep us from knowing how sick he was. And I had gone back to playing along. *Who were we trying to fool?*

On the road the next morning, Mom insisted we stop at the visitor center just inside the Idaho border. Dad would have preferred to continue driving until we either peed on the seats or reached our destination. The friendly receptionist gave us coupons that read, "Free Taters for Out-of-Staters." We'd grown potatoes in the garden, so a free potato should not have been a big deal. But that day, the buttery "Idaho Baker" I ate sitting next to Mom and Dad at a picnic table behind a farm market tasted like precious candy.

By the time we arrived in West Yellowstone, Dad was wobbly-kneed. He needed a nap, but we had arrived too early to check into the hotel. He sat in the car until he had gathered his strength, then took out his camcorder and wandered up and down the main street videotaping the wild-west-styled buildings. He moved slowly, struggling to catch his breath. Walking beside him, I told myself the altitude was making him gasp. In part, it probably was. At the end of the street, he stopped and handed me the camcorder. He used to wield it with no problem, but now it was too heavy for him to hold for long.

As he surveyed the street, empty of tourists, a misty expression spread across his face. He looked disappointed and very sad. Our eyes met and then he looked away.

"It's the end of the season," he said. I chose to assume that he meant the end of the tourist months in Yellowstone, but my gut registered the larger meaning.

Beyond him, I saw Mom signal that we could check into the hotel. I tapped him on the shoulder. He turned and began to trudge toward her. His back was sloped and, for the first time, I thought that he looked like an old man.

Mom, Dad and I had traveled together several times after I reached adulthood. I never asked for my own room unless one of my significant others was with me. In therapy, when Joan and I discussed the trip, she recommended separate hotel rooms. I'd dismissed the idea as if she were suggesting a private jet. "Mom's paying. I don't need anything special."

But Joan convinced me that, at least once we got to Yellowstone, I should have my own room. Unlike the other towns we blew through, Mom, Dad, and I would spend several days there. We would all need some space.

Despite my being thirty-four years old, when I imagined telling my mother I wanted my own room, my insides quaked as if I were asking for the moon. A much younger and less healthy part of me saw it as betraying and abandoning them by leaving them alone with each other, as if they needed my protection.

But time was running out. This was my chance to break the pattern. I had picked up the phone and told my mother I needed a room of my own.

She wasn't surprised or even displeased. "You'll need time alone by then," she agreed, which I heard as, "I'll want time with your father."

Once we checked in, we all succumbed to the need for naps. Our rooms had an adjoining door. If I wanted to be social, I could leave it open, but I told Mom, "If it's closed, please knock." She agreed. Safe in the knowledge that I had privacy if I needed it, I voluntarily left the adjoining door ajar. After I closed my eyes, I heard Dad quietly moaning. I got out of my bed, nudged the door open further, and peered into their room.

Mom snored softly on the little sofa across from the bed where Dad lay on his back with his mouth open. Sometimes he babbled when he napped, but today he made low groans. On his left side, beneath his golf shirt, a bulge the diameter of a golf cup rose and fell with his breath. At the highest point, it stuck out a quarter of an inch from the rest of his ribs.

The tumor.

My breath grew shallow and my vision blackened at the edges. I backed out of the doorway, inched the door closed, and dropped to the bed. I wrapped my arms around myself and silently rocked back and forth.

We had talked about it. I had read about it. I had even written about it, but when he stood or sat, his shirt concealed it. I hadn't seen it, until now.

When I called Ed that night, I tried to explain how faint I'd felt when I saw the tumor, but words couldn't capture it. Was I the only one who didn't know how sick my father was? How much longer could I deny it?

We spent the next two days in Yellowstone National Park seeing whatever Dad wanted. Old Faithful sprayed up out of the ground and shot above our heads right on schedule; the paint pots, those caldrons of nasty chemicals in vibrant colors like an artist's palette, bubbled out of the ground in front of us; the upper loop, pine groves, and aspens with mountain backdrops surrounded thousands of acres of plains. The park layout allowed Dad to view all the scenery from his driver's seat without ever leaving the car.

On the second day as we left the park, the cars ahead slowed to a stop. Dad stuck his head out the window to look and said, "There's a dozen cars backed up ahead of us." While we were stopped, I took the chance to write in my journal. I recorded how, on the flight over, I had looked out the airplane window at the clouds below and the blue sky above and asked whatever divine presence there might be to give me the strength to be real. Unlike my previous trips out west, for the most part we had all stopped pretending everything would be "just fine." My habit of slipping into denial wasn't completely gone, but I saw improvement.

The traffic began to move and we inched forward. I set down my journal and looked up to see a herd of more than twenty bison alongside the road near the car ahead of us. Dad slowed the car to a crawl.

The bull stood off to one side, its enormous scrotum hanging low. As Dad inched the car forward, one cow and then a second stepped calmly in front of the car. Mom sucked in her breath. The bull turned and began walking toward us. I wondered if the people in one of the other cars had tried to feed them.

The beasts continued to surround the wagon. Dad's window was still down and a cow sniffed his mirror. He slowly began to roll up his window. Before he could close it completely, she stuck her snout through the opening, but retracted it when the rising glass touched her chin.

Enormous, woolly, yet sweet faces peered in at us through every pane. Mother grew pale and clutched the edge of the seat. My head spun with excitement.

In the vast acreage of Yellowstone, we humans were on the bison's turf. The road was a tiny paved ribbon through their land. It was their forest and their plain and their rivers and their streams. They made the rules.

I picked up my notebook again and wrote about how cancer is like that, too. When it chose our family, we entered a foreign zone. We didn't speak the language. The doctors tried to translate, but they weren't natives. We were up against something bigger, stronger, and wiser in the ways of its land than us.

The bison could pass their nights in this wilderness, forage for food among the grasses, and know which water to drink. You didn't see them going for a swim in any of the scalding, stinky geysers.

Cancer creates its own landscape, which sometimes includes radiation, chemo, surgery, and nearly always pain. The patients, families, and friends don't visit this territory by choice. They wind up there between a movie and an ice cream sundae, or dressed up in high heels, riding their boyfriend's motorcycle to a party, or swinging a golf club on a January day. The symptoms come and the language changes and nothing is ever the same.

"Hand me the camcorder," Dad said in a calm, even tone. "Slow."

I slid the black bag from the floor beside me, eased the machine out and handed it to my father who began recording the huge curly heads. One of the cows rubbed her side against the fender. When the car rocked, Mom gasped. Dad continued to film; I continued to take notes. The bull slowly walked toward our car and sniffed the hood before continuing across the road. The cows followed. When the road was clear, Dad passed the camera off to Mom, put the car in gear, and edged forward. When he was a few feet ahead of the first cow, he punched the accelerator and tore toward the exit. Mom was still clutching the camera when we reached the Three Bears Lodge.

On our last day in the park, I noticed Dad holding his side more. He also snapped at Mom while we packed the car. When Mom stepped back into the motel, he said to me, "I think my cancer's getting to her. She's really scattered." I started to ask if he was angry or disappointed that our visit was nearly over. I knew I was. I could feel my heart beating faster than normal and I had trouble looking at him. But when I opened my mouth, nothing came out.

We drove through Canyon Village, Upper Falls, and Sulfur Caldron then stopped at Lake Yellowstone for supper. When we sat down, the overcast and cloudy sky with the Tetons rising sharply in the background gave the lake a dark and foreboding look. But as we ate, the sun broke through, sparkled the water with twinkling stars of light, and transformed the snow on the mountain tops into a frosty glaze.

I remember little about the trip back to their house in Arizona, except that Dad let me drive so he could sleep. My father did not relinquish the wheel by choice, but his body no longer gave him the option.

Somewhere in the middle of Utah, I remembered the movie *Thelma and Louise*. I thought of telling my parents, "Let's just keep driving." I could see us flying into the Grand Canyon with me at the helm, Mom dozing in the back seat, and Dad snoring beside me. I let the thought pass and steadied my hands on the wheel.

CHAPTER 20

CANCER COMMUNE

The night before I flew home from our "trip of a lifetime," Mom showed Dad and me a video for a cancer center in Mexico. As we watched, Dad shifted in his recliner then stared at the floor. When he looked up, his eyes and nose were red.

Later, over a basket of chips at a Mexican restaurant down the road, Mom asked, "What did you think, Gene?" As she spoke, she fidgeted like a candidate in a job interview.

"It's so much money," he said looking down at the table.

"We're talking about your life," I said. The fiesta music was too cheery. I wished they would turn it off. Later, I would wonder if I'd sounded supportive or as if I was trying to twist his arm.

"What if we spend all the money we've got and it doesn't work?" Dad said.

Mom looked at me, her eyes pleading. I reached for another chip.

She faced Dad. "If you don't believe it will work, it won't."

With his eyes glued to the chip basket, he replied, "It might not work even if I do believe."

The next morning, I got on the plane not knowing what Dad would decide.

A few evenings after I flew home, Mom called with an update. Some friends had suggested the Cancer Treatment Centers of America in Tulsa, Oklahoma, and Mom had convinced my father to go. Dad had started out behind the wheel headed for the Center, but within a few hours he couldn't stay awake. Mom drove the remaining 1,150 miles with him asleep in the passenger seat beside her.

What Mom didn't know as they sped along Route 40 was that Dad was fading in and out of consciousness. The cancer eating his ribs had begun to dump large quantities of calcium into his bloodstream. As she drove, he could have slipped into a coma before they reached Oklahoma and never regained consciousness. Later, with mixed emotions, I wondered if that might have been the kindest outcome.

The Center doctors immediately counteracted the calcium poisoning with a twelve-hour infusion. Dad also agreed to cisplatin chemotherapy and morphine patches.

Ten days later, Mom called again. Dad had gradually stopped eating and his weight and white blood cell count had plummeted. Back in June, Dr. Grecula at Ohio State had advised against chemo, and Dad had seemed confident in his decision to refuse it. I wondered if he regretted changing his mind and whether anything I'd said had tipped the scale. With his "trip of a lifetime" behind him, had the reality hit that his life might soon be over as well?

When Mom called again in mid-October, her voice sounded strained with fear and exhaustion. She wanted my sister, brother, and I to come. Dad had told her he didn't want any more chemo. "I'm afraid he's going to die soon," she said. I got on the next flight.

As the plane descended into the still green Tulsa landscape, I spotted fringes of shrubs and trees amid rolling hills. Ed had stayed home with the dogs. My mother was prone to exaggeration and neither Ed nor I believed Dad would die right away, especially not at the Cancer Center. Plus, Ed thought Dad's trip to Tulsa unnecessarily delayed the inevitable. But he would never second-guess Dad. He wasn't in his shoes.

When I cried from the fear of losing Dad, Ed put his arms around me and said, "It's all happening perfectly." I sometimes mistook his radical acceptance for coldness. It was different from my father's stoicism, but seemed just as stern. I was torn between believing Ed and his clear-eyed realism and clinging to a sliver of hope that Dad might tolerate treatment. Most of all, I wanted to honor Dad's wishes. He had chosen to go to the center and receive medical intervention. I got off the plane determined to stay open-minded and see what happened.

The Tulsa branch of the Cancer Treatment Centers of America was a sort of cancer commune. The building on the campus of Oral Roberts University was a converted 1970s dormitory that still wore that era's earth tones. Each floor had patient rooms surrounding a common living area with TVs and sofas. Family members could rent hotel rooms on the floors above.

As I approached, Mom and Dad sat on a sofa in the living area. The sight of him disoriented me. It was nearly 4 p.m. and he was in his pajamas, robe, and house slippers with a black-and-white "Will Golf for Food" ball cap on his head. It would take time for me to get used to him wearing pajamas before dark, though part of me doubted I ever would.

Mom's hug was fierce. She gripped me with bony fingers and her polished nails dug into my back. She was stranded on a desert island and I was one of the savages she hoped would help her build a boat she could row to safety. She didn't let go.

When she finally released me, I turned to Dad, who said, "Sorry if I don't get up." I bent down and wrapped my arms around him. Wisps of his thinning blond hair stuck out from beneath the cap.

"Guess we're not golfing today," I said.

"Nope," he shook his head.

I didn't know what else to say. Without golf between us, I wanted to disappear, or run.

"Is that a cafeteria?" I asked pointing to a room filled with tables.

"You eating?" I asked Dad.

"Everything tastes like metal."

I sat on the sofa next to him and asked how things were going at the Center.

"They're treating me alright," he said, shifting uncomfortably.

I leaned toward Mom. "He behaving?"

"This is the first day he's felt well enough to get out of his room and watch TV," Mom said, pointing to a closed hospital room door.

"I can't follow the TV. My brain's mushy," Dad explained.

"You could still walk around," Mom said.

"Walking's good for you," I agreed.

Mom nodded too enthusiastically.

"If you want to," I added.

Several other patients, mostly men, and their wives, drifted past. Mom introduced me. One woman, the wife of another lung cancer patient, joined us. Her red-haired toddler granddaughter cantered out of the grandfather's hospital room, circled our chairs a few times at a full gallop, then settled at her grandmother's feet. The grandmother handed her a large doll.

The sixty-ish woman explained to me, "Now that my husband is stable, we come here each month for chemo." She absent-mindedly ran her fingers through the young girl's hair while she explained that her husband was weak after treatment, but doing "pretty well" by the second week.

After dinner, Mom and I listened to a woman in an expensive suit lecture from behind a podium in a small conference room. Her brass badge bore the initials "R.N." after her name. "At Cancer Treatment Centers of America," she said, "We're here to give our patients and their families hope." I listened skeptically as she explained that the staff prided themselves on taking extreme measures to preserve patient life. "We're not in the death business," she said.

Later, while Dad slept, Mom and I sat in stuffed chairs within view of the open door to his room.

"He nixed chemo?"

Mom's eyes filled. "I don't know what to do," she said and began to cough.

I moved the tissues to the end table next to her.

"He's not eating," she added between coughs.

I asked if he was still drinking the nutrition beverages. I thought they were supposed to help maintain his weight. Mom looked away then down. She began to list all the classes she was taking at the Center: nutrition, chemo, and intimacy during cancer.

"Sugar feeds cancer," a nutritionist had told her. "Those drinks are loaded with sugar."

Remembering the six-pack of nutrition drink cans we carried in the golf cart cooler all summer, I grimaced. I could see Dad raising can after can to his lips.

"He's got to start eating," I said, again noticing that sinking inside. If we had found this place earlier, would it have made a difference?

Amy and Jim arrived the next morning. When I came down to greet them, they were sitting in the recliners watching golf with our parents. The PGA Tour Championship was being played at Southern Hills Country Club just across town. Shouldn't we pack Dad into the car and take him down to watch? But Dad was nearly too weak to stand. When he took a shower the day before, Mom had stood in the stall with him because he was afraid that he would fall. He'd slept the rest of the day.

I hugged Amy first, then Jim, who stands 6'4" tall and is built lean like our father. After a quick release, Jim pointed to a new Ohio State ball cap he'd given Dad.

"This is a great hat," Dad said. "It's a shame I won't be golfing today."

At lunch, we ate lettuce salad, steamed vegetables, and pasta. Dad sat with us but barely ate two bites.

The toddler's grandfather and his family stopped to say hello. The man pushed an oxygen canister and had a clear tube inserted into his nose and wrapped around his head.

After the family had seated themselves at a table far across the room, Amy motioned toward the grandfather and said, "We met his wife. She told us he does pretty well three weeks out of the month."

Dad laughed. "He told me he's sick three weeks out of four. The week he gets the chemo, he's sick as a dog and has to live in this place. The second and third weeks he starts to recover. By the fourth week he's pretty good and then it's time to start all over."

Jim turned to Mom, "Does he seem to be getting better?"

"Well, he's not dying," she said.

I wondered if the man was dying, but just at a slower pace than my father. This experience had broadened my definition of the word. As if he read my thoughts, Dad snapped, "He can't play golf," and that closed the subject.

After lunch, Dad returned to his room to sleep. A case manager ushered Mom, Jim, Amy and me into a small conference room where she promised the oncologist would see us soon. After half an hour, Whitecoat Number One, a tall, wiry, man in his mid-fifties, flew into the room on a wave of self-importance and briskly explained the "cancer management plan." It included: chemotherapy, pain medication, adjustments to Dad's diet, counseling for both Mom and Dad, and "management of any contingencies."

"Contingencies?" Jim asked.

"Side effects of chemotherapy. Nausea, infections, weight loss. You know, general body trauma."

Mom stared toward the doctor, but her eyes had a faraway look. Jim reflexively put his hand on top of hers.

Amy cleared her throat, ran a hand through her short blonde hair, and said, "Are there any other options?"

Whitecoat One shook his head. "This is the best treatment we have."

Mom nodded.

"He's scheduled for another round of chemotherapy next week, but . . ." His voice trailed off.

I jumped in. "I thought he didn't want any more chemo?" I turned to Mom, but she was staring at a blank space between two paintings.

Jim scowled. Amy looked at Mom and then down at the table.

Whitecoat stiffened, "That's what he said last week. Patients are often confused about their treatment options."

"We haven't talked to him yet," Jim said.

"I'll talk to him in the next couple of days as well." Whitecoat One said, then looked at his watch. "I'm due in another meeting. You have my pager number."

Then he blew out of the room.

The case manager poked her head in. "The gastroenterologist will see you shortly."

After a few moments of silent waiting, Jim said, "Maybe we should bring him back to Ohio for treatment at the James. We can take care of him there."

Mom looked stricken, "Ohio? In the winter?"

As she spoke, the door slowly opened and Whitecoat Number Two entered. He shook each of our hands. "It's nice to meet you, under the circumstances."

My stomach relaxed. My brother, sister, and mother leaned forward.

Whitecoat Two opened a file folder and scanned it before speaking. "When patients undergo chemotherapy, nutrition can become problematic. His weight has dropped to a critical level. My job is to find a way to meet his nutritional needs." Whitecoat Two explained their methods.

"Dietary will meet with him and we'll try pharmaceutical intervention as well."

"Medications?" Jim asked.

"Our most successful is Marinol."

"What does it do?"

"It's a derivative of the marijuana plant."

"Pot?" I asked. Jim rolled his eyes. When Amy giggled, her turquoise blue contact lenses made her eyes sparkle.

"Well-known for its appetite-enhancing properties," Whitecoat Two agreed with a smile.

We all laughed and again, I sensed the tension ease.

"We'll only resort to surgery if those interventions are unsuccessful."

"Surgery?" I said, back on guard.

"A gastric tube to deliver food directly into his stomach."

When I was in college, a close friend of Dad's had a feeding tube before he eventually died of cancer. Dad described sitting by the man's bedside pumping cans of liquid food through a tube in his side. "The stuff smelled awful," Dad explained. "If I ever get that bad, just take me out behind the barn and shoot me."

My family members looked sullen. My head shook, *No, no, no!*

Whitecoat Two looked at my mother, who sniffed softly at the end of the table, holding my sister's hand. Mom looked at my brother, then turned to Whitecoat Two. "What happens without the feeding tube?"

"Starvation."

The word hung in the air.

My throat closed. *He's going to starve to death anyway*, I thought. That's what the cancer books I had read said.

"Have you talked to Dad about this?" I asked.

"We'll discuss it if it becomes necessary."

Did any of the doctors intend to ask Dad what *he* wanted? Or did they only want us to sell their plan to Dad?

After the whitecoat meetings, Amy and I found a Wendy's restaurant and brought Dad back his favorite, a double with fries and a Frosty. He took a few hopeful bites and then handed it back to her.

"It doesn't taste right. Maybe they don't make them the same way here."

I offered him the Frosty. He trembled as he took a tiny sip from a straw.

His face puckered. "Tastes like metal." That was the problem. His system had been flooded with the precious metal that women clamored to have their wedding rings forged from. Everything tasted like platinum.

That night, a nurse brought his pills, which included a round, white gel capsule in a little paper cup. "What's that?" Dad asked.

"Marinol," the nurse replied.

"Pot," I added. This really was the cancer commune, complete with marijuana. "We hope you'll wake with a fierce case of the munchies."

Within half an hour, Dad fell into a deep sleep.

Amy, Jim, Mom and I watched television in one of the living areas. During a commercial break, Jim said that we needed to be firm with Dad.

"He doesn't seem to realize these are his only options."

I countered, "We can't force him to do anything."

Mom turned down the TV. "I don't think he knows what he wants."

"Maybe we should ask him," I said, wondering why no one seemed interested in Dad's thoughts.

Amy shook her head, "Why does it have to be so complicated? It's all . . ."

Jim broke in, "It's not complicated. He simply needs to follow the doctors' orders."

I watched my brother, a high-level executive in a large corporation whose job was to remedy emergencies with clear directives. Like the doctors, Jim's frame of reference didn't automatically include asking Dad what he wanted. We all knew this was an emergency. You told folks what to do and they complied. The idea of asking people their desires probably seemed naive and vaguely annoying to him, like static in the background of a radio station he was straining to hear.

When Jim was in college, he had moved out of our home after refusing my father's order to pick up rocks in the back field during exam week when he needed to be studying. And now, he was trying to save the father he'd nearly lost years before.

Jim turned to Mom. "He'd have a better shot if you both come back to Ohio, closer to us."

Mom began to cry. My sister and brother comforted her as tears welled in my own eyes. I couldn't catch my breath. I stood, walked down the hall to Dad's room, and looked in his door window. Asleep on his back with his head turned slightly to one side, his mouth gaped open. My father's mortality swept over me. Was it possible to fight and let go at the same time?

I remembered my final night in Arizona, the look of panic on Dad's face, and Mom's tears as we watched the video from the cancer center in Mexico. I thought about the Columbus oncologist who, back in June, had warned my parents about the side effects of chemo. As predicted, Dad could no longer eat, walk, or enjoy life. He couldn't golf, either. To my father, lying in a hospital bed, tied to a feeding tube, was not living.

And I remembered Solo, the one-winged eagle in his locked cage at the Raptor Center. Dad's door wasn't locked, but it was closed.

Somebody had to open it.

The next morning, Dad told me he'd had nightmares.

"Terrible dreams. Thought I died and woke up in Hell." I wondered if he ever dreamed about playing golf and if it wasn't always a nightmare to wake up and find himself in a body that could no longer do what he loved.

He had told the nurse he didn't want any more of the "white pills."

"But are you hungry?" I asked.

"I've been starving for days, but the crap they're feeding me tastes like shit."

A little later, several dietary staff members arrived to discuss high-protein, high-calorie shakes they hoped Dad could tolerate.

"We can make any flavor you'd like," a perky college intern said. "Strawberry, mocha, green eggs and ham."

I put my hand over my eyes as Dad grimaced. "How about something simple," I suggested. "Plain old ordinary chocolate."

"Coming right up," she said over her shoulder as she bounced out of the room.

"Green eggs and ham?" Dad asked. "Are they trying to kill me?" Dad was losing two or three pounds a day. His mood was bad and he seemed confused. He was convinced the food at the Center was to blame.

"It's not the food," I explained. "The platinum messed up your taste buds." He shook his now nearly bald head. His hair had fallen out almost completely in the week I'd been there and only a few strands of his former flaxen locks remained.

"My buds are fine," he said, licking his lips and sticking out his tongue. "They just can't cook worth a damn."

Throughout the day, the intern delivered shakes of various flavors: chocolate, coconut cream, banana, orange, each of which my father rejected. Finally, after he had nixed peach, he told her, "Can we try this later?" and closed his eyes.

I followed her dejected figure out to the hallway. "The platinum fouled up his taste buds," I said.

"They warned us in school, but it's so discouraging." She sighed and carried several of the discarded drinks away.

I returned to Dad's room. He shoved the peach shake at me. "You want this?" Dad said.

"You trying to poison me?" I asked. Dad laughed. I pushed it toward him, "Try another sip."

"Whose side are you on?" he said. I threw the drink in the trash.

That afternoon, while Dad slept and Jim took a walk, I sat with Mom, Amy and the lung cancer patient's wife, who showed us photos of her other grandchildren.

"Does your husband ever want to give up?" Amy asked.

"At first he didn't want any part of it," she explained. "But now, he wants to live."

I nodded then said, "The chemo made our dad so sick. He says he doesn't want any more."

The woman turned, first to look at me, then shifted so she faced Mom directly. With a vigorous shake of her head, she said, "If he doesn't want it, he shouldn't have it. Every bite, every pill, every trip here has to be his choice. If it isn't, it won't work."

Jim and Whitecoat Two approached the living area and the doctor asked to speak to Mom. The grandmother stood, "I'll see you all at dinner."

Jim sat while Whitecoat Two turned toward Mom. "Our interventions aren't working. He's lost three more pounds."

Mom sighed heavily then looked at Jim.

"We've scheduled the surgery for tomorrow," Whitecoat Two continued.

"Dad agreed to it?" I asked, confused.

"We'll explain it to him in the morning."

The anger that had been simmering in me welled up.

"Excuse me," I said, then stood, and strode away leaving my family to listen to the doctor calmly soothe them with his explanation of the procedure. His voice faded as I walked down the quiet hall toward the elevators. Tears stung my eyes and I wiped my nose with the back of my hand. The big clock on the wall read 3:50 p.m. I had a telephone therapy session with Joan in ten minutes. I boarded the elevator and studied the numbers as it carried me to my room.

Lying on the double bed, I dialed the number. When Joan answered I explained what had happened in the conference room the hour before.

"No one asks Dad what he wants."

"Have you?" Her voice seemed thin and far away. I wished I were sitting in the blue chair across from her so I could see her brown eyes and gauge her mood from the tilt of her head.

"No."

I imagined myself storming into the conference room, turning over the table, and taking the doctor out with one punch. In my head, I turned to Mom and pointed my finger at her. "Even you don't care what he wants."

But I knew that wasn't true. Mom looked so scared. She could not imagine her life without my father. It had all happened too early. She had always been the sick one, the one to be taken care of.

I wondered if, subconsciously, Mom had called us to Tulsa hoping we could convince Dad to have more chemo. Had some desperate part of her really thought we could change our stubborn father's mind? Mom couldn't imagine her life without my father. She'd never lived alone for one day of her life. I pictured her in that Arizona house after he was gone, rattling around in silence, calling me every night.

Joan, unaware of my thoughts, interrupted them.

"I doubt anyone else is going to ask what he wants."

"Should I?"

"Only if you're prepared to honor whatever he says . . ."

After a brief pause she added, ". . . and ready to accept any flack that comes from stepping out of your usual family role."

I closed my eyes. She'd suggested what I'd been avoiding.

"What I really want is for someone to walk into Doc Whitecoat Two's office and say, 'We've scheduled you for a gastric tube insertion tomorrow morning. Don't eat anything after midnight.'"

Joan laughed. "Not gonna happen."

After the call, I imagined talking to my father, face-to-face. No golf jokes. No TV as a distraction. Just the two of us.

I dried my eyes, took the elevator down to the main hallway, then stepped out the door into the fall Oklahoma air. The overcast sky was gray like Ohio. I wondered if Dad would be there soon. He and Mom originally planned to come home for a short visit the week of Thanksgiving, which included his birthday, but now he didn't look fit to travel to the bathroom.

As I walked the trail around the building, my sister slowly approached. We all seemed to be in low gear. She and I sat on a bench overlooking a small pond.

"You alright?" she asked.

"I'm pissed. I can't believe these doctors have those meetings without him. It's like he's a child or something."

"The doctors just want what's best for Dad and Mom."

"They're only interested in how long he lives, not how well." I remembered the first night's lecture when the woman stood behind the podium in her expensive suit and said "We're not in the death business."

I turned to Amy. "Do you really think he should have a feeding tube and then more chemo?"

She shrugged, "If he doesn't, he will die."

My frustration turned to panic. Nearly shouting, I said, "He's going to die anyway!"

"I know, but . . ." she swallowed hard and turned away ". . . I prefer it to be later than sooner." Amy had been Daddy's first little girl. After she graduated from high school, she and our father had driven to work together for years at Ohio Bell. She had married and moved away, but Dad stayed in touch with her by letter—letters he never wrote to me or my brother. When Amy's marriage failed, she had brought her young daughter back to Ohio, to the farm, to live in the shelter of Dad's care. Now, he would be gone.

"I haven't been able to spend enough time with him this summer," she whispered. Her full-time job, classes at Ohio State, and raising her daughter had prevented that.

I couldn't imagine how she felt, but I was beginning to know how I did. "I don't want him to die either, but . . . he can't play golf . . ." I gulped back tears. "He can't even watch golf!"

Amy reached for me and we held each other for a few moments before she went back inside. I stayed, closing my eyes and listening to my own breath. *What a faint thing, these inhales and exhales that we take for granted.*

When I thought my legs could hold me, I headed indoors, walked to Dad's closed door, and looked in through the window. His white blood count had dipped and he'd been moved to an isolation room with special ventilation. When he saw me, he smiled and motioned for me to come in. I washed my hands in the little sink outside his room, donned a mask, and opened the door.

"What's up, Pops?"

"Just lying around," he said.

I told him I needed to talk about something serious.

"Oh no," he said and we both laughed.

I explained about the Whitecoat meetings and that the doctors wanted to put in a feeding tube. "They've scheduled it for tomorrow morning." From behind my mask, I felt so far away. It crinkled when I talked.

"How'd you find out that?" he asked.

"Secret doctor powwow."

"Was your mother there?"

I nodded, "All of us, um, except for you."

He looked around the room then back at me. "What do you think?"

"I want you to do what you want."

He looked away again, now out the window. I imagined from his vantage he could only see the gray autumn sky.

"I don't want to be fed pablum the rest of my life. I want to eat hamburgers and milkshakes and drink a beer."

I hesitated then said, "Even a beer would taste like crap now."

He frowned. "Is everyone ganging up on me?"

"Not quite." I leaned forward. "I'm on your side."

He looked at me with doleful eyes. He reminded me of Maxine, our black lab who had perfected the puppy dog facial expression to plead for anything I was eating. He searched my face, as if checking whether I meant what I said.

Suddenly angry, as angry as a man without one remaining ounce of energy can be, he raised his voice and spat, "Tell the doctors I'm done. They can keep their platinum and their lousy protein shakes and their feeding tube!" Then, he sunk in a heap of exhaustion. "Tell them that," he whispered.

"I thought you should be in the meetings, but no one seems interested in my opinion." I didn't add that as the youngest in the family I often felt invisible, ignored.

"The one I have to tell is your mother," he said.

I nodded vigorously. "She's scared."

"And I'm not?"

We both began to cry. I hadn't seen him cry outright since that day back in May at the cancer support group at Ohio State. I don't know if he ever returned to that group. I never did either. Over the months golfing and on the trip to Yellowstone, we had stuffed down, laughed around, and raged away these tears, not showing them to each other since.

I gulped and said, "Tell me what you want and I'll do what I can."

"I just want to go home."

"To Ohio?"

"Hell, no!" he said, as if I had suggested that he go to Pluto. "Arizona. Home. It's been ten years since I've spent a winter in Ohio. I can't imagine going through one now."

"I'll do what I can. In the meantime, stall."

"What the hell do you think I've been doing?"

Now we were laughing. I hugged him carefully then started to stand, but he tugged my hand.

"You're quite a gal," he said, then gave my fingers a little squeeze.

My face flushed and I looked over the top of the mask into his eyes. "You raised me."

I met Mom, Jim, and Amy out in the family room and told them about my conversation with Dad.

"And?" Mom leaned forward.

"He doesn't want a feeding tube."

"You couldn't talk him into it?" Mom asked.

"I didn't try."

Her eyes filled, her body drooped, and she bent her face toward the carpet.

Amy sat very still as if she'd absorbed a blow.

Jim asked, "Does he understand what that means?"

"Yes," I said. "He does."

Jim's mouth tightened and he turned away.

The next morning, Dad still hadn't eaten. When Whitecoats One and Two converged on him, he was ready. "I don't want to be hooked up to some tube the rest of my life, however short that is."

Whitecoat Two looked puzzled, "You'd only be hooked up to it when you had to eat. The rest of the time you would be free to move around."

"If I can't eat, I might as well die," Dad said. Then he turned to Whitecoat One. "I don't want any more of your platinum either."

The doctors looked crestfallen. Whitecoat One turned to Mom, said "There's nothing left for us to do," and both doctors swept out of the room. Mom cradled Dad's big hand in both of her small ones while I stared at the linoleum squares. It was almost time to go home.

Dad slept the rest of the day. I worked one of the jigsaw puzzles in the common area. That night, I went to Dad's room and sat on his bed. I was flying out in the morning. "You'll be home soon," I reassured him.

"I'm so tired," he said. How many times had I watched this scene in movies, this line whispered from the dying patient's lips, but now it was *my* father in the bed.

"We're not in the death business," the well-dressed woman had said.

Well, I thought, that's the only business Dad has left.

"We'll figure out how to take care of you," I told him.

"And your mom too?"

I assured him that Mom would take care of him, too.

"No. I mean you'll take care of your mother."

Take care of Mom? Hadn't we all taken care of her our whole lives? Until Dad's illness, she had been the "sick" one. But this would be different. Dad wouldn't be there as a buffer. We would be on our own with her.

"Of course," I reassured him. We would figure it out.

Earlier that afternoon, I had called Joan again to tell her I'd spoken to Dad. I choked up when I shared that he had called me "Quite a gal."

She was silent for a moment then said, "Did you hear what he was saying?"

"Yes," I told her. "It went all the way through."

In the morning, Jim joined me in Dad's room so I could say goodbye before I headed to the airport. He and Amy would fly out later that day. But the respiration team came in to give Dad a treatment, and cut our goodbye short.

"Be good!" I teased.

With a shaky hand, he pointed to the scrubbed technicians. "You're as bad as these guys. No one wants me to have any fun!"

I waved him off. "I'll call when I get home."

Jim noticed the sun coming up and opened the mini-blind so Dad could see the tangerine-streaked sky. Dad's face lit up.

"Just watch the sun rise while they work on you," Jim told him.

As I turned to leave, I caught sight of the poster Amy and I had hung on his wall the day before. It too was a sunrise. It read, "Trust in God may not make the mountains smaller, but it will make the climb easier."

THE BACK NINE
NOVEMBER 1995 TO JANUARY 1996

You can't win them all, but you can learn from every experience.

—Phil Mickelson

CHAPTER 21

I NEED MY GLASSES

In the days following my visit to Tulsa, the plan for Dad's return to Arizona changed. Despite my parents' distaste for Ohio winters, since my father couldn't golf anyway, they both decided it made sense for him to spend his final months in Ohio close to his family. Even though he wanted to be cremated, he also wanted a viewing with the Catholic ritual of "praying the rosary" and the full Knights of Columbus ceremony. If he died in Arizona, it would be no easy task to get his body back to Ohio. He needed to come to Ohio now.

The physicians in Tulsa would only release Dad to another doctor, so Mom called one of the oncologists Dad had seen at Ohio State. Mom and Dad would fly to Columbus and Dad would be admitted to The James. The hospital was only a ten-minute drive from our house and Ed and I had a spare bedroom. Mom could stay with us while Dad was there. The same friends who had recommended the Cancer Center offered to fly to Tulsa and drive my parents' wagon back to Arizona.

At the beginning of November, Mom and Dad flew from Tulsa to Columbus. To fortify myself for their arrival, on the way to the airport I stopped at a candy store in Bexley and bought several pounds of wrapped chocolates, butterscotch (Dad's favorite), and other sweets. In those days before September 11, 2001, you could still meet passengers at the gate. Amy and Jim were waiting in the molded plastic chairs. I hefted the bag of goodies and said, "We don't drink. We don't smoke. We don't sleep around. We've got to get through this somehow."

I reached into the bag, pulled out a walnut caramel, then handed the bag to Amy. My brother Jim, the only one of the family with a shred of willpower left, at first waved it off, but succumbed when the gate attendant announced that the plane had arrived.

We stood and waited. After nearly everyone had exited the plane, I saw the attendant backing towards us and Mom beyond. "There she is," Jim said. I began to wave, then thought better of it. We crowded around the jetway door. Eventually, the back of Dad's head came into view. His figure grew larger and larger until finally his wheelchair was out the door. The attendant turned the chair around and there was Dad, in pajamas on a weeknight, tied to his IV drip, beaming up at us.

"Sorry to drop in on you like this," he joked. *Had he been practicing that line the whole flight?* Careful of the IV, we took turns hugging Dad first, then Mom, and passing the bag of candy.

The wheelchair attendant gave us a few minutes before whisking Dad away to the waiting ambulance. Amy and Jim took Mom to the hospital.

As Ed and I drove home, reality began to sink in. Dad and Mom weren't home for a holiday. It wasn't a family reunion or summer vacation. No one was playing golf. It was winter and Dad's clubs had stayed behind in Arizona. He wouldn't be borrowing anyone else's. He'd turned in his long-necked Budweisers for morphine and the pull cart he'd pushed for a walker.

He still had his sense of humor, though. At least we had that.

The next day, Mom and I sat in Dad's hospital room at the James Cancer Center and listened to yet another oncologist give Dad the same advice. *What had we expected?*

He asked Dad, "Are you sure you don't want to give chemotherapy another try?"

"It's no way to live," Dad said, pointing to the port in his shoulder and the tubes in his arm. "I can't even golf." He faced the doctor. "Besides. Nothing tastes right. If a man can't eat, he can't live." He did not look at Mom or me.

"I'll write the orders," the doctor said. He shook Dad's hand, then Mom's, then mine, and left.

Silence filled the room until Dad said, "I guess that's that," as if he had swallowed the hemlock. Mom and I stood on either side of his bed and held each of his hands. I did not look at Mom, only Dad. He did not cry and neither did I.

Hospice. The word so final. Even though it had been seven months since his initial diagnosis and some part of me knew this outcome was inevitable, the word made me wobbly.

I excused myself and found a pay phone to call Ed. In Tulsa, Mom, Dad and I had talked hypothetically about Mom living with us if they came to Ohio. But we thought Dad would be in the hospital. We had all agreed we would do what it took to take care of Dad at home. Ed would be at work during the day, and my father mostly slept now, so it would essentially be me and my mother. Still, I wanted to confirm Ed's willingness. He heartily agreed to the arrangement.

Jim was very worried about the impact on my mental health, especially if Dad died in our house. I was still seeing my therapist, attending group, going to recovery meetings, and meditating regularly. I didn't know how I would fare, but was prepared to find out.

We moved the double bed from the guest room into the basement and two men came to set up the hospital bed. Before Dad arrived, Ed suggested that we turn the hospital bed to face the window. As I stepped out to move the other end of the bed, Ed pulled it so quickly away from me that the wheel banged into my toe. "Shit! What are you trying to do?"

"Don't you want his bed moved?"

"For Christ's sake!" I yelled. "Can't we move it slowly?" It irked me that the bed lay at an odd angle, pointing out from the corner. That placement didn't bother Ed and he did not apologize for hitting my foot with the bed. *Would this mood, set minutes before Dad's arrival, permeate my parents' stay?*

Once the ambulance drivers had wheeled Dad in and arranged him on the hospital bed, he stared out the window. The only sound was the electric oxygen machine humming in the corner beside the bed. Ed, Mom, and I let him rest.

For the first few days I sat in the wooden chair next to Dad's bed and watched him breathe. The air moved in and out of his mouth in rasps, like sandpaper against soft wood. I also wrote in my journal, recording the details of his presence along with my conflicting thoughts. *Is this really it? This is taking forever! Did I do the right thing in Tulsa?* When I could relax, I napped. Sometimes, Mom joined us in his room, but she was still worn out from the Cancer Treatment Center ordeal and slept a lot. When Ed was home, he sat in Dad's room with me.

When Dad did speak, his voice was raspy and weak. If we weren't in his room or at least near the doorway, we couldn't hear him call. A few years before, I'd begun collecting bells. My parents had leaped on this. They'd brought back bells from Mexico and bells from Arizona and bells blessed by the bishop in Chicago. I sorted through my collection, found a silver one that had a pleasant tone, and showed it to my father. "Ring this when you need us," I said.

He wrinkled his nose and gave the bell a stern look. I imagined he wouldn't want to call us like servants. But the next time he was in pain and couldn't get anyone's attention, he rang it.

Listening became my duty. The faint tinkling of the little silver bell meant I could finally do something. To prove my love? To earn his love? I wasn't sure. But when the ringing bell woke me in the night, when it stirred me from a daydream or a nap, whenever it called, I snapped into action.

One morning while I was still in bed, I heard Mom go into the bathroom. A moment later, Dad's bell rang. I bolted up and opened the bedroom door just as Mom exited the bathroom. Without a second thought, I surged ahead and beat her down the hall to Dad's room. She arrived, a few steps after me, dejection on her face. At first, I felt a flash of relief, but when I saw her sad eyes, the sting of shame replaced it.

I was not perceptive enough then to realize why she wouldn't, couldn't sleep on the bed we had moved out of the guest room and set up in the basement. Still so unsure of my father's love, I wanted to be the one Dad wanted. My insecurity blinded me to her needs. A decade would pass before I understood why she chose to sleep on the brocade sofa in our living room steps away from his door. Only once my love for Ed deepened to a place close to what hers must have been for my dying father would I understand that she too needed to answer that bell, to be helpful, to do something, *anything*, in the face of her powerlessness.

I wanted to be the confidante, the helpful nurse, doting daughter. It seemed as if I were the wife of two men, sleeping in bed with Ed and then caring for Dad in the bed down the hall. Ed usually slept through my night-time nurse runs and was at work for my day-time duty. In the evenings, I sometimes allowed Ed to answer the bell.

One night when Ed heard me roused by the bell, he grabbed my arm. "Let your mother get it." But I could not. I struggled free to go to my father's aid.

That bell was my gate to power, a signal to launch the energy that sat swirling in my belly, throat, and mind the rest of the time. When Dad rang that bell, I could act. Go to the kitchen. Open a fresh, cold can of generic root beer. Measure a small dose of liquid morphine. Hand it to him in a plastic cup. Watch him chug it. Then quickly hand him the cold can of root beer and watch him gulp that to wash away the bitter taste. Then I was done.

"Is there anything else?"

"No."

"A pillow?" "A foot massage?" "Anything?" I was tempted to add, "A crack upside the head?" the way he had when we were children and wouldn't say what we wanted.

And so it went. Hour after hour, day after day, as he lay in the hospital bed in our guest room under the close watch of the

Crimson King maple and the birds that called it home. Outside, the leaves on every other tree turned and fell, but day after day, the maple held its deep, maroon leaves, leaves that would eventually turn brown, but remain until long after he was gone.

Shortly after Dad arrived at our house, Mom began to shop at Kohl's, a nearby department store, nearly every day. She brought in full sacks of shopping one day and carried the same sacks out the next. I didn't ask what she was shopping for. I assumed she needed winter clothes. My sister had loaned her a coat, but our pants were too long for Mom and our boots too big.

I didn't mind her absence. After those first few days, I hadn't spent as much time in Dad's room except to give him his liquid morphine mixed with root beer or meet with the hospice nurse when she came. It had become difficult to stay in his room. I picked at my cuticles, looked out the window, and checked the clock too often. I could easily write in the next room or do dishes in the kitchen. Sometimes, I was able to lie down and rest. But sitting still or even reading in his room agitated me. I felt like a cat, jumpy and tired at the same time.

But one day when Mom was gone, I vowed to spend as much time with Dad as I could. I meditated in his room while he slept and sat with him when he was awake. He didn't want to talk. He just stared out the window rubbing the wide part of his thumb across the tips of his fingernails. They were long and dirty.

He saw me watching and said, "If I could see better, I'd cut them."

I offered to trim them for him, but he said he would ask the nurse.

"I can give you a manicure," I said.

"I've never had a manicure."

"'bout time you started!"

I smiled, happy to have a project, something to do besides sit and watch him stare out the window. I was used to working beside him, helping him, handing him tools, handing him a golf club, watching him make something happen.

I retrieved clippers and a nail file from the bathroom, then put some soap in a little dish and ran warm water over it just like Madge on the old Palmolive commercials. I wanted to tell him, "You're soaking in it," just like she did, but I didn't know if his brain could even handle that. I would have to keep my joke to myself. We all used that green dish soap out of the plastic bottle—his mother, my mother, me. And now, I was going to soak his nails in it. I laughed at my very-inside joke then carried the equipment into his room on a tray.

"This won't hurt, will it?" he asked.

"Only if you move."

"I hurt every time I move anyway so this won't be any different." We both laughed. I loved our dark humor and the special bond it formed between us.

"So don't move," I said.

He held out his right hand. I lowered his hospital tray with my "instruments" toward him so he could put his right hand in the little bowl. "Put your fingertips in the dish for a few minutes to soften everything, then we'll get to work."

"Just like Madge," he said. "I suppose it's Palmolive."

"Only the finest for you," I said, overjoyed that he wasn't too far gone to remember the commercial.

A minute or so later, I pulled his hand out and said, "Put your other hand in there and I'll work on this one." I dried it then got out the clippers.

"Hey! Those are toenail clippers. Don't you have a little pair?"

I hadn't even thought about it. Unlike Mom with her array of nail tools, I always cut my own fingernails with these huge clippers, but he was right. "You sure are choosy," I said, lowering his hand back in the dish to accompany the other one. I went to the bathroom and found the small pair of clippers.

As I walked into the room, he said, "Did you sanitize those?"

"Yep. I swished them around in the toilet."

"Good," he said. "You can never be too careful."

I picked up his hand again, dried it, then began to gently clip his flat, thin nails. I wondered if his bones, now probably riddled with cancer, were similarly distressed. He lay very still and closed his eyes, relaxing his hand completely in mine.

"My mother used to trim my nails," he said. "A long, long time ago."

After a few minutes of my clipping and filing, his breath became soft and rhythmic. I continued, cleaning the grime that hadn't soaked away, and wondering why I hadn't noticed how long his nails had gotten. The simplest things, things we take for granted, can make such a difference.

A few times, he woke with a start, the same way he had startled awake when I was small and Mom sent me to wake him from a nap. He jumped a little, grunted, "What? What?" and looked at me puzzled as if I were in the wrong place.

"It's me, Dad," I said. "Nita."

"Oh. Oh," he said and turned toward the window. "I dreamed I'd died."

"What was it like?"

"Like the farm. Green and rolling. So beautiful."

If there was a heaven, I hoped it was like the farm only better, that it was everything Dad loved about that land and more, and everything he loved about golf and more.

When I finished his last pinkie nail, I laid his hand down and said, "All done. How do they look?" He held them out in front of him and then rubbed his thumbs across them.

"This one's still a little rough," he said holding out the fourth finger on his left hand. I picked it up and carefully filed down the corners.

"How's that?" I asked.

"Just right," he said. "That feels wonderful."

It had been so intimate. His big hands in mine, his fingers in mine, one by one. I'd never really looked at his hands, the long fingers, the flat nail beds. I'd never noticed the way the moons on his fingernails curved. I wondered if he and Mom held hands a lot when they dated, if she had grown to know the curve of his fingers the way I now knew Ed's. So much I didn't know.

I wish I had set up a tape recorder from the first day he'd come home that summer, when part of me knew he was dying. I wish I had pumped stories out of him. I wish I had questioned him like an attorney, cross-examining him until I learned every detail of his life, not giving up until I knew who was related to whom and what pictures were of whom. I wish I hadn't given up until I had all the stories and all the song lyrics and all the details of everything. Now that he was at our house, the questions I thought to ask arose in the stillness while I watched him sleep or in the middle of the night when I could not ask. I didn't have the foresight to write them down and they remain unanswered.

One morning, when I walked into Dad's room, he had a wide smile on his face. He had dreamed that he and Pete, that Appalachian carpenter who'd helped Dad with the church's CCD building, had been playing showboat rummy in heaven. "I'm so happy to know I'll see Pete again," he said. I liked thinking of heaven as one big poker game: queens and follows, baseball, five-card stud with deuces wild and jacks better to open.

When I peeked in on him another afternoon and saw him smiling, I whispered, "Dreaming again?"

"I'll go to see my father," he said, pointing to the end of the bed. "He's waiting there for me." I didn't know if he meant his own father or God. A priest had come to give him communion the day before and I wondered if that had influenced his dreams.

After he had lain in the bed for weeks, he told me he dreamed that he had been trapped in a shopping mall.

"A fate worse than death," I said.

"Yes," he agreed. "And this mall was enormous. We couldn't see the end of it." Pete had been in this dream, too.

"Pete doesn't like to shop either," I said.

"No," he agreed, the excitement rising in his tone. "But get this! We were shopping for golf clubs." The thought of Pete, a man who had made fun of Dad's love of golf, shopping for clubs made me laugh out loud.

"The worst of it," he continued, "was that we couldn't find our way out. Signs everywhere pointed to exits, but there were no doors. All I wanted was a way out, but there wasn't one." He didn't seem to catch the poignancy of this message, but I did.

Another day, as I approached his room, I heard him and Mom arguing.

"I need them," he said.

"I'll read it for you," she answered.

When I walked in, they stopped talking. Dad was sitting upright in bed, a posture he hadn't taken in days. Mom had the thick phone book open on the bed next to him.

Dad spotted me and explained, "I need to call Berwanger and tell him I won't be in for a few days." Dad had worked for a man named Berwanger at Ohio Bell, although, if I recalled correctly, he hadn't been Dad's boss for many years before Dad retired.

"Really?" I said, doing my best to play along.

"And I need to talk to your mother alone," he said.

I nodded and left the room, but Mom was on my heels.

"He's losing his mind," she said. "I told him he doesn't work anymore, but he won't hear it."

We walked back to his room and I said, "I'll call for you, Dad."

"No Dammit! Why doesn't anyone understand. I have to be the one to call." He slouched back down in the bed. I motioned for Mom to come back into the hall with me.

"I think he's right on schedule," I told her. During the days when I sat in his room, I'd read the books *Final Gifts* and *How We Die*. When I read how the dying sometimes flash to the past, it comforted me and my body relaxed. *He needs to do this.* I also read about how the dying may need to do penance or make contact with people already dead. *Yep*, and *Yep*, my mind confirmed. If he was "right on schedule" I might survive what I could no longer deny was coming. I might survive losing him.

Once I had shared this information with Mom, she began to search for his glasses. He hadn't worn them in a month and neither of us knew where they were. When she found them, he put them on and began flipping through the thick white pages.

After a few minutes he said, "I'm so tired and these glasses don't seem right. Do I need to have my eyes checked?"

I said, "You probably do, Dad. Here, let me look for you." Now he gave the phone book up willingly. I said, "Who do you want to find?"

"Just call work for me," he said, then repeated, "I need to talk to your mother alone."

Half an hour later, Mom came out to the kitchen and explained that Dad was worried about a set of extension tree trimmers—long olive-green poles with a saw on one end designed to cut tree limbs out of the way of phone lines. He had "borrowed" them from the Bell System and never returned them. Mom and I didn't know if my brother had them or if they were still in the barn on the farm. "He's afraid he's going to burn in hell if he doesn't pay someone for those damned tree trimmers," she said angrily. Of all the questionable things he'd done throughout his life, the trimmers came into his mind as the one thing sure to prevent him from passing through the pearly gates. "All these years and now he wants me to fix it," she said.

I nodded and tried to reassure her.

I found my father's desire to make amends for not returning the tree trimmers curious while also endearing. He had an odd relationship with honesty. A rule follower in many ways, he also bent the truth at times. To some rules, he adhered hard and fast. Other rules, including some unwritten rules I respected, he regarded as mere guidelines.

In the barn, years before, I'd watched him burn up not one, not two, but three Craftsman drills while trying to enlarge a tractor wheel hole by using a grinding stone hooked to the end of a drill bit. Each drill overheated, so he swapped them in and out of the freezer. When, after two days of this brutal treatment, they all finally died, he took them back to Sears and got three brand-new drills under their lifetime warranty. "No questions asked," he said, shining his charming grin. When I protested, he shrugged. "That's what the warranty says!"

◦ ◦ ◦

As I watched Dad lie in the hospital bed in our guest bedroom, I pondered his need to absolve himself of the tree-trimmer situation. Our ranch house on the farm was full of items Dad had picked up from Ohio Bell over the years. Until now, I never wondered if he had "borrowed" the many telephones he brought home. And what about those drills? So brazen! Shame would have ripped a hole in my stomach if I had tried to return three drills I had knowingly ruined. To my father, there were rules and then there were *rules*!

My detached analysis of his dreams and his sudden need for truth-telling might have seemed absurd to Mom. But it helped me cope. If, according to the books, Dad was "on course," things would be okay. I'd spent my life studying, being the best student I knew how. I was going to be the best student of Dad's death. I'm surprised Mom didn't tell me to shut up. I would have if I was her. Someone should have told me to put down the books and wake up, to spend more time sitting beside my father and listening. Instead, I reverted to what I knew best: study. Learn what to expect and everything will be fine.

In the end, he and Mom agreed that she would send money to a charity to make up for the value of the tree trimmers. I don't know if she ever did.

CHAPTER 22

ALL DOGS GO TO HEAVEN

On any given day when I walked into Dad's room, our two dogs were keeping him company. Astro, the fluffy white bundle of American Eskimo dog energy, settled herself in a donut-shaped bundle next to the oxygen machine while Maxine, the big black lug of a Labrador retriever, sat sentry beside Dad's bed, often resting her head near his hand for a bit before stretching her long black body to its fullest length at his bedside. In the mid-afternoons, I could hear the three of them snoring from clear out in the kitchen.

Their bedside vigil brought to mind one afternoon when I worked at the consulting firm. The receptionist had buzzed me as I sat at my desk writing a research memorandum.

"Your Dad's on the phone."

Despite his decades of work at the phone company, he hated talking on the phone. I steadied myself then picked up the receiver.

"It's a good thing you've got a phone in your basement." His resonant voice came across the wires, reminding me of the phones he had installed at the farm in every room, including the bathroom and the barn.

Dad was staying with me for a few days, painting the shutters, soffits, and trim of a house I'd recently bought.

"What's wrong?" I asked.

"Max has me trapped."

When I left that morning, I'd put Maxine and Astro in their crates in the basement. I didn't want to worry about them getting loose every time he opened an outside door. Maxine would have simply followed him around, but Astro—a white fluff-ball, flying-streak escape artist—would have been two counties over before he knew she was gone.

At the back of the house, there were three doors at the top of a small landing: one to the kitchen, one to the garage, and the third to the back yard. On a break, intending to let the dogs out to relieve themselves, Dad had come in from the garage, closed the door behind him, and gone down the stairs without first opening the back door. When he let the dogs out of their crates, they ran up the stairs. With all three doors closed, the dogs were now stuck on the landing.

When Dad began to come up the stairs, Astro had run back down, but Maxine, normally the calm, quiet, docile one, had bared her teeth and growled.

"Did you try taking off your ball cap?" I asked.

"No luck. She's pissed."

"Actually, she's just scared."

"I tried sitting down on the steps and calling her. She won't budge. I'm afraid she'll bite me."

Max did have a fierce side. She had once flattened a store clerk who opened the back of my station wagon to load our dog food. Max couldn't see me behind the man. She flew over the rear seat and put him on the ground.

"I know you're busy, but can you come let me out? I've been down here nearly an hour and need to go to the bathroom."

"Oh my god Dad! Were you going to stay there all day?"

Silence.

I laughed. "I'll be right home."

Maxine had long since forgotten her animosity toward my father. She responded to his illness by lying beside his hospital bed, remaining in his room except to eat, drink or go outside. One day, when I was sitting with Dad and the dogs, sort of meditating, sort of spacing out, listening to all of them snore, I waited for Dad to wake. When he seemed alert, I asked, "Did you and Mom ever think about getting a dog when you moved out west?"

I expected him to say something practical like, "It's tough to keep a dog in an RV," or, "We didn't have a yard in Bullhead City," both of which were true. Their golf course home had a small square of gravel with a few cacti that Dad tended, but no place for a dog to roam the way Dad thought dogs should.

Instead, he let out a loud groan.

"Do you need Roxanol?" I asked.

"No," he said. His face had reddened and tears slipped from the corners of his closed eyes.

He took a deep breath, then said, "That was the hardest thing. When I had to take Missy to the vet . . ."

When I was in law school, Mom had told me that Missy, the last dog they had on the farm, had grown too old and feeble to walk. "It was tough on your father," Mom said. Until this day, Dad had never mentioned it.

The tenderness and pain in his reply made it difficult for me to breathe. From where I sat, I could see Maxine sleeping. I turned toward Astro's white curl of fur and watched her chest rise and fall a few times. Spending time with the dogs had softened him.

I put my hand on his arm and said "Oh, Dad," expecting that to be the end of our conversation.

But he continued. "I buried her under the pines with Puppsy."

Now, the blood rushed to my face. I stifled a sob and said, "With Puppsy?"

I'd never known what happened to her body after the accident. Mom had ushered me into the house and, other than to express distress that I wasn't getting over her death quickly enough, Dad pretended it never happened. I never asked.

But he had buried her.

All those years ago, by tending to Puppsy's body after he ended her suffering, my father had shown his love the way he knew how: through action. I just hadn't known. I could forgive Dad for what I had thought was a mistake but was actually a kindness. An icy spot in my heart I thought I'd resolved earlier in the summer melted completely. He did understand after all.

"Maybe I'll see Missy again, soon," he said. Then added, "Maybe all the dogs."

An image of a canine pack bounding toward him formed in my mind: Puppsy, Ginger, Lady, Tiny, Sunny, Skeeter, Tony, Bouncy, Missy. All the dogs we ever had.

"Maybe, Dad," I said. "Maybe all the dogs."

Chapter 23

Funereal Sprite

One day toward the end of November, I strolled the aisles of Meijer, the big-box store, where I'd come to choose Dad's birthday present. *What do you buy for a man who only has a few weeks to live?*

In the past, Dad's November 26th birthday had been swallowed by Thanksgiving. This year, his birthday was also overshadowed by its finality. Dad wasn't exactly grateful to be alive. Most mornings when I walked into his room, he greeted me with, "Guess I'm still here." Had he and Mom not gone to Tulsa, he would have died in early October shortly after his "trip of a lifetime." Because he fought back, he was now spending long winter days staring out the window of our guest room.

I rolled the wobbly grocery cart past the men's clothing (*he only wears a hospital gown*), past the fishing gear (*he is bedridden*), past the Edy's butter pecan ice cream that he ate every night before his diagnosis (*now he eats nothing*), until I found myself in the sporting goods section. I winced at the sight of a scarlet and gray golf bag, abruptly turned my cart, and pushed it out of the department.

In the lawn and garden section, I stared at bags of grass seed then bent over the cart and moaned quietly as I thought of our days mowing together, as well as the times he pointed out blades of grass I'd missed. I also remembered asking for grass seed to help Dad tend the golf courses once my resentment had cooled. I pushed the cart on, away from these memories.

To complicate things further, for Mom, Dad's approaching birthday was not something to celebrate. When Dad retired, they chose to receive a higher monthly company pension that would end when he died. "A bad bet," she called it when she reminded us that she had never been completely comfortable with this arrangement. After Dad's diagnosis, the full reality dawned on her and, at first, she refused to talk about it.

Regardless of these issues, I wanted Dad to have some joy. I remembered Christmases when the right gift earned his childlike grin. Buying him a present was also the proper thing to do. And, at this point, I wanted no regrets.

When I told Mom I was contemplating what to get him for his birthday, she fumed, "He doesn't need a goddamned thing!"

My eyes widened and my jaw clenched. I waited, hoping her rage would pass.

"I don't feel like celebrating when he cut me out of his retirement like that," she said. "I didn't ask for this. And he didn't ask me what I wanted."

Dad insisted that Mom had signed off on the plan. "I've got the papers to prove it."

Regardless of who was right, when he died, she would be left with Social Security as her only pension.

Later, when Amy visited Dad at our house, my sister—family preserver of traditions and slaughterer of sacred cows—also brought up Dad's birthday.

"Mom! This is probably his last birthday," she said. "I'm sorry about the financial situation, but he deserves a gift."

Mother frowned, then sighed. "I suppose we could give him something."

At Meijer, my eyes landed on a little plastic feeder with a brown top and brown perches. Dad frequently consulted *Birds of North America* to identify rare birds. When I was growing up on the farm, he hated sparrows and house finches so much that he trained me to scare them with that BB-gun. But he loved the goldfinches just as fiercely. Despite it being winter and the more colorful birds still remaining cozy in their warm southern homes, I imagined the feeder, filled with finches, hanging from the branches of the Crimson King maple outside Dad's window.

I picked up the box and looked at the price. I wouldn't be able to stand looking at this feeder after Dad died. How much money did I want to spend? My thoughts felt sticky, treacherous, guilt-laden. *What birds are still here in November? What if the wrong birds come? What if he hates it?* I looked at my watch. I'd been in the store more than an hour.

I put the little feeder and a small bag of thistle seed in the cart. I tossed in a small wire suet feeder and a square of thistle suet for good measure, then turned my cart toward the cashier line.

A few days after my shopping trip to Meijer, Jean, the hospice nurse, showed up ahead of her regularly scheduled day.

Normally a pleasant, chatty woman, she skipped the pleasantries and told my father, "I'll help you with your pants," as she began to take down his pajama bottoms.

"What for?" he asked.

"I need to put your catheter in." Jean had a gentle face and she spoke softly, but today, her hands moved more quickly than normal.

"I never agreed to that," Dad said, glaring first at her then me.

"I thought Mom . . ." I stumbled on the words. "I thought you had agreed."

He shook his head firmly. When he tried to yell Mom's name, it came out as a hiss. "Get your mother," he said quietly.

When Dad first came to live with Ed and me, the hospice team had brought a bedside commode which we put in his room. As the weeks wore on and he weakened, he needed help. If he needed to relieve himself, I asked Mom or Ed to assist him and left the room.

But a few days before when I came home from a meeting, my mother explained that Dad had almost fallen when she'd tried to get him on the commode. She told me she had asked the hospice nurse about getting a catheter.

"Did you talk to Dad about it?" I'd asked.

"I will," she assured me.

I walked down the hall and called for mom. "In here, honey," she sang from our master bedroom at the rear of the house. I turned into the doorway and froze.

Before our full-length mirror, my mother stood dressed head-to-toe in black, complete with a black, veiled, pill-box hat. Kohl's shopping bags littered the floor and our bed. When she saw me, she touched the hat then did a perky little pivot. Her eyes twinkled.

"How do I look?" she asked.

My mother looked like a funereal sprite.

Should I laugh? Scream? Hug her?

She had been married to this man for more than forty years. The Kohl's sprees that began with a quest for winter clothes and turned into daily trips had culminated in this.

As I stared at her, I could nearly see the pompom-wielding cheerleader she had been in high school. An icy sensation spread through my chest. There was no cheer for where we were now.

I started to step toward her, then remembered Jean and Dad.

"Did you ask Dad about the catheter?"

She turned back toward the mirror and adjusted the veil on the front of her hat. "I told him we were afraid he would fall."

"Yes, but did he agree?"

Mom turned toward me again, now exasperated. "He's going to fall!"

I longed to scream "He's terminal! He's gonna die from something!" but bit my tongue.

Mother and I were both weary and it wasn't my job to lecture her, even if I sometimes thought she acted like a child. She probably wished she were a child and that a benevolent parental force would save her from this nightmare. I'd had similar thoughts myself.

She removed the hat and began to turn it in her hands.

I wanted to run down the hall and out through the front door, to leave my parents to resolve this without me.

Instead, I took a deep breath. Then, in a steady tone—the kind of voice Harri, the group social worker, used with unstable clients—I said, "Mom, Jean's here. She wants to put in the catheter, but Dad says he didn't agree to it."

Her face crumbled. She carefully placed the hat in one of the plastic bags. "I'll be there in a minute."

I returned to the guest room where Dad lay on the bed naked from the waist down, his flaccid penis limp against his leg. I averted my eyes and started to turn away, but Jean said, "I need your help."

Should I wait for Mom? No. She might not come.

I turned back and asked the wall above Dad's head, "You okay, Dad?"

He said, "Jean says it'll be easier on you and your mother."

I held the bag while Jean inserted the catheter. Dad grimaced and groaned even though Jean had given him some extra pain medicine. When she was finished, she gave him another dose and together we pulled up his pajama bottoms.

As Jean began to show me how to change the bag, Mom walked into the room dressed in a pale aqua sweat suit. When Dad saw Mom, he reached for her hand.

CHAPTER 24

FAMILY CONFERENCE

During my parents' stay at our house, Mom and Ed argued. They fought over whether the air filter machine made the living room where Mom slept too cold, whether Dad needed oxygen all the time, and especially the house temperature.

The thermostat hung on the wall outside the spare bedroom I used for an office. One morning, I heard Ed and Mom arguing and poked my head out to see if I could, once again, mediate their dispute. "It's too cold. He's freezing!" Mom said. Ed rolled his eyes, frowned at me, and walked away. After he left for work, Mom returned to the device and poked at it to increase the temperature. I knew both Mom and Ed were struggling over more than just the heat, but their picking at each other left Dad and me on the sidelines together. If they fought in Dad's room, he and I locked eyes. Sometimes, he winked. More often, he gave me a forlorn look and closed his eyes as I tried to herd them into the hall.

Now that my father had a catheter, he also had to use a bedpan. Later that morning, Mom and I cleaned another overflowing pan, washed his bottom, and changed the soiled sheets. The morning before, my sister had helped clean one of the worst messes, but she worked full-time, had a teenage daughter, and lived forty-five minutes away. The hospice workers also helped three days a week. They bathed Dad and change his sheets, but my father's bowel movements seemed to coincide with their days off.

To exacerbate things, Mom's chronic cough had deepened into a hoarse rattle that wouldn't let up. Her sinuses were swollen and she had a sore throat.

That afternoon, she announced, "We're going to have to put your father in a nursing home if he lives much longer."

She had repeatedly threatened to call the hospice social worker and make this request, but today, she was circling the phone. When she reached for the receiver, I said, "Let's get some extra help."

"Do you have any idea how expensive private nurses are?"

I admitted that I didn't, but I couldn't imagine Dad would last much longer. He hadn't eaten anything in weeks and drank only canned root beer. I didn't know how long it took a six-foot, two-inch man to starve, but I didn't think this would go on for months.

When Ed called to check in, I told him that Mom wanted to put Dad in a nursing home. He shouted down the line, "She just doesn't want to take care of him! Does she know what nursing homes are like?" I'm not sure what I had expected, but I hadn't anticipated my normally stoic husband to start watching my mother like she was the enemy, positioning himself between her and Dad's room as if Mom was intentionally setting out to make Dad miserable.

I was a referee, the equal sign in the equation of my family. When necessary, I morphed into a plus or minus sign, shape-shifting to avoid conflict and carry the weight of their competing desires. I thought I needed to be Lady Justice with her scales, balancing them all on separate trays, keeping everything fair. But my arms were tired and we still had a way to go.

By the end of the day and after many calls, Mom arranged for Dad to visit the Kobacker House, a hospice center, for a few days of respite. "They won't keep him," she said wearily as she packed a tote bag.

When the social worker finished talking to Mom on the phone, she asked to speak to me. "We're worried about your family's stress level," she said. "You might not be able to care for him properly. This respite is as much for *you* as it is for your father."

As she spoke, I began to cry. We had promised to care for him *at our house*. If he left, that meant we had done something wrong. I thought we had failed him.

When the ambulance arrived, I frowned after the attendants who carried him away and watched the doors close behind him.

The hospice facility, then housed in a Tudor-style mansion, reminded me of the large, new homes on the back route to New Albany that Dad and I admired as we drove to have brunch after Sunday mass. Dad loved Tudor houses: beige stucco, manicured lawns, wood windows framed with wooden grids, cement driveways, and simple landscaping on large lots. He dreamed of building one on our farm. Warmth filled me when I imagined him finally getting his sprawling house, his own personal mansion.

The facility's golden retriever and I became instant pals. He smelled me over, sniffing our dogs' scents with every hello. But his greeting didn't erase my discomfort. On our first visit, the social worker had announced that she wanted to have a family meeting before Dad would be allowed to return to our house. A few days after Dad arrived at Kobacker House, Mom, Ed and I gathered with the social worker in Dad's room. A bright winter sun shone through the sheers as we sat on the love seat and Victorian-styled chairs.

The social worker began, saying that Dad had raised some concerns about whether we could take care of him. Dad looked calm, but Mom's face was tight. She stared at the lamp next to Dad's bed.

Ed asked, "What makes you think that?"

"Gene, would you like to tell them?" the social worker responded.

"You're all so grumpy," Dad said.

I stifled a laugh. We were exhausted. It was amazing we hadn't killed each other.

Dad looked first at Ed, then at Mom. "And you two are always arguing."

How had he known? When Ed and Mom fought, I had ushered them out of his room and closed the door. Dad's eyesight may have gone, but his hearing was fully intact.

Mom saw her opportunity. "I'm not sure we can take care of him," she said to the social worker.

Ed turned on her, "There's three of us, Ellen. We've been managing just fine." Mom's face tightened even more, then she burst into tears.

"That's what I'm talking about," Dad said to the social worker.

I stared at a painting of a vase of pink and beige roses. It was so calm and peaceful. I wanted to crawl inside it. The silence spread through the room like a bubble until I wasn't certain there was enough air left to breathe.

Then Ed walked to the edge of the bed and put his hand out to Dad. "I'm sorry Gene," he said. "We want to do whatever it takes to care for you."

Early in the summer when Mom and Dad stayed with us before their Airstream was ready, I had overheard Ed and Dad having a heated political argument. The two most important men in my life sat at nearly opposite poles on the political spectrum. Watching from the kitchen that looked over the family room where they stood, I froze, awaiting the outcome. After a few moments of back and forth, Dad shook his head, stood, and walked into the living room. When Ed believed something deeply, there was no "agree to disagree."

But now, as we sat with the social worker, Ed's posture was soft. My husband might be opinionated, but he was a man of his word. If he said he was all-in on helping Dad in whatever way was needed, he meant it.

Dad's eyes filled the way they had in the cancer support group we'd all attended early in the summer, only months before—months that now seemed like decades.

The social worker began to ask questions. After a twenty-minute discussion, Ed agreed to let up on Mom, and Mom agreed to take more responsibility for Dad. *Would their promises hold?* I was uncertain, but the following afternoon the doctor released Dad to return to our house.

※ ※ ※

The days continued to pass. Each morning, I walked into the guest bedroom and sat in the straight-back chair to watch him sleep. The sound of his regular breathing, so foreign a few months before, had become familiar. During these hours, I wondered how, not so long ago, he could have driven the ball clear across the creek of the first hole at Wilson Road. How had my strong, handsome father, been transformed into this withering old man with a sinking mouth and dark, crusty eyes. And I wondered what next summer would be like without him.

In the middle of December, as the days wore on and my father didn't die, I bought a computer program that would supposedly calculate a person's biorhythms. The box alleged that the biorhythm charted your cycles of physiological, emotional, and intellectual well-being. I began to check Dad's biorhythms daily, and for future dates as well. I wanted to see if they would tell me when he would die, but I didn't know how it might show that. Would his biorhythms be low? High? Would they plummet off the chart? I wanted to know the future, to be prepared.

And I wanted to be the one to say, "I knew it would happen today."

When something happened, good or bad, Mother and I both had a habit of saying, "I thought that would happen," or, "I just had a feeling." Neither of us would say we had the feeling before things happened, and so it looked like we were just saying it after the fact. I really did get gut feelings about things. Often, I ignored them. They were sometimes wrong and I didn't want to look like a fool.

But I didn't have any intuition about when he would die. I wanted the biorhythms to alert me. I imagined us keeping vigil by his bed, sitting there with a candle lit, but the biorhythms offered no relief.

For the same reason, I also secretly read tarot cards, laying out the Queen of Wands and the Knight of Swords. But the tarot and biorhythms just made my thoughts spin and my insides shake. I put them away and went back to Dad's room to watch him breathe.

CHAPTER 25

TURKEY DAY

Three days before Dad's actual birthday, Thanksgiving arrived with chilly sunshine and a houseful of family. Jim and Deanna, their three children, Amy and her daughter Jamey, Ken and Paul, plus Mom, Dad, Ed and I filled our small house.

Due purely to chance, I had spent more time with Dad since his diagnosis than anyone else apart from Mom. We'd golfed all summer, gone on that "trip of a lifetime," and now he and Mom lived with Ed and me. Jim and Amy both worked full-time and had children. Jim traveled for work and Amy was finishing her degree. Jim's children had visited a few times, but Jamey had insisted she wanted to remember her grandfather as healthy and hadn't come by until this gathering. I'd gotten the best end of the deal.

My father never asked whether anyone was coming to visit him. He'd always put his work and school first. Even dying of cancer, he didn't expect his relatives to drop everything to see him. Still, I worried I had hogged Dad. So, each time the doorbell rang, I greeted the guests, showed them to Dad's room, then paused only long enough to take in his smile before I stepped out and let them have their moments with him.

Dad informed us that he wanted to "ramble out to the family room and stare at the 'idiot box'" as he called the television. Ed and I roped extensions of oxygen tubing down the hallway as Dad rolled along on his walker. Once in front of the television, he became uninterested.

"Everything looks funny," he said. "I can't really follow the game." He sat up just long enough to eat a sliver of pumpkin pie, the first food he'd had since Tulsa. I felt a glimmer of hope at him wanting to eat, but quickly realized it was false. He was still dying. But I loved that for one day he could enjoy pie.

After fifteen minutes, he used his walker to creep back down the hallway to the bedroom. I followed, winding the extra length of hose the way he taught me to wind the orange extension cord in the barn. Paul helped Mom get my father back into bed and before I had finished winding the cord, Dad was asleep.

With our patient securely tucked in and snoring, Paul asked if I would be willing to look at a legal writing project he was doing for law school.

"Of course!" I said. Because Paul lived in Indiana and was busy first with college and now law school, we didn't get to spend much time with him. From what I had seen, he was eager, smart, and, unlike me, not afraid of conflict. He would make a great lawyer. This seemed like a chance to connect.

For the most part, my decision to leave my job as a legal partner satisfied me, but a tiny part of me believed I had something to prove, especially to those in the legal profession. Research and writing had been my specialty so I jumped at the chance to help. Paul brought me the legal note and returned to the family room while I reviewed it.

I attempted to read, but grew disoriented. I scanned the same sentence three times. The legal terms were familiar. I'd written tons of briefs and memoranda, but the words stared back, mocking me. Neither Paul's writing nor his logic was at fault. Between the antidepressant fog and my jumpy, broken brain, I couldn't focus enough to follow the concepts he presented. The words slid through my mind as if it was full of holes.

Fifteen or twenty minutes passed and he reappeared at my office door. I handed the note back to him and said, "Looks fine to me."

Not satisfied with my simplistic response, he began to ask me about his argument. He laid the cases he had brought on my desk. I picked them up and again tried to read. When I got to the end of the first sentence, I could not remember what it said.

"Tell me your argument," I said. He did. I heard familiar words, but could not follow what he was saying.

"I'm sorry, Paul. This wasn't my area of law and I'm having trouble reading cases right now." He looked puzzled, but accepted my answer.

"Thanks, anyway," he said and turned away.

I closed the door behind him and stared at the desktop. I'd been so eager to prove I was still in there somewhere. My attempt and failure confirmed that I had no business setting foot in a law firm any time soon.

Later, Paul helped me turn Dad, a cumbersome but necessary task to prevent my father from getting painful bedsores. Paul listened and followed my lead. He didn't seem to mind that I couldn't help with his legal writing. I hoped he didn't think any less of me because of it.

In the afternoon, Ken stepped away from the football game to help with the dishes. When Dad rang his bell, he followed me down the hall to Dad's room. While I gave my father his liquid morphine, I asked Ken about his job and any golf courses he had played.

"We hit Blacklick Woods this week," Ken said, mimicking a golf swing. My older stepson loved the sport and golfed regularly with friends.

"Have you played it?" Ken asked my father.

"Sounds like fun," Dad said. "You folks go on. I can't get out of this bed," he added, oblivious to the fact that it was below freezing outside and no one was going anywhere.

"Another time," Ken said, and returned to the family room.

⛳ ⛳ ⛳

Ken had endured a front-row view of my mental health decline. When he first moved in with us, shortly after he graduated from college, I still practiced law, drove the fancy car, wore the fancy clothes. Then I was on leave, and then in the psych ward. A few months after I was released from the ward but still in the partial hospital program, Ken found an apartment and moved out. Of course a grown man with a busy job would want his own place. But I worried that my mental illness hastened his departure. The timing was telling. Specifically, I wondered if his absence was precipitated by an event that happened the year before, on the day I'd come home from the psych ward.

After Ed brought me home that day, I drove to my regular recovery meeting then out for bagels with some other group members, the way we usually did on Saturdays. Hours passed as we laughed over the odd horoscopes and unusual personal ads in a local paper. By the time I got home it was nearly two o'clock. I opened the door between the garage and the family room to find Ken slouched on the sofa gazing absently at the television. When he didn't look up or acknowledge me in any way, I said, "Hi," and went to the bedroom, hoping to find Ed.

I walked through the house and didn't see him, so I returned to the family room and asked, "Where's Ed?"

Without taking his eyes off the TV, Ken said, "Out back," in a flat, but ominous tone that chilled me.

I flung open the door to the back yard. Ed sat in a lawn chair on the grass, his back facing the door, with one dog on either side of him. Both dogs stood and turned toward me, but Ed didn't move. I walked around the chair to face him. His eyes were closed.

I knelt. "I'm so sorry," I whispered.

He opened his eyes. They were bloodshot and tears leaked out.

"I'm so sorry," I repeated. I could count on one hand the times I'd seen Ed cry.

"You were gone so long," he said. "I didn't know where you were."

I stood and put my arms around him.

Ed and I went back into the house, but Ken was gone.

I don't remember if Ken had to work that day or if he simply left, but only then did I begin to see how much my mental illness was impacting those around me, including Ken. I wish I had brought it up with Ken right away, but I didn't.

* * *

Now, months later at Thanksgiving with our family, I thanked Ken for coming and reiterated how good it was to see him. He seemed surprised and shrugged.

"It's turkey day," he said. "No way was I gonna miss out on pie."

I wanted to tell him I understood if he had needed to distance himself from my mental illness back then. But the way he brushed it off now told me he'd moved on, even if I hadn't. It was my turn to let it go.

Late in the day after nearly everyone had gone, Dad woke again. Amy answered his bell and gave him some pain medicine. When I heard them, I carried his gifts into his room.

"It's almost your birthday," I said. "I got you a present."

He began to laugh, then winced from the pain in his side. "Stop. You're killing me."

"Um, in case you haven't noticed, you're dying anyway."

"Yeah, but does it have to be this painful?"

"I'll try to take it easy on you."

He smiled and closed his eyes.

The few remaining family members gathered in the room. As I pulled out the bird feeder box and the bag of seed and suet, I remembered my dilemma in Meijer and reminded myself that, regardless of his response, I had done what I wanted by getting him a gift.

"It's not much," I said, then gently set the items on the side of the bed, careful not to touch his ribs.

He opened his eyes. "A dying man doesn't need much." I handed him the box and he stared at it. "What is it? I don't have my glasses."

"A birdfeeder."

He screwed up his face. "What am I going to do with a birdfeeder?"

"We'll put it in the tree out front where you can watch the birds."

"Hopefully I'll die before they come."

"Well, I'll put it in the tree anyway and we'll see who wins, you or the birds." That made him laugh again. I pulled the feeder out of the box and showed him. "It's kind of cool, see-through plastic. I got a suet feeder too."

"The squirrels will love that," he snarled.

My chest tightened, but I didn't respond to his pessimism. The hospice nurse had warned me and the books confirmed, "Their tact goes first." They were right.

"I'm going out right now to put it up."

"Suit yourself," he said, with a big grin.

I glowed inside at having given him something he might not like. Even if he didn't offer an inch of praise, for once I was fine with that. And, I was pretty sure he loved it.

I got my coat and stepped into the frigid sunshine. When I was done, I knocked on his window. He gave me a thumbs up and that goofy smile.

Back inside and stripped of my winter gear, I told him, "Now, we wait."

"I'm waiting every day," he said closing his eyes. I stared at his bony feet. The opaque toenails stuck out from under the sheet.

"Do you want me to cover your tootsies?"

"That would be nice."

I tucked the sheet and the light blanket under his long feet, noticing the blond hairs on his toes as I did. In a few minutes, his breathing became regular. Thinking he was asleep, I turned to leave.

"Thanks," he whispered.

I leaned over the bed and kissed the top of his nearly bald head.

CHAPTER 26

ICE STORM

The day after Christmas, we woke to trees sparkling with a crystalline layer that glittered against a cloudless blue sky. I heard Ed turn on the shower. Then, something clicked and the lights went out. A "beep-beep-beep" came from Dad's room and he started to ring his bell. The oxygen machine was signaling the power outage. I ran to get the portable tank and hauled it into Dad's room.

Before I could turn it on, Ed came in and asked if Dad wouldn't be alright without it for a few minutes. He needed to light some candles to see to finish his shower and get ready for work. Oxygen itself is not flammable, but the hospice nurse had explained that oxygen intensifies and supports combustion. In the presence of oxygen, any type of open flame such as a candle could easily ignite other things and a fire would spread more quickly. To keep us safe, I intended to follow the rules.

But I was also grumpy and tired. Mother and I were both fighting colds. *Did Ed just want to prove Dad could breathe without oxygen?* He and my mother had continued to argue this point long after the family conference. On the other hand, the bathroom where he was dressing had no windows. With the door closed, it was pitch dark, so I agreed. Ed showered and dressed quickly. When Dad said he was having trouble breathing, Ed blew out the candles and I swapped Dad's oxygen line to the portable tank.

Without electricity, we also had no heat. Ed left for work and Mom and I layered Dad with blankets. Mom called the electric company, American Electric Power (AEP), then bundled herself in blankets on the couch. I piled blankets from our bed onto the floor in Dad's room to try to sleep, then closed myself in with both dogs, hoping our collective bodies would keep the room tolerable. I considered climbing into the hospital bed with Dad so my body heat would keep him warm, but what was left of his ribs was excruciatingly painful to the touch.

AEP had promised Mom that the electric would be back on in fifteen minutes, but after several hours we still had no power. Dad was in pain and wanted us to adjust the bed so he could get more comfortable, but it was electric. I gave him more liquid morphine mixed with root beer and Mom and I turned him on his side. His pain eased for a while, but when it came back it was worse.

An hour later, despite more promises from AEP, the power still wasn't on. Mom had already phoned the hospice nurse, but called again. We donned our winter coats, gathered every blanket and bedspread from every room in the house, turned Dad again, then spread them all across him. Another hour passed before the nurse supervisor arrived. When she heard Mom's heavy cough and my raspy voice she said, "I bet you both have strep. There are plenty of beds at Kobacker. Let's get him out of here so you two can get well."

Because Dad had that respite visit a few weeks before, approval took yet another hour and the house temperature dropped to 55°F. Mom returned to the sofa and I headed back to Dad's room to wait on the ambulance. Astro was curled in a little white pile at the foot of Dad's bed while Maxine sat beside it with her long black head resting gently on the edge. Dad lifted his fingers to pat the top of her head.

"Good dog," he mumbled.

She turned soft eyes toward his face, but didn't move away. As I walked past her around the end of the bed to a chair on the opposite side, her eyes followed me.

"She really likes you, Dad."

He murmured.

I found it hard to believe Maxine was the same dog that, years before, had trapped him at the bottom of the basement stairs for over an hour. She continued to sit calmly, head resting gently enough that it didn't hurt his cancer-ravaged ribs. As the guest room cooled even more, Dad grew quiet and Max stretched her long body out on the floor near him. His breath continued to rasp in and out of his mouth, but his shivering stilled and he stopped responding to my questions.

We were losing him.

I looked again at those two sweet dogs. It was nearly impossible to believe that, not long before, we had come so close to losing it all.

In the seven months before my father was diagnosed with cancer and the four days that followed our first wedding anniversary, depression, anxiety, and panic attacks had continued to shrink my world. Not only had I swapped the Volvo for a Toyota, I'd traded the four-bedroom two-story for a perfectly-sized suburban ranch home, where Ed, Ken, Astro, Maxine, and I now lived. I only left the house for psychotherapy, therapy group, recovery meetings, and class. I felt like a mouse stuck to a glue trap, trying to pull my legs free. Every move made them stick harder. I had trouble sleeping and the medicine I took for insomnia either didn't work or made me so drowsy I slept through the day.

Thursday, September 29, 1994, the morning of the day I would enter the psych ward, I'd woken with my usual headache and looming sense of dread. I managed to get myself as far as the family room floor. Maxine snuggled against me and put her paw on my arm. Astro let me pet her white fur, but did not lie down. As usual, she was in motion, trotting around Max and me. As I sank further into the carpet, she stopped long enough to sniff my unwashed hair.

In a cottony fog, as if someone was wrapping me up and shuttling me away to somewhere safe, I remembered the times I'd pulled my car to the berm on the highway because panic had forced the air from my lungs. I remembered walking past my office to the bathroom to empty my stomach before being able to go in. And I remembered the clock I imagined was ticking down the days until my disability leave would end and I would have to go back to the law firm.

Stretched out on the carpet with my face pressed into the Berber pattern, I let my thoughts melt. I'd been struggling for so long. As I lay there, what seemed like a solution floated through my head as if it were a movie.

In my mind, I saw myself open the door that leads from the family room to the garage. I called Astro and Max, opened the hatch of the Volvo station wagon. Eager for a ride, they hopped in. I got in and turned on the motor. As the engine kicked in, light from the closed garage door window shone through the car windows. With the car running, I got out of the front and crawled in back with the dogs. The seat was all the way down and their tails wagged. Astro bounced, jumping on the car doors, and looking out the window as if to say, "Where we going, Mom?" I lay down on the black nylon carpet with the blanket I kept in the car. With much difficulty, since Astro kept jumping on it, I spread the blanket over me. All the while the engine purred, spreading exhaust through the garage.

As my daydream continued, we settled, Maxi beside me and Astro eventually lying down a few inches away. One by one, we slept. Astro first, her breath slowing, a cough or two, then her body still, her tail uncurling as she lay flat out on her side, calm and relaxed. Then, Maxi stretched to her full length and moaned a little sigh. Finally, I fell asleep with them, lying there until we were all three gone, all three sleeping, forever. No pressure. No guilt. No emotion. No thought. Just, the end.

Then, the phone rang.

I opened my eyes to see not the black carpet of the car, but the cream Berber of the family room. When I sat up, the dogs stirred. If I wanted to put this plan into action, I couldn't be interrupted. Instead of answering the call, I got up and picked up my date book to confirm the morning was clear.

The page read, "11:15 - Joan." The clock on the stove read 10:55.

Therapy! In twenty minutes! If I didn't show, Joan might try to find me. Still wearing the same blue jeans and ratty gray sweatshirt I'd worn for several days, I grabbed my purse, opened the garage door, got in the car and backed out, pushing away the potentially fatal daydream I'd just had.

When I arrived at Joan's office in such a disheveled state, she saw the reality I'd been trying to hide. I stared at the multi-colored carpet in her office and remembered the Berber carpet rough against my cheek. I imagined how the nylon carpet of my car might have smelled. When Joan asked how I was, I let my daydream spill out. I told her about the car and the dogs, how Astro would die first because she was the smallest, then Maxi, then me. The words seemed far away, as if they were coming from somewhere outside me. She listened to this, and my admission that I'd called suicide prevention six times. Then, she summoned the psychiatrist who recommended my hospitalization.

*　*　*

In the months since, as I made my way through days in the hospital, weeks of the partial hospital program, months of individual and group therapy, and my father's cancer diagnosis and grim prognosis, I frequently remembered that morning. I remembered it every time I played with the dogs. I remembered it every time Ed and I made love. And I remembered it every time I met my father on a golf course: the warm rays of the sun on my skin, the breeze blowing through my hair, his gestures, his voice.

Now, as I sat shivering in the frigid guest room near Maxine, Astro, and my dying father, it seemed impossible to imagine I ever believed that ending my life was the only option.

Even after decades of therapy, recovery work, meditation, and introspection, I still don't understand what makes a mind snap. So calm. So quiet. Just "I'll load the dogs into the car" as if I were contemplating a trip to the park.

Was I a monster? I came so close to killing not only myself, *but the dogs, too!*

What was I thinking?

Therapists, friends, and family have offered theories. Perhaps I saw Astro and Maxine as my responsibility and a painful reminder for Ed that I thought he would be better off without once I was gone. Maybe I considered they would be a burden to him. Or, worst of all, I might have selfishly wanted their canine comfort as I ended my pain.

But the truth is simpler and more terrifying.

That morning, there was no logic, no emotion, no gut sense. I was on autopilot.

That morning, I did not "think" at all.

Yes, there was a monster. A lethal, deadly force: *mental illness.*

Chronic, severe, recurrent depression had me so firmly in its grasp that I almost took two of the most precious beings in the world down with me.

The power of an unhealthy mind is terrifying, the way it can attack, the same way cancer attacked Dad. A malignant cell in his lung waiting, possibly ten years, to spawn, then bouncing quickly to his ribs before he even felt the first pain. We were both nearly over the falls before either of us saw the rapids. I would survive. He would not.

In our guest room chair, as I listened to my father's shallow breath rasp in and out and stared at our dogs, a thought broke through like a single ray of sun on a cloudy day: *I want to live!* Not only did I no longer want to die, I actually wanted to live.

Of course, I didn't want Dad to die. But that, I knew, was inevitable.

The ambulance arrived half an hour after the hospice nurse left. When the two men gently loaded my father's blanket-draped frame onto the cart, carried him through the freezing house, and rolled him out through the garage into their warm vehicle, Dad was already in a coma. His mouth hung open like a drawer.

After the ambulance drove away, Mom crawled into Dad's hospital bed and pulled the remaining layers around her. I covered her with a blanket and tucked her in. I carried the remaining bedding back to our master bedroom and crawled under my own blankets.

The power came back on that afternoon, but the hospice facility kept Dad. Heading into New Year's weekend, Mom and I both still had bad colds. The previous respite had been for my father. This "respite" would be for Mom, Ed, me, and the dogs.

CHAPTER 27

QUITE A GAL

On New Year's Day, when Ed and I walked into Dad's hospice room, my father dozed on and off through the Citrus Bowl pregame as Mom, Jim, and Deanna watched the program. After the hospice team rescued Dad from our frigid house, he had been unconscious for several days then slowly rose from his coma. His return seemed like a minor miracle. It was as if he had been frozen and, once thawed by the hospice workers, brought temporarily back to life. Although sallower than I remembered and napping, he was otherwise conscious, propped up with a pillow tucked behind his head. Dad hadn't worn his glasses in months and his medication distorted his vision, but when he wasn't asleep, he appeared to be watching the game.

"Hi Dad," I said, walking toward him. His eyes continued following the images on the screen but he smiled when he heard my voice. "He still knows us," Mom whispered when I hugged her. She looked pinker than she had in days.

I had spent the weekend in bed and still had a ragged cough, but we were a family of avid Ohio State fans. When I was growing up, our family spent autumn Saturdays watching Buckeye football while Dad explained the rules. I knew what "third and long" meant before I could talk. Despite feeling rough, I didn't want to miss the family gathering around the TV set to watch Ohio State take on Tennessee. Amy arrived and perched next to Deanna on the love seat at the end of Dad's room.

The sportscasters droned on relentlessly about the slippery playing field. Rain captured by the television microphones sounded like tiny hammers. They pounded my heavy head and heart. Ohio State had lost the Big Ten title to Michigan, their all-time rival. Dad was dying. Even Eddie George winning the Heisman Trophy meant nothing this year. An image of Dad in his scarlet and gray Ohio State golf shirt and matching gray pants flashed through my mind. I shook it away.

I stole glances at the snow-covered garden outside Dad's room. Before I arrived, someone had pulled in extra chairs and the number of people made the room stuffy. Probably too many for Dad and certainly too many for me. It was such a sharp contrast to the quiet days I'd enjoyed alone with him at our house.

Dad stirred and muttered. Mom wet his parched mouth with water from little sponges on sticks like lollipops. The nurse came in and asked Dad, "How's your pain?" He stared up at her, but didn't speak.

Mom said, "He's been moaning a little," and the nurse left.

When Tennessee tied the game, Dad turned to Mom and, with stunning lucidity, asked, "You get that beer?"

Mom replied, "I'll be right back," pulled on her coat and left.

The rain pouring down at the bowl game made the television screen seem fuzzy while the crowd at the game roared.

Had I heard correctly? I thought Dad had all but stopped drinking in solidarity with my mother giving it up. I hadn't seen him take so much as a sip of alcohol since he'd had that beer on the golf course early in the summer.

My eyes widened involuntarily when Mom returned carrying a bottle in a brown paper bag. She gave me a stern look. "He wanted a beer, so I got one." She strode to his bed and held the package like a gift where he could see.

Speaking mainly to Dad, Mom said, "The man looked at me strangely when I told him I just wanted one beer."

Amy chuckled.

"And then," Mom continued, "I asked him to put it in a bag!"

Jim shifted uncomfortably in the chair next to Dad's bed then shrugged. "How else are you going to carry one beer?"

From somewhere outside myself I heard my own too loud, forced laughter.

"I bet nobody even has a church key," I said, also too loudly.

By joking about the lack of bottle openers in our family—a family that doesn't drink anymore—I was trying to let this all be okay. But I thought Dad drinking a beer was a very bad idea and that judgmental streak betrayed me. My reasons were hazy. He was on so much medication. We were in the hospice house. I tried to counter those thoughts, telling myself to relax and have fun. Dad wanted a last beer. A dying man's request. Why not?

In fact, I was more concerned by the fact that my mother had gone to a carry-out and bought it. When you've stopped drinking because you put your car "out to pasture" a few too many times, buying it for other people is usually a bad idea. Under ordinary circumstances, I doubted that my now sober-several-years mother would succumb to the temptation to drink again, but her husband of forty-five years was dying. A chill swept through me as my mind played a scene of Mom tipping the beer to her lips.

My family had hardly spent a holiday together since the early 1980s when, on a Christmas Eve, Amy's then husband made a drunken comment about my brother's children.

What followed was utter chaos as the house erupted with shouting, shoving, and threats of violence. Mom, already intoxicated, crowned the evening by picking up a handle of Southern Comfort, chugging a large gulp, tucking the bottle under her arm, grabbing the keys to the old Ford pickup, and shouting, "I hope you all have a merry fucking Christmas!" Then she threw open the side door and dramatically tromped out into the knee-high snow.

When Dad came out of the bedroom where he'd been fighting with my brother, he ran after her. But she had locked herself in the truck. He returned for the spare set of keys and hauled her, screaming and crying, back to the house where he put her to bed.

All these years later, despite her sobriety, I imagined her returning to the carry-out for her own supply once Dad's single beer in
the hospice room was gone. I saw myself coming home to find
her passed out at the kitchen table next to a fifth of Mattingly &
Moore. The room began to look as gray as the TV screen.

"It's a twist-top," Mom said, beaming and happy to be the
helpful center of attention.

She opened the long-necked Budweiser and poured a quarter of an inch into a plastic medication cup. She sat the bottle
on his tray table and tipped the cup to Dad's lips. He made a
smacking sound and nodded. As Mom sat the empty cup next to
the beer bottle, the nurse returned carrying a little brown bottle
of Roxanol, the same liquid morphine we gave Dad at our house.

"I see nothing," the nurse said when Mom tried to stuff the
beer back into the bag. Mom giggled. The rest of us looked away.

"Time for pain meds," the nurse told Dad, standing over the
bed. She also held a can of root beer that beaded with sweat. She
turned to Mom. "How much do you normally mix with this?"
With her free hand, Mom used her thumb and forefinger to show
an inch. The nurse poured a measured amount into a plastic glass.

As I watched Mom and the nurse, my throat clogged with
emotion. I wanted to lighten the mood to distract myself and everyone else from the sadness. And, I wanted my family to think I
didn't care about the alcohol.

I cleared my throat and said, "Hey! Why not put the morphine in your Budweiser?"

No one laughed.

I turned back to the television. Before I could refocus, Dad's
voice, strident and stronger than I'd heard it in weeks, cut through
me.

"What the hell business is it of yours!"

My face grew hot and tears filled my eyes. I nodded, stood, and walked slowly toward the door.

None, I thought. *It's none of my business.* And a torrent of self-deprecating thoughts flooded my mind.

Before I edged out of the room, I looked toward my father, but his eyes had closed.

As I escaped into the hall, I imagined the nurse pouring an inch of Budweiser over the morphine and Jim handing her one of the plastic spoons from the night stand. I could almost see the nurse stirring the morphine and alcohol concoction, then Jim lifting Dad's head so he could drink from that cup.

Before I'd taken more than a few steps down the hallway, Dad's door closed again and my sister put her hand on my shoulder.

"You okay?" she asked.

I nodded then burst into tears.

Amy wrapped her arms around me. "He wasn't talking to you," she said. "He thought it was the nurse."

That idea had floated through my mind, but my gut said otherwise. His filter was entirely gone.

"He knew it was me and meant exactly what he said."

My sister held me for a few minutes. I gave her a squeeze, and said, "You're missing the game." She smiled, released me, and returned to Dad's room.

My arms felt like leaden bags as I stumbled the rest of the way down the hall toward the hospice center's sitting room.

When I graduated from college, Dad had driven me and my belongings in our red Ford pickup from Ohio University in Athens to Columbus, where I was headed for law school. I was leaving behind the place where I'd first shaped my identity, as well as that townie lover I probably wouldn't see for months. I began to cry before the truck crossed the Athens County line.

An hour and fifteen minutes later, when Dad took the curve at the I70-71 split in Columbus, I was still weeping. He turned and spat, "What the hell is the matter with you?"

Trying to stop the tears made me cry harder. Between gulps of air, I said, "I just left everything behind."

My father glared at me with disgust. "I left Ohio Bell after more than thirty years without so much as a backward glance. What's your problem?" In that moment, I believed that he didn't understand me at all and never would.

Dad hadn't thought writing was a decent career and when I finally found the courage to tell him I intended to go to law school, he had accused me of staying in school to avoid getting a job. And, until I proved otherwise, he hadn't been able to imagine me as a lawyer, either.

Years after I graduated from law school and was practicing, I learned that Dad's middle brother, with whom he fought for much of his young life, had also attended law school. Dad told of how my uncle, their mother's pet, teased him mercilessly, once provoking him to the point that my father threw a hatchet at him. The blade missed my uncle's head by inches. Afterwards, he taunted Dad for missing.

Another time, after Dad had spent hours whittling a toy rifle, his brother saw it, picked it up as if to admire it, then broke it over his knee. Enraged, Dad grabbed a chisel, threw it, and hit his brother in the forehead leaving a lifelong scar. With age, the brothers mellowed and reached a semblance of peace. But I always sensed that my father held my uncle at a distance.

I certainly didn't have my uncle's guile. And I was nothing like the attorneys who had ended Dad's career at Ohio Bell. "The lawyers cut a deal," he said of his early retirement. It hadn't been a "deal" at all; it had been a demand. Ohio Bell had just transferred Dad back from Cleveland, I had left for college, and Mom was drinking her fool head off when he received notice of the reduction in force. No wonder the word "lawyer" made him mad.

According to my father, I didn't even have proper attorney attire. He made that clear after I made the mistake of asking him if I looked like a lawyer when I'd gotten some new clothes.

Eventually, thanks to Ms. Z28, I got the right wardrobe, but I never had the temperament. At least not according to my father's standard. As he saw it, I lacked both the stomach and spine for the job.

Had Dad seen the irony? His youngest daughter, who was so much like him, wanted to follow in the footsteps of the brother he detested. Meanwhile, the only actual attorneys he knew had ended his career.

❦ ❦ ❦

I entered the hospice house sitting room with waves of hot anger flooding my body and confusion clouding my head. I sank into one of the wingback chairs, put my head in my hands, and stared at my boots. Too tired to cry, I let my breath slow on its own and sensed my abdomen move in and out. My mind also slowed.

Given the fact that I was no longer practicing law, Dad might have been right. I had to admit that, at least when I was in my 20s and trying to decide on a career, my father might have known me better than I knew myself. Maybe we were so much alike that he could see what I hadn't.

"Dummy," I had heard him yell at himself on the St. Albans course.

"Dummy," I'd chanted to myself in group.

Did it infuriate him to see himself in me?

Or, was this his final attempt to care for Mom, to protect her from my criticism?

Regardless of the reason, Dad's cutting words contained an entire conversation he and I sidestepped all summer by joking around instead of dealing with the truth. I'd tried to sound nonchalant, but my sentiment was the opposite—another version of "happy camper." He had called it out.

During those months on the golf course with him, I'd begun to live again. He helped me not want to die. I could return the favor by helping him live his final days with gusto. *What did it matter if Mom bought him a beer or if he mixed that beer with morphine?*

If I had mixed beer with my medication or my mother had taken even a sip, it would have been suicide. Despite my anxiety, a deep part of me knew neither of us would do that. I had chosen not to die from my mental illness. My mother and I had both chosen not to die from alcoholism. My father didn't have those options.

He was actually, honest-to-god, going to die and I was petrified.

We were out of time.

I raised my head and remembered bumping along cart paths with him on golf courses in three different states, spilling coffee and nutrition drinks along the way. I remembered Mom and I giving him Roxanol mixed in root beer five times a day for weeks.

And, I remembered Tulsa.

"You're quite a gal," he'd said in the "cancer commune" when I'd sided with him against the doctors. I didn't need the orange pin from partial hospital to tell me, "You did good." I had it straight from Dad.

As I lifted my body out of the chair, I felt lighter.

Part of my quest on those golf courses had been to find out if he loved me, was proud of me, admired me. I had disappointed him and he disappointed me. Regardless, we still loved each other.

In Tulsa, when his voice flowed with admiration, I had replied, "You raised me." When Joan asked if his words landed within me, I said they had.

But I had also learned something even more valuable.

Even if he doesn't know who I am, *I know who I am*. And even if he doesn't love, respect, and admire me, *I love, respect, and admire myself*. That would sustain me long after he was gone.

In the bathroom, I splashed water on my cheeks, and looked in the mirror. Out loud, to my puffy, red face, I said the words.

"You're quite a gal."

I walked back to his hospice room where my family still gathered and the game still played. Everyone looked up. I smiled, then took my seat. When the Buckeyes scored again, we all cheered. In the end, Ohio State lost. But I had won something that could never be taken away.

CHAPTER 28

A VERY PRIVATE ACT

The call came at 9:45 a.m. on the fourth day of January when I was in the lobby of the mental health center waiting to be summoned for therapy.

Phoning from our house, Mom sounded calm. Serene even. "They don't think Daddy will make it through the night."

"Should I come home right away?" The idea of being present for my father's final breath held a strange attraction for me, but I wasn't sure I could endure witnessing it without a therapy session to prepare me. Despite the hospice nurse's prediction that he would die during the night, I feared Dad wouldn't make it until we got there. I didn't want to miss the main event.

"Do what you think is best," Mom said.

Fifteen minutes later, after a rushed therapy session, I was in my car, laser-focused on getting Mom to the hospice facility before Dad died. We needed to hold his hand, to let him go, together.

Adrenaline zipped through my arms and legs as I drove to our house to pick up Mom. I rolled into the driveway and honked the horn. I thought Mom would be on the fly, but she did not come out. I struggled with the car door then strode into the house.

My mother stood in the living room completely still, frozen in place as if she'd fallen into a trance while standing. In front of her sat several grocery bags filled with clothes.

"We've got to go!" I shouted, then bundled her into the winter coat Amy had loaned her and grabbed the bags.

"Come on, Mom," I urged, more gently.

Finally, with a long sigh, she picked up her purse and slowly moved toward the door.

"It's okay Mom. We're on our way, now."

But we had lost two hours since the nurse's call. The ache of dread filled my body as if I was about to miss a filing deadline. I wanted to put my foot to the car floor, but Mom sat silently beside me, locked in some place I couldn't access. We hit every light red. I did my best to remain calm and drive sensibly while, inside, I screamed.

I thought Mom would surely snap awake when we reached Kobacker, but she shuffled to the building and down the hall as if she were drugged. When I realized I was more than five yards ahead of her, I slowed, and took a few deep breaths to calm myself. I turned the corner of the hallway that led to Dad's room and a nurse walked out of his door, her smart smock too bright for the gray winter day. I waved and she nodded. Out of the corner of my eye, I saw the house golden retriever napping by the nurse's station and slowed a little more.

Mom continued to move as if she were under water. So I stepped into Dad's room ahead of her, then stopped. His face was gray and the energy around his bed had an eerie calmness. I wheeled around, almost knocking Mom over.

"I think he's gone," I said.

Not waiting for Mom's reply, I strode after the nurse.

Wasn't this the event he and I had been training for? The final round? Wasn't this what all those Thursdays on all those golf courses and his "trip of a lifetime" was supposed to lead to? Hadn't those days in Tulsa followed by weeks of keeping vigil at his bed, stationed in a straight chair in our guest room, been practice for a single instant, the final exhale?

Had I missed it?

I called to the bright smock, "I think my dad's dead."

She turned, eyes wide.

I pointed to his room.

She didn't run, but she walked with purpose.

"I was just in there," she said, exasperated. "He was breathing."

I believed her. It was just like him to hear us coming and sneak off before we had a chance to make a scene. He wouldn't have wanted to bother anyone.

Or maybe he had miscalculated. Maybe he thought we would come right away. Should I have skipped therapy? Should we have come immediately when the hospice nurse said he had taken the infamous "turn for the worst"?

I walked into his room a second time and put my hand on his arm. It was still warm.

In this stillness, I relived the mornings I had awakened to silence, walked slowly down the hall to his room, peered in at his gaping mouth, and watched his chest to figure out if he was still alive. No more need to guess. My father could have been one of the stone markers on any of the courses we had played. A stone in the sun, but a stone nonetheless.

I reached for Mom's hand as the hospice nurse put her stethoscope to Dad's heart and then lifted his wrist to check for a pulse. My mother must have been holding her breath. When the nurse began, "I'm so sorry . . ." Mom exhaled a little gasp then began to cry softly.

She looked up at me like a child. "Gone?"

In my head, I heard my father's words, "And your mother?"

I put my arms around her and she shuddered tiny, inaudible sobs.

"Maybe you should sit down, Mom," I said, gently guiding her to the sofa where I had napped with Dad the afternoon before. Mom slid onto the cushions, leaned sideways against the back of the sofa, and stared out the window.

I returned to Dad's bedside and put my hand back on his arm. It was beginning to cool. *He's really gone.* I stood by his body staring at that gaunt, gray face, and let the flood of tears roll down my cheeks.

Jim and Amy soon arrived. I let a wall support me as my 6'4" brother leaned against Dad's hospital bed and wept, openly. He mumbled, "I keep thinking of him digging those fence-post holes under the blazing summer sun. So humid," he said, choking out the words. I'd never seen Jim cry like this. Given the some-times-rocky nature of their relationship, the depth of his emotion caught me by surprise. *He, too, truly loved our father.*

As Amy held Dad's hand, I imagined her remembering their hours together driving to and from Ohio Bell, time she cherished. After a few moments, she hugged Jim then pulled up a chair next to Mom, and me. Here we were, the remaining members of our now seemingly much smaller family.

None of us thought this ox of a man, a man who would walk across the bottom of a swimming pool rather than flunk a class, would ever succumb. Our father thought otherwise and left qui-etly. There was no bedside vigil, no waiting for him to go. We'd had nine months to do that. The nurse probably heard his last breath, that final exhale. Then, no more inhale. Not a labored or heavy breath, just one slow exhale and it was over. Nine months of hospitals and doctors and radiation and chemotherapy—over. Nine months playing golf again and again as if it were the last time—over. No more need to keep score. It was that simple. He just stopped breathing.

Missing Dad's death haunted me. I relived the scene as if I could make a different choice, fly back in time to the moment just before he was going to die, jet myself into his room, and change the ending. But Dad knew how much I wanted to be with him and how much of a toll his illness had taken on Mother and me. I believe he sensed the exhaustion, with both of us fighting colds and the weather so icy. He had seen us drag ourselves into his room hour after hour, day after endless day. And so, moments before we arrived back to the hospice house from our night of rest, moments before we walked into his room, he went . . . with-out us.

Dad's solo exit was not unusual. Loved ones often slip away when no one is around. They wait until you are fast asleep, step out to get a sandwich, smoke a cigarette, or relieve yourself, and then, they take their leave. The hospice social worker said, "You can close your eyes for a moment or two and open them again to find them gone. Dying is a very private act. I think most people want to do it alone."

When I told Mom about my angst over missing Dad's death, her response stunned me. "I don't think I could have withstood watching him die."

She had been relieved to miss the very moment I was trying to ensure we were both there for. I had wanted what I wanted. It never dawned on me that Mom might not want the same thing. When she explained this, my mouth filled with sour shame at how much I had tried to control things.

And unlike me, it would be just like Dad to know that Mom couldn't have taken it if she'd had to watch him die. He had spared her that last moment, that last gasp when she could no longer do anything for him. He knew Mom better than any of us.

Perhaps he thought he knew me better, too. Perhaps he wanted to protect my mental health. While I can't say how I would have held up seeing his last breath, I thought I was prepared. I'd been growing toward his final exhale from the day he first said, "It's in my bones."

* * *

While I may have missed his physical death, I witnessed the death of his golf game. Back in September when my parents and I arrived in Arizona after our trip to Yellowstone, the day before I was due to fly back to Ohio, Dad and I headed to the Chaparral golf course to play what we knew, but didn't say, would be our final nine holes. On four, as we passed their house, we waved at Mom.

Dad played badly. He hit most of his drives short and pulled his putts, an unbelievable decline from the championship golfer he had been on Wilson Road just five months before. When he putted out on the fifth hole, his hands shook. He stopped taking practice strokes.

On six, Dad drove first, from the men's tee box, a short hop shot that he topped and hooked after wincing and groaning audibly from the effort. Then we pulled the cart up to the women's tees.

I hit a solid drive, demonstrating the steady improvement I'd made all summer under his tutelage. The ball flew long and straight, sailing through the air. It caught a current and made that sweet whooshing sound of a well-hit ball, the sound I often heard Dad's drives make much earlier in the summer. We watched it soar.

I couldn't stop staring, waiting, willing it to drop. It sailed onward. I glanced at my father. A deep sadness, a faint recognition, something inconsolable crossed his eyes as he watched my ball continue to fly through the air. All those months on the links, in the hottest summer in several decades, we'd worked on my game with him telling me, "Keep your head down. Keep your arm straight. You hit it exactly where you aimed it." But now, his eyes looked dark and empty.

I turned back toward the fairway and located my ball: a white dot halfway up, just beyond the white dot that was Dad's ball. The picture didn't compute. Dad's ball was six feet closer to us than mine.

A few awkward seconds passed. I looked back at him and then at the ground, waiting.

"You out-drove me," he said.

"Lucky hit," I tried.

He wouldn't have it. "No. It was a good, solid drive."

I had no therapeutic phrases to pull out of my psychological top hat. "You taught me well," was all I could manage.

"You learned well," he said, then added, "I'm really tired. Mind if we call it a day?" I didn't mind. We picked up the balls, got in the cart, and drove back to the clubhouse in silence.

CHAPTER 29

HE KNEW HOW TO DO THINGS RIGHT

The day of Dad's funeral dawned with sunshine and more ice. On the drive from Columbus to Johnstown, Ed and I inched our way across recently salted roads and marveled at how the shimmering, frozen coating had transformed the bare limbs of trees into sparkling visions.

At the funeral home, we each had a moment to say our last goodbyes to Dad's body. Mom stepped up first, dressed in the same head-to-toe black funeral garb, complete with veiled hat, that she had modeled the day Dad's catheter was put in. Our "funereal sprite" whispered a few private words, touched his arm, then stepped away. Her outfit and demeanor preserved her feisty personality while also honoring the solemnity of the occasion.

Jim approached next, then Amy.

When my turn came, I knelt by the casket. Up close, I could clearly see that the empty body in that fancy box was not my father. The vibrant energy I normally sensed in his presence was absent. *Dad really was gone.* I shuddered with that recognition. When I could not stop crying, Ed came to my side and guided me toward the door. I turned back for one last look and saw my niece, Jamey, approaching the casket for her final goodbye.

When we walked into the Catholic church, I scanned the pews, amazed. All four of my former law partners and many recovery friends had braved the ice storm to attend. Each of them knew what I'd faced to get to this day.

Father Ron, the priest whom Dad had worked for on the CCD building, had also served my parent's parish during the last year I was in high school. He told of my dad's adventures trimming the shrubbery at the parish property. "I have never seen greenery trimmed so precisely. If there was one little sprig of shrub sticking up, Gene would track it down and trim it with the very edge of the hand trimmers so that the whole shrub was exactly the same height. You could have put a level on that shrub and it would be plumb." Dad had also spent a summer painting the front of the church. "I don't know how many coats of paint are on that wall, but I know it's perfect," Father Ron said. "Gene knew how to do things right."

I caught Ed's eye and stifled a laugh. Father Ron had captured Dad perfectly.

My father spent my entire life trying to "improve" us. I'm sure if anyone asked, he would have insisted he loved us exactly the way we were, but his actions said that everything I did was just a little not right.

After one of my flute recitals, he said I played just fine, but that girl who played the trumpet solo was really grand.

"I sure like the trumpet," he proclaimed. I had even chosen the wrong instrument.

When he helped with my algebra homework, he didn't like how I laid the problems out on the page. A frugal environmentalist at heart, I was trying to save paper. When I explained, he said, "There's plenty of trees. Just look out there!" and gestured toward our fifteen acres of woods. I burst into tears at his suggestion that we might cut down those exquisite oaks and maples to make paper for my algebra homework. He stared at me, baffled. "It's just paper," he said and turned back to the problems.

At the time, each of those exchanges had seemed like a pummeling. But remembering it all today made me smile. *Another example of Dad being Dad!*

Every game my father and I played on the golf course was an opportunity for him to give me a lesson. It never dawned on him that we were keeping score of entirely different things. I was there for the sunshine, the trees, and the time with him. If I had tried to explain, he would have said, "A thing worth doing is a thing worth doing well."

When he stood behind me and put his arms around me to help me with my grip and stance, I could feel the urgency in his hands. He would pull my arms around in a circle the way they were supposed to go. He had needed me to get better.

By the end of the summer, when he tried to guide me that way, the resentment I'd previously felt had vanished. I didn't even tense. *This is who he is.*

I also stopped admonishing myself for my lack of skill or accusing myself of stupidity. But I did not ignore him. I'd had a year and a half of heavy-duty therapy, was no longer working in a profession where the difference between good and good enough could get you fired, and had come close to killing myself even when I wanted to live. Instead, I simply agreed with him.

"You're right," I said. "I hit it right where I aimed it, but what a great shot it was!" He shook his head, but remained silent. I knew what he was thinking. "It would have been a great shot if you'd hit it in the right direction."

This became my new practice. He would tell me what I was doing wrong and I would tell myself, and sometimes him, what I was doing right.

It annoyed him that his efforts did not improve me more quickly. I *was* getting better, just not the way he intended. The more we played and the more he criticized me and himself, the less I cared. I chuckled when I topped the ball and laughed out loud if I hit it into the water.

Eventually, my humor rubbed off on him. One day late in the summer, when we first got into the cart, I cheerily showed him an extra sleeve of balls I'd brought "just in case."

"This game is too expensive for you if you're gonna lose that many balls," he snarled, trying to play the stern parent. It was no use. I was already giggling. He couldn't keep a straight face and began to laugh along with me.

EPILOGUE

I picked up the urn, a tin can really, from the funeral home. It was gold-tone metal, about the size of a potato chip can. I secured it in the front seat of my car with the seat belt. At home, I carried it down the basement stairs and set it on the workbench, where I looked at it for a while.

Dad.

Mom had agreed to share my father's remains with my sister and I. I had offered to separate his ashes into three equal portions. My brother, who thought we three women were morbid, declined his share.

Two Folgers decaffeinated coffee cans, the one-pound kind with plastic lids, already sat on the bench. One can had a worn label that read "flavored." I hadn't thought ahead to get something more appropriate, so I had emptied the coffee from our freezer into Ziploc bags. I'd thought of putting the ashes themselves into Ziploc bags then decided against it. They didn't seem strong enough to hold a man who had stood over six feet tall. And the thought of putting him in a Ziploc bag disturbed me. I had decided on the coffee cans and had carried them with a measuring cup down to the basement earlier that day.

Dad's hammer, drill, sander, and router were tucked in slots beneath the bench. On a shelf to my left sat the little bird feeder, his final birthday present. The birds had come, but after Dad died I could neither bear to see it hanging from the tree nor give it away. In the basement, Dad's intangible presence was everywhere and I couldn't think of a better place to divide his tangible remains.

I continued to stare at the large tin for a few minutes, afraid to open the lid. A vague Halloweenish fear of dead things seized me, but I couldn't have told you what I was afraid of. A small chill ran down my spine, the kind you get when you watch a scary, late-night movie with your best friend in a dark room after your parents have gone to sleep.

I told myself, "It's just a can full of ashes," and wriggled my shoulders to shake off the creeps. Then, I tucked my fingernails under one side of the lid, gingerly pried up the edge, pulled the lid off, and set it upside down on the bench. I laughed out loud when I saw that the tin contained a plastic bag—not a Ziploc bag, but a plastic bag just the same—secured with a large twist tie. A thin beige powder covered the inside of the lid and the top of the plastic bag. It took a moment for me to understand what I was looking at: ash and bits of bone and some indeterminate things that didn't seem like they could possibly have ever been my dad. "Dad is escaping!" I thought, a little giddy, but he would have approved of the joke.

I took a deep breath, undid the twist tie, and began scooping cremains into the two coffee cans while leaving a portion in the original tin. As I tried to keep the thirds even, I remembered Dad's mother, a large German woman who, to make certain we each got the same amount, had weighed the apples, candy, and popcorn squares she gave us at Christmas.

I wanted to keep some part of what remained of my father's physical body. But once I finished dividing his ashes, I didn't know what to do with my share and I didn't really want to think about it. He hadn't wanted a gravestone or to be buried, so I filed the can with the "flavored" label on it in the bottom drawer of my metal filing cabinet.

Although I had these ashes, I wanted something I could look at to remind me of him. I don't believe that he ever was his body. His body had only been a satchel that carried around what he really was. It had been a tool that his energy used to dig post holes, swing golf clubs, and give me those rare hugs I so desperately wanted. Perhaps the Catholic upbringing I thought I'd left behind made me believe I needed a remnant, something to hold onto so I would not have lost him completely.

Five years later, while unpacking knickknacks after Ed and I moved to a new house, I found a two-inch-tall, clear-glass pitcher-shaped perfume bottle with a stopper. I cleaned the tiny glass container, pulled the green Folgers can from my file drawer, and filled the bottle to the top with some of the grayish silt. Powdered Dad. Just add water. If only it were that simple. I sealed the tiny pitcher with plumber's putty, what Dad always called "pipe dope."

I sprinkled some of the rest of Dad's ashes in Sedona at Oak Creek Canyon, near the spot where so many years ago he reached for me the moment I had begun to cry. At our successive homes in Taos, New Mexico, and Upper Arlington, Ohio, I remembered his hands working the earth at the farm as I mixed some of his ashes into the dirt each time we planted a new tree. I also spaded some of his ashes into the ground at the base of the crimson king maple that still stood outside the window of the guest room of our house in Dublin, Ohio, where he lay in his hospital bed the final months before he died.

My mother sprinkled some of her portion of the ashes in Oak Creek in Sedona where she and Dad had vacationed when they first visited Arizona. And she had some of his ashes placed beneath a tree she had planted in Dad's honor on the golf course in Bullhead City.

My sister sprinkled her portion around a pair of thirty-foot blue spruce trees at the edge of the back field at the farm—the same trees under which my father had buried the bodies of so many pets, including Puppsy, Missy, and some of my niece Jamey's cats and dogs. The year after my sister sprinkled the ashes there, lightning struck both trees. They died, fell, and rotted. The spot where the trees once stood now lay fallow. No sign that the trees ever lived remains. In 2002, six years after Dad died, my mother sold the farm.

I still have the little perfume bottle. It sits on a shelf in my office next to a photo of the farm and a tree-shaped collage frame that holds photos of Dad, Mom, Jim, Amy, and me, all taken when I was about six months old. For eleven years, the remainder of my third of his ashes sat on a shelf at the back of my closet, still in the green decaffeinated "flavored" coffee can. They remained there until Mom died, when their ashes were combined.

🌢 🌢 🌢

Decades after his death, my memories of my father are fading. I cannot close my eyes and see his face anymore. I cannot hear his voice. Behind my eyelids I can only capture the edge of his smile, the crinkle around his eyes, the way he shifted his weight from one foot to another before he drove off the tee. I wish I could touch him one last time. I don't remember how he smells. I do not have him whole. I do not really have him at all.

But sometimes, when I am afraid, confused, lonely, he comes to me.

In March of 1996, two months after Dad died, the *Dog World* article was published and I began another, this one for *Dog Fancy.* The following year, I sold my golf clubs and Ed and I moved to Taos in the mountains of northern New Mexico. I thought the 353 days of sun and the writing workshops I'd begun to take would heal my depression for good.

One night when Ed was working the late shift, I began to feel a friendly presence, as if someone was standing next to our bed. I thought Ed had come home. But my sensations didn't match the "wifely radar" feelings I get when Ed is nearby. I kept my eyes closed and called Ed's name anyway. No one answered, but the calm feeling stayed.

I opened my eyes and peered into the dim light. A shadowy shape loomed, tall, and fuzzy around the edges. I rubbed the sleep from my eyes and it disappeared. But when I squinted, I could still see the form, like a hazy cloud beneath my eyelids.

"Dad?" I asked the empty room. The warmth of his embrace flooded through me. I tried to hold onto it, but it faded as quickly as it had come. I rolled over and cried myself back to sleep.

Another evening, also when Ed was gone, I sat meditating cross-legged on our living room sofa. The deep dream of what Taos would be had collided with reality. The jagged mountains, dry dirt, and prickly vegetation of our high desert town disturbed me. I missed my Ohio friends and couldn't pull myself out of the doldrums. I dreamed daily of driving my car off the Rio Grande Gorge Bridge, but continued to meditate because that was what I knew how to do. Now, unlike before, when suicidal thoughts rose, they were mild and passed quickly.

That evening, Astro and Maxine had settled into their meditative snores and I was following my own breath when a warm wave passed in front of me. I opened my eyes as Astro lifted her head and looked in my direction, but not at me. I closed my eyes again, but the presence did not move. The warmth was familiar, friendly, and gentle.

"Dad?"

The warmth grew.

"What am I supposed to be doing?"

"Just go for it."

I didn't hear the sound of his voice, but I experienced the meaning of his words, an echo of what he'd said in Sedona. Back then, I hadn't been ready to take them in. But over the past few years, I had internalized his message completely. Still, a little fatherly support wouldn't hurt.

"I'm afraid," I said.

"Don't let anyone stop you. It's alright."

I was crying now, shuddering and letting the flood of tears and wracking sobs come.

"Just go for it. It's okay. Everything is alright."

Again and again, I felt his voice as clearly as if he stood before me.

What I didn't know as I sat basking in this warmth was that Ed and I would soon move back to Ohio, my mental health would eventually stabilize, and I would go on to write several books.

As Dad's presence repeated the phrases, I let them wash over me. After a bit, I began to say them out loud: *Just go for. It's okay. Everything is alright.* I already knew they were true.

When the words stopped, I waited. Slowly, the warmth began to fade. I opened my eyes. Astro was asleep again.

"Thank you," I said. And he was gone.

THE END

ACKNOWLEDGMENTS

First, foremost, and always, overflowing love and gratitude to Ed. Deep bows to him and everyone listed below, as well as the many I certainly forgot:

Amy Ax Eisenbach, Jim Buddelmeyer, Deanna Buddelmeyer, the late Sally Settles, the late Salty Settles, Ken Sweeney, Paul Sweeney, George Eisenbach, Mark Buddelmeyer, the late Jamey Ax, each of my family members near and far, Sensei Sean "Koho" W. Murphy, Tania Casselle, Natalie Goldberg, the staff of Mabel Dodge Luhan House, Goldberg loop, Writing Loop, Shutupandwrite loop, all the Goldberg workshop participants, Wendy Drake, Krissy Grimshaw, Mary Michael, Tim Kolb, Ted Stone, Jamie Figueroa, Lora Fish, Shirley Hyatt, Pat Snyder, Candace Hartzler, Shannon Jackson Arnold, Lynn McNish, Nancy Golden, Dhanu Sant, the late Mary Christensen, Tonya Malench, Mitsy Andrews, Karen Burry, Sharon Mast, Marie Radanovich, Joy Schroeder, Taryn Paige Mullins, Leslie Robinson, Cheryl Peterson, Martha Crone, Laura Staley, Sammi Soutar, Krista Hilton, Sally Stamper, Alison Hazelbaker, Mary Yost, Sydney Schardt, everyone at the late, great National Novel Writing Month, Anne Delekta, Suzanna-Charlotte Anderson, all of my coaching clients, the Writer's Roundtable participants and all the participants of all my classes, Meg Hartenstein, Senath Rankin, Deborah Ann Guy, Karla Rivers, Michael Wilson, Matt Betts, Valerie Chandler, Mickie Kreidler, Jenn Bonito, Lisa Wooley, Cynthia Rosi, Elizabeth Nasser, Paula J. Lambert, M.J. Abell, Steve Rockwell, Julie Workman, Cora Spring Moon, Debbie Russell, Cheryl Leutjen, the late Anna Kvinta, Priscilla Gill

McGovern, Jennifer Rogers, Jenny Combs, Christy Feamster, Cassandra Madden, Julia Lada, Sara Barry, Meegan Chalfant, Constance Frey Chappelear, Sam Jordan, Debbe Yakubowski, Jay Wilkins, Adam Meyer Darlin, Jim Wittenmyer, all the Meditating Peacocks, everyone at One Breath at a Time, Saturday Afternoon Live, the ex-problem drinkers who shall remain anonymous, Erika Holycross, Maureen Thompson, Judi Firchow, Nancy Stapp, The late Jill Tibbles, the late Ruth Friscoe, Stephen Shelton, the late Beverly Swerling, Elizabeth Statmore, Jennifer Pooley, the late Nancy Zafris, Brenda Knight, Jeanne Simonoff, Lisa Loeb, Carol Ford, Mariana Damon, Karen Winston, Karen Baldwin, Saundra Goldman, Vaunceil Strassenburg Kruse, Victoria Pope Hubbell, Jeanne Weinberg, Jenn Wood, Lori Wostl, everyone from the 2005 class of Write to the Finish, The Johnny Depp Society, the Taos writing group, Michelle Huff, Jackie Coggin, Lisa Seepaw, the late Ruth Ross, Anne, Fiona Thompson, Deb Saine, Jill Blixt, Sonya Feher, Sherry Hardage, Roma Arellano, Abby Alexander, the late Brenda Mantz, Feroza Jussawalla, Marilee Burton, Aomawa Shields, Memphis Holland, Sonja Lillvik, the late Barbara Moran, Barbara Levinson, Gary Feuerman, Suzanne Steinberg Lynne, Deborah Santana, Debbie Eisenberg Merion, Robin A. Sheerer, Nathanael Worley, Barbara Mertus Munyon, Judith M. Ford, Laura Flett, Hadiyah Carlyle, Celeste Krueger, Christy Bright, Jennifer Bodaken, Marsha Kite, Marja-Riitta Vainikkala, Bill Addison, the late Ryder Finnegan, the late Dr. Gwendolyn Teekell, Sharyn Dimmick, Nancy Canyon, Neola Mace, Laura Goldin, Abby Ross, Deanna Goodrich McMain, Flo Holt, the late Elaine Sutton, Trudy Goodman, Lorraine Lener Ciancio, Marina Salazar, Susie Ekberg Risher, Laura Kooris, Vivian Lewin, Pamela McDowell Saylor, Dorotea Mendoza, Chrystal Chissell, Sarah Getz, Deby Dixon, the late Bob Chrisman, Jan Marquart, Katrina Davidson, Belinda Griffin, Judalon Manes, Martha Geany, Becca Syme, Susan Bischoff, Crystal Shannon, the folks at Better Faster Academy, 750words, Marion Roach, Dinty Moore, Lisa Cooper Ellison, Claire Taylor, Wendy Dale, Tim

Grahl, Lorin Oberweger, Marcia Rose, the late Holly Lisle, the late Father Ron Atwood, Goddard College, Clockhouse West Writers, Aimee Liu, Victoria Nelson, Diana Gould, Darah Cloud, Neil Landau, Michael Klein, Paul Selig, Erin Fristad, Ellen Baileybrown, Lisa Haneberg, Alison James, Shel Graves, Katharine English, David Rask Behling, Wanda Grace, Annie Keeling, Myeesha Moncrief, Sidney Williams, Isla McKetta, Julie Sayres, Shanti Elke Bannwart, Priya Sheleen, Penny Johnson, Cyndee Mady, Tammie Burnsed, Jill Schmaedeke, Rachel Roman, Kirsten Dixon, Jana Bourne, Carol Despeaux Fawcett, Patricia Busbee, Ann Hedreen, Tracy Vicory-Rosenquest, Jennifer Brennock, Dani Boss Wilson, Roxana Arama, Nikki Kallio, John Schimmel, Sue Ann Colvin, Walidah Imarisha, Elaine Flory, Cody Luff, Kenny Fries, Jan Vallone, Les Lamkin, Thomas A. Thomas, Sophie Davis, Drew Dillhunt, Ellen Welker, Marcia Casey, Matthew Tan Ebnet, Ann Graham Walker, Meredith Bailey, Kakwasi Somadhi, Mel Michaels, Amy Nicole Collier, Roshelle Amundson, Stephanie Pilar Peirce, Natasha Oliver, Dawnelle Wilkie, Lori Pohlman, Michael Weinstock, George Obermiller, Timothy P. Brown, Icess Fernandez Rojas, Christy Lochrie, Kat Good-Schiff, Sabrina Rongstad-Bravo, Sam Moore, Radha Botofasina, Kij Johnson, the late Teri Crane, the late Julie Geene, Jonathan Kiner, Donna Hartley, Ray Pantle, Leslie Parisi, Katrina Stonoff, Rami Ungar, T. Scott Purvis, Faith Van Horne, David Wilson, Sally Vallat, Sue A Back, Jenn Houck, Debora Hysell Nichola, Gea, Lissie Faye, Lynette, Solveig, Tank, Sam, Brewster's Coffee, Colin Gawel and the staff at Colin's Coffee, Crimson Cup (Clintonville), Tim Blair and the staff at Market District Kingsdale, Elaine Brill Paris, Evie and Luna, Tom and the staff at Stauf's Coffee Roasters, Barnes & Noble (Easton & Lennox), the late Caribou Coffee (Upper Arlington), River Road Coffee (Granville), Panera (Mill Run), Wired (Taos), Cafe Tazza (Taos), The Tea House (Santa Fe), The Coffee Loft (Gatlinburg), The Bean (Taos), Cloud Cliff Bakery (Santa Fe), Santa Fe Baking Company, Santa Fe Hotel, 1012 espresso (Port Townsend), The Taos Library, the quiet rooms and the amazing librarians at Dublin, Hilliard, and Whetstone Libraries, Columbus Metroparks, Hyatt Place Dublin, the folks at Ship Print eSell (Upper Arlington), Dog World, Dog Fancy, Country Living, The Taos News, Greater Columbus Arts Council, Ohio Arts Council, Chaz O'Neil, Dr. Joan Williams, the late Harri Amurgis, Lori Biesiada, Dr. Belinda Gore, Janice George, Mary Simonini, Dr. Richard Davis, Psy. D., Dr. Dean Kirkendahll, the staff and professionals at United Behavioral Health, Beth Scherer, Bethany Dwinnell, Dr. Darrin Bright, Dr. Anne Albers, Dr. David Sabgir, Dr. Sanjeeb Bhattacharya, Russell Nohelty, Cherry Poteet, Carol Fey, Catherine Heid, Theresa Rittinger Schaefer, Cathy Huston, Martha Sweterlitsch, the late Suzanne Stasiewicz, Nancy Erickson, David Blaugrund, John Herbert, Jon Gabel, the late Keith Mesirow, Jennifer Jones, Ruby Renshaw, Emily Journey, Bill Estep, Ellie Nowels, Rich Warren, James Kingsland, Kelly and the design professionals at 100 Covers, The BookLife Prize, Publisher's Weekly, Gabe Howard, James Dodson, the late Yolanda Scott, Julie DeBord, Jeff Henderson, Donna Poland, Sue Henderson, Grace Gregg, Helen Hill, Peggy Dunn, Jamie Moran Kirby, Lynne Johansson, Laura Holzhauer, Shari French, Connie Bowman, Devon Whittaker, Kristin Mainzer, Brenna Rudd, Jessica Baldwin, Shellie Lloyd, Julia Meeker, Stephanie Klinger, Anne VanBuskirk, Gail Sadler, Morgan Stutz Bonito, Robin Rizek, Kathy Henderson, Deirdre Pifer, Connie Manno, Maryn Marshall, M.J. Picard, Tiffani Myers-Wilson, Heather Bechtel, Mandy Still, Katy Hite, Jackie Schilling, Mishelle Lynch, Brian Johnson, Michael Petrovich, Stephanie Clark, the late Mary Ditty Hill, Sarah Steiner, Richard Basile, Amy Fouch, Laurie Bilovesky, Fred Girtsch, everyone at Fleet Feet Columbus and Marathoner in Training, Heidi Williams, Arian Williams, Brandie Richardson, Mensur Sejfovic, The late Chuck Franklin, CPA, Anthony J. Provenzola, Brian Matthys, Chris Gardner, Cameron Ladd, Jenn Loeffler, Ryan Smith, Vance Quatez Bennett, Carl Zimmerman, Demi Huang, Jungwoo Oh, Suha Cho, Sungjin Lee, Syed Mustafa, Dennis Lee, Riney

Lochmann, Scott Campbell, Cindy Carvour, Bill Gallagher, Dr. Leif Smith, Psy.D., John Xavier Perez, J.D., Stephen H. Dodd, J.D., Scott Light, Christie Casaday, Chris Svec, Christy Bertolo, Jim Karam, Nolene Murembeni, Ben Welcher, Matt Pflieger, Quinn Gardner, Jimmy Miscovich, Don Oates, Lowell Bowdle, Michael Loftis, Keith Hanson, Luke Bumgarner, Adam Huddle, Kota Tanaka, Naoki Kojima, Ryan Searle, the folks at Premier Asphalt and Concrete, Kevin Moran, Corey Moritz, Craig Norton, Bill Watkins, everyone at IACE Travel, the folks at RWK Services, the RJK Roofing guys, everyone at Honda Kaihatsu Americas, the Ventra Health folks, and everyone else at Americenters Dublin, Kevin Nestrick, Steve Barnhart, Mindy Deer, Tracy at Broadview Golf Course, Vida, Rachel, Mark, Gail, John, Scott, Julie, and all the neighbors, as well as Puppsy, Lady, Tiny, Ginger, Sunny, Skeeter, Tony, Bouncy, Missy, Venir, Tootsie, Mandy, Aspen, Maxine, Astro, Bodhi, Morgan, Scarlet, and any other being or institution that ever cheered me on.

ABOUT THE AUTHOR

Nita Sweeney is the bestselling author of five books including the award-winning memoir *Depression Hates a Moving Target: How Running with My Dog Brought Me Back from the Brink*. Her work on mindfulness, movement, and mental health has been featured in the *Wall Street Journal, Men's Health, Woman's Day, bpHope, AARP Magazine, First for Women*, and *Psych Central*.

A mindfulness coach, certified meditation teacher, ultramarathoner, certified running coach, and retired attorney, she knows firsthand the power of showing up for yourself and for those you love even when it feels impossible.

Nita lives in central Ohio with her husband, Ed, and their yellow Labrador retriever, Scarlet, not far from the golf courses where many of the events in MEMORIAL took place.

A GIFT AND A REQUEST

Thank you for reading! As a small gift, please download your free copy of *Three Tools for a Happier, Healthier Mind* by visiting nitasweeney.com or scanning this code:

If MEMORIAL resonated with you, please tell anyone who might want or need it about the book, ask your favorite bookstore and library to order it, and leave positive reviews on any of the bookselling sites. These actions mean so much!